Praise for *Demystifying Outcomes* *International Educators*

"As educational study-abroad programs have become more diverse, it has become more challenging for international educators to ensure quality and assess student learning outcomes. In this important book, Darla Deardorff stresses the importance of well-designed and fully equipped assessment programs, and she provides critical reference material for us to use as a basis for our assessments."—**Shingo Ashizawa**, Professor, Toyo University, Japan

"With characteristic practical bend, Darla Deadorff reviews current work on assessment of student learning and applies it to intercultural education. The book is of interest to professionals in international education interested in familiarizing themselves with assessment and intercultural learning."—**Veronica Boix-Mansilla**, Principal Investigator at Project Zero, Harvard Graduate School of Education, United States

"In the service of international outcomes assessment, this book provides an accessible introduction to the uninitiated, reassurance to the intimidated, and new insights to the accustomed practitioner. An indispensable book for international educators who recognize the value in demonstrating the transformative results of their work to their campus constituencies." —**Harvey Charles**, President, Association of International Education Administrators

"Dr. Deardorff's book is an invaluable resource for institutional leaders concerned with assessing global competencies, an increasingly critical area of learning for students in the twenty-first century."—**Jenifer Cushman**, President-Elect, Association of International Education Administrators

"This will be an enormously useful book for international educators. Thoroughly grounded in the literature and in good practice, it addresses the imperative of assessment in a clear, user-friendly, and practical manner."—**Madeleine F. Green**, Senior Fellow, International Association of Universities and NAFSA: Association of International Educators

"Strategic internationalization has rapidly become one of the most significant trends within higher education. With precision and purpose, Dr. Deardorff provides a rigorous and flexible model to measure, evaluate, and showcase key student-based outcomes associated with international education initiatives. With its focus on inputs and approach, her work helps us measure outcomes and impact (what counts in international education), and makes an invaluable contribution to the community."—**Clay Hensley**, Senior Director, International Strategy & Outreach, The College Board

"Assessing outcomes and impacts from internationalizing higher education, especially those related to student learning, is essential to demonstrating payoffs from investing scarce time, money, and effort in international education. This book is timely in presenting a number of salient issues needing attention in order to produce valid and useful assessment results about international education."—**John K. Hudzik**, Professor, Michigan State University, United States

"Internationalisation of higher education is evolving and is becoming a definite academic field. To develop it further in an academic discipline, a book like this, written by one of the most experienced researchers in the field of assessment of higher education internationalisation, will guide future studies by practitioners and other researchers. It could synchronise the outcomes of future studies that in turn should influence the development of philosophies that will guide higher education internationalisation."—**Nico Jooste**, Professor, Nelson Mandela Metropolitan University, South Africa

"Deardorff takes what can be a burdensome, albeit necessary, process for any education abroad office and breaks it down into practical, practicable chunks. For those who have long wanted a roadmap for outcomes assessment in international education, this book is a must-have resource."—**Amanda Toler Kelso**, Executive Director of Global Education Office for Undergraduates and Assistant Vice Provost for Undergraduate Education, Duke University, United States

"It is certainly time to pay more attention to the impact of internationalisation on student learning outcomes in universities and colleges. The practical resources and guidance presented in this book will be welcomed by many working the field."—**Betty Leask**, Pro Vice-Chancellor, Teaching and Learning, La Trobe University, Australia

"Without outcomes assessment it is very difficult to make a more compelling case in favor of international education. The new publication authored by Darla Deardorff provides a comprehensive, easy-to-read, and refreshing view on this important topic. A necessary reading for international education practitioners."—**Francisco Marmolejo**, Tertiary Education Coordinator, Education Global Practice, The World Bank

"Globalization is changing the way the world works, and colleges and universities around the world must prepare their students to be successful in a global economy. This excellent new publication provides practical and valuable advice on how to measure the impact and outcomes of campus-based international education initiatives."—**Daniel Obst**, Deputy Vice President, Institute of International Education

"This is a terrific book that will be enormously useful to international education professionals who are involved in the important work of assessing student learning outcomes."—**Brian Whalen**, CEO, Forum on Education Abroad

Demystifying Outcomes Assessment for International Educators

Demystifying Outcomes Assessment for International Educators

A Practical Approach

Darla K. Deardorff

Forewords by
Trudy W. Banta and Hans de Wit

STERLING, VIRGINIA

Published by Stylus Publishing, LLC
22883 Quicksilver Drive
Sterling, Virginia 20166-2102

The Civic Engagement VALUE Rubric, Global Learning VALUE
Rubric, and Intercultural Knowledge and Competence VALUE
Rubric featured in appendix E were developed by the Association
of American Colleges & Universities and are available for
download at www.aacu.org/value-rubrics.

Library of Congress Cataloging-in-Publication Data
Deardorff, Darla K.
Demystifying outcomes assessment for international educators:
a practical approach / Darla K. Deardorff ; forewords by
Trudy W. Banta and Hans de Wit.
    pages cm
Includes bibliographical references and index.
ISBN 978-1-62036-127-6 (cloth : alk. paper)
ISBN 978-1-62036-128-3 (pbk. : alk. paper)
ISBN 978-1-62036-129-0 (library networkable e-edition)
ISBN 978-1-62036-130-6 (consumer e-edition)
1. Educational evaluation. 2. International education. I. Title.
LB2822.75.D43 2015
379.1'58–dc23

                                                        2014040491

13-digit ISBN: 978-1-62036-127-6 (cloth)
13-digit ISBN: 978-1-62036-128-3 (paperback)
13-digit ISBN: 978-1-62036-129-0 (library networkable e-edition)
13-digit ISBN: 978-1-62036-130-6 (consumer e-edition)

Printed in the United States of America

All first editions printed on acid-free paper
that meets the American National Standards Institute
Z39-48 Standard.

First Edition, 2015

10 9 8 7 6 5 4 3 2 1

To my husband

Contents

Foreword 1

Trudy W. Banta

Darla K. Deardorff is uniquely qualified to contribute an important text on outcomes assessment for international educators. A review of her curriculum vitae reveals that the topic of her dissertation in pursuit of the doctorate in higher education administration from North Carolina State University was "The Identification and Assessment of Intercultural Competence as a Student Outcome of Internationalization at Institutions of Higher Education in the United States." And since receiving her degree, virtually all of her professional positions and activities have involved international education. Deardorff has coordinated an international studies center at Duke University, advised Duke students applying for Fulbright Scholarships, and designed curriculum and materials for cross-cultural communication courses and English-as-a-second-language teacher training courses at Duke. She manages an online community for scholars and practitioners on intercultural competence. And for the past decade she has served as executive director of the Association of International Education Administrators. In recent years her work has increasingly become focused on outcomes assessment in her field.

My own doctorate is in educational psychology, with an emphasis on the measurement of program outcomes. I quickly focused my work on program evaluation, and after applying my measurement skills to evaluate programs as diverse as early childhood intervention strategies, year-round school calendars, and nutrition education, I realized that virtually any field could utilize assessment skills. So when states initiated performance funding initiatives for colleges and universities in the 1980s I discovered yet another arena that called for my experience and expertise in program evaluation. Darla K. Deardorff is a pioneer in applying similar experience and expertise in a new area: international education.

Deardorff knows the audience for this book very well—consulting as she has with many institutions in the United States and accepting invitations to provide keynote addresses and to participate in seminars in countries as widely dispersed as Australia, Costa Rica, Italy, and Japan. She understands that, just as is the case with most other disciplines, professionals in the field of international education have deep knowledge and experience in promoting student learning during study abroad and other internationalizing activities, but they have very little knowledge or experience in evaluating student learning or program effectiveness. Yet in this age of accountability, these faculty and staff understand that they must demonstrate the effectiveness of their activities.

Deardorff estimates that more than 140 questionnaires and inventories have been developed for the purpose of collecting indirect evidence of the outcomes of international education. That is, these instruments are designed to assess the attitudes, opinions, and experiences of students, faculty, administrators, host families for study abroad, and others associated with international education. But Darla K. Deardorff knows that this indirect evidence, while valuable in creating a complete picture of outcomes, is insufficient. We must have direct measures of student learning and program effectiveness: What can students actually *do* as a result of their international experience? What evidence can be cited that tells us if a program is accomplishing the goals set for it?

The author's Introduction to this volume is an essential starting point for readers interested in finding an overview of purpose and content. Deardorff quickly acknowledges that the book is not for assessment professionals. Instead it is aimed at international educators who have no background in assessment but understand that they must provide credible evidence of the effectiveness of their work and who need an accessible introduction to the application of evaluation techniques in their field.

In her text Deardorff emphasizes the basic steps that are essential in planning assessment approaches. Helpful appendices contain numerous examples specific to international education. Chapter 9 gives readers good advice, relevant for any discipline, about providing leadership for outcomes assessment. And I recommend particularly chapter 10, which contains a most thoughtful agenda for future research in international education assessment that also has implications for other fields.

For international educators seeking a primer on outcomes assessment in their field, Darla K. Deardorff has provided an excellent resource. In future years we can anticipate additional significant contributions to the assessment literature from this competent scholar.

Trudy W. Banta
Indianapolis
September 2014

Foreword 2

Hans de Wit

INTERNATIONAL EDUCATION IS ALL ABOUT THE WHY, WHAT, HOW, AND OUTCOMES

In comparison to 25 years ago, when international education was still a rather marginal and ad hoc issue on the agenda of higher education institutions, international dimensions are now increasingly driving more higher education leaders' strategies at the (inter)national and institutional levels. The *Fourth Global Survey on Internationalization of Higher Education* of the International Association of Universities (IAU) confirms that trend (Egron Polak & Hudson, 2014). Not only have at least 70% of universities around the world developed an internationalization strategy, 16% have incorporated internationalization as a key component of their overall institutional strategy and vision, an indicator of the mainstreaming of internationalization. And the top-ranked finding (32%) for the benefits of internationalization is *student's increased international awareness and engagement with global issues*, followed by *improved quality of teaching and learning*. These findings give an optimistic picture of the relevance of international education in the current higher education environment, of its increased comprehensiveness, and of a perceived focus on what students should learn in order to be able to work and live in this globalized society. Other results from the survey, though, make clear that when it comes to action, priorities are different. *Outgoing mobility* (29%), *international research collaboration* (24%), and *strengthening international content of curriculum* (14%) are the three foremost internationalization activities. These conclusions illustrate that output (more study abroad, more publications) is still far more important than outcome (internationalization of the curriculum and learning outcomes).

This quantitative input and output approach to international education is still rather dominant. These directives are key in what I have described as the misconceptions of internationalization of higher education (de Wit, 2011). Outgoing mobility, by far the number-one priority action in the IAU survey, in its most optimistic calculations reaches approximately 20% to 25% of the total student body, thus leaving out the large majority of students. One also cannot assume that study abroad as such automatically enhances students' intercultural and international learning outcomes. Although studies on the impact of study abroad indicate a positive impact on civic engagement, identity, and employability, they also make clear that this impact is much higher when embedded in an internationalized curriculum and learning environment—before, during, and after the experience. We need to understand better the outcomes of study abroad but also the intercultural and international competencies of the large majority of students who do not travel abroad.

Outcomes assessment is one of the key priorities we need to focus on in international education in the coming years, as it makes us accountable for what we are doing, while providing us with better insight in the kind of impacts it has on students, faculty, and policy. Still, leaders do not give outcomes assessment high priority. They like the quantitative output targets approach more than qualitative outcomes assessment, as the quantitative approach is concrete, less debatable, and less expensive. But an outcomes assessment adds more relevant information to the quantitative data, gives more tools for improvement and enhancement, and for that reason needs increased attention.

For these reasons, a practical guide on outcomes assessment for international educators is much needed. As Darla K. Deardorff writes in her first chapter, "Outcomes assessment in international education is in its infancy." This book provides a blueprint that not only demystifies the topic and focuses on doing assessment but is also practical and digestible, giving an at-a-glance list of frequently asked questions—all important signals for what international educators need on this topic. The danger of such an approach is that readers might assume that by digesting the rich amount of information contained in this book, they will have the "silver bullet" for answering all their questions on outcomes assessment in international education. For that reason, Darla K. Deardorff—who, with her long list of books and articles on intercultural competences and on outcomes assessment, can be considered as a leading expert in this evolving field and thus the appropriate person to write this guide—in her introduction emphasizes that many different perspectives on assessment exist and a one-size-fits-all volume cannot work.

I have been and continue to be involved in several different assessments in international education, at the regional, national, institutional, and program levels, and in many different contexts (see, for instance, Aerden, de Decker, Divis, Frederiks, & de Wit, 2013). Successful international education policies and practices are based on providing answers up front to the following key questions: Why, what, and how do we assess on an ongoing basis the impacts *and* outcomes of international education? Darla K. Deardorff addresses all these matters in this text.

Hans de Wit

Director, Centre for Higher Education Internationalisation (CHEI), Milan, Italy;
professor of internationalization, Amsterdam University of Applied Sciences,
The Netherlands; research associate, Nelson Mandela Metropolitan University,
Port Elizabeth, South Africa

REFERENCES

Aerden, A., de Decker, F., Divis, J., Frederiks, M., & de Wit, H. (2013). Assessing the internationalisation of degree programmes: Experiences from a Dutch-Flemish pilot certifying internationalisation. *Compare: A Journal of Comparative and International Education, 43*(1), 56–78.

De Wit, H. (2011). Internationalization misconceptions. *International Higher Education, 64*(Summer 2011), 6–7.

Egron Polak, E., & Hudson, R. (2014). *Internationalization of higher education: Growing expectations, fundamental values.* Paris: International Association of Universities.

Acknowledgments

This book is inspired by many colleagues in international education. Thanks to all who asked questions and shared insights, and who care so deeply about student learning.

I want to express deep appreciation to those who reviewed this book, especially Trudy Banta, Duane Deardorff, and Kathryn Rosenbaum. Appreciation is also expressed to John von Knorring and colleagues at Stylus for their amazing support throughout this project. Thanks also to Kaylee Deardorff and Shaun Deardorff for their encouragement and patience during the writing of this book.

The author and publisher also wish to thank the Association of American Colleges & Universities and the American Council on Education for permission to reproduce their copyrighted material, as well as Matt Serra, Duke University; Charles Calahan, Purdue University; and Tara Harvey, Council on International Educational Exchange, for their contributions to appendix F.

Introduction

Are you tasked with assessing education abroad programs and exchanges? An international or global course? An international students' program? An orientation? An overseas internship program? A service-learning abroad course? An intercultural on-campus program? An online program in international education?

Do you need to know where to start with outcomes assessment?

Do you want to make sure assessments efforts are effective, given all that goes into assessment?

This book is a practical guide to student learning outcomes assessment in international education, no matter your particular area. The concepts and materials can apply across the different contexts of international education, including formal and nonformal settings. Presented in a clear and accessible manner and assuming no prior knowledge of assessment, this book takes readers through the process of "doing assessment," with particular emphasis on setting up the assessment, since the setup and approach are key to making assessment efforts successful. For readers already somewhat familiar with assessment, much of this material will be a refresher and can serve as a check to ensure quality assessment work. This resource is written primarily for international educators, since there is typically little formal training in assessment for professionals in this field and even less time to read the plethora of assessment books that already exist. Parts of this book may be useful to colleagues in the assessment field wanting to understand more of the complexities in assessing learning outcomes in international education. Those in international education and assessment are encouraged to work together since each group has unique expertise that can be effectively utilized through collaboration. Based on over a decade of work with international education programs and higher education institutions around the world, this publication serves as a foundation for effective assessment in international education. Although this book reflects a predominantly U.S. perspective, readers from different geographic and cultural contexts may find this information helpful. In many ways, this resource channels the learning from these institutions in different parts of the world as well as from assessment experts to create a guide for those who wish to understand and use effective outcomes assessment in the international education field. After going through the materials in this publication, you will be ready to put together an effective assessment plan, or tweak an already existing plan, in your area that will result in a solid assessment strategy yielding the results that you and your learners need. This book does *not* present an exhaustive list of assessment instruments (resources in the back provide guides for finding that information) nor does it offer lots of concrete examples, except for those in the appendices. Consider this more of a blueprint for developing and improving assessment efforts in readers' specific international education contexts. I have discovered through the years that international education colleagues find this kind of foundational information helpful in demystifying the assessment process as a whole as well as being useful in either getting started on assessment properly in their unique context or in ensuring the effectiveness of the assessment work they're already doing.

Given that international educators are busy professionals with much more than assessment in their portfolios, this book is meant to be more practical and "digestible," so that readers find it useful. Much of this book focuses on setting up and planning for assessment, maximizing assessment results from an initial investment in the planning process. Here's an analogy for the importance of preparation: Think about preparing for a hiking adventure. You'll generally have a more successful experience if you prepare adequately with a map, compass, water, proper hiking shoes, and so on than if you just start walking. In the latter case, you may encounter more difficulties and could end up anywhere. Remember, *the success of outcomes assessment efforts depends on how much work and effort are invested from the very beginning.*

Given this focus on preparation, chapter 1 frames international education assessment in terms of approaching assessment as well as provides an overview and the context for the rest of the volume. An at-a-glance list of frequently asked questions is featured in chapter 2, which provides a road map to materials in the book. Chapter 3 highlights key aspects that make outcomes assessment in international education unique in relation to other types of assessment in higher education. Chapter 4 outlines fundamental assessment principles that should underlie any assessment effort, regardless of context (study abroad, global curriculum, etc.). Chapter 5 provides a holistic approach to outcomes assessment, while chapter 6 discusses practical steps in getting started in assessment. Chapter 7 outlines how to develop an assessment strategy through an actual assessment plan which takes into account the process of implementation. Chapter 8 discusses some common pitfalls and lessons learned in outcomes assessment in international education. Chapter 9 explores the role of leadership in international education assessment, which is essential to assessment success. Chapter 10 looks to the future in international education outcomes assessment, including issues and questions that still need further examination, along with new ways to think about outcomes assessment that result in a paradigm shift for international education and assessment. Appendices include a suggested list of standards adapted to international education outcomes assessment, a selection that highlights examples of assessment in international education in a variety of contexts, a detailed discussion on assessing intercultural competence, and resources. International educators may want to start with appendix A, for example, which includes practical worksheets that you can use to guide your assessment efforts as you put together an assessment team and bring others at your institution on board with assessment efforts.

While this book could be read all the way through, many readers will most likely pick and choose chapters that meet their needs, which means that key points are reemphasized throughout the book so that some chapters or sections can be read independently. Thus, those who choose to read this publication from cover to cover will find some necessary repetition in order to accommodate those readers who choose selected chapters based on their own needs and contexts.

International education has many outcomes. This book focuses primarily on student learning outcomes assessment, since learning outcomes—what students know and are able to do as a result of completing a course or program—have been recognized as the ultimate drivers of internationalization (International Education Association of South Africa, 2014). Furthermore, the focus is primarily on how to approach and prepare for outcomes assessment, since the preparation is crucial to effective results. International education operates in diverse settings, and a rich variety of programs and organizations are involved in providing learning experiences that help today's learners be better prepared to live in the global century. With this diversity comes many different perspectives on assessment and the recognition that a one-size-fits-all approach will simply not work across these different contexts. Thus, this book is focused more on the foundational basis for assessment, ensuring that a common starting point exists for assessment efforts.

CHAPTER 1

Framing International Education Assessment

Let's start with some assessment myths that occur within international education:

- Myth 1: Pre-/post- surveys are sufficient for assessment.
- Myth 2: It's fine to just start collecting information and then figure out later what to do with the results.
- Myth 3: There's one best tool to assess outcomes in international education programs.
- Myth 4: It's best to develop the program first and add the assessment in later.
- Myth 5: One person or office can do the assessment.
- Myth 6: International educators should agree on one standardized tool that everyone can use.
- Myth 7: Outcomes assessment is the same as program evaluation.

This book is written to debunk some of these myths, and hopefully by the time you've finished, you'll see why these seven statements are indeed myths. (See appendix A for a handout you can use to explore these with colleagues.) If you're reading this book, chances are that you have an interest in assessing international education outcomes. The purpose of this resource is to provide the basics of assessment for professionals and faculty in international education, regardless of the program or context. The following chapters help to demystify outcomes assessment by distilling the vast assessment literature into the more relevant points for international education professionals—from staff in study-abroad and international student offices to academics teaching complex global or intercultural learning outcomes in their courses. The contexts may range from assessing international programs on campus—such as student orientations, international week, and housing programs, to assessing education-abroad programs, to assessing global learning generally within the curriculum, to leading institutional internationalization efforts.

Assessment often generates some initial responses, all of which are quite normal reactions:

- Assessment—What's that?
- Assessment—I don't know how.
- Ignoring it.
- Negotiating with or encouraging someone else to do it.
- Complaining about it.
- Losing sleep over it.
- Looking for the easy way out (one pre-/post- measure will take care of it, right?).
- Doing it.

Perhaps you recognize yourself in one or more of these responses. Remember that all of these are normal responses to assessment. In the end, "doing it" is the desired response, which means doing assessment well with meaningful results that are useful to learners as well as to the program and institution. Regardless of the responses to it, educational experts agree that assessment, especially of student learning, is here to stay. For example, accreditors continue to insist on evidence of students' knowledge, skills, and abilities. Employers continue to value performance beyond knowledge. Governments, parents, students, and even the general public continue to call for evidence of return on investment. And the field of international education has come late to the concrete assessment of student learning, instead relying for far too long on metrics around numbers—number of participants, number of students going abroad, even the percentage of students who score a certain way on a survey or inventory, and so on. Numbers are certainly important, but there's much more to assessment. This book synthesizes key information in the assessment field for international educators. The goal is to provide a basic foundational guide that will enhance assessment efforts, which should be viewed as *ongoing* efforts versus a discrete process to complete. This assessment primer will help ensure that the time and resources invested will not only be effective but yield the desired results in terms of improving student learning and strengthening international education efforts. Ultimately, the goal is to better equip you with knowledge and tools to work with others in effectively assessing the learning outcomes of international education efforts, both in and out of the classroom.

TERMS

Let's start with some basic definitions.

What is assessment? *Assessment*, simply put, is the systematic collection, review, and use of information about student learning (Driscoll & Wood, 2007; Palomba & Banta, 2011). According to assessment expert Robert Thorndike (2005), outcomes-based assessment is about expectations, and stakeholders need to identify desired results, performance, and products. Note that assessment in the context of this book does not refer to grading or assigning a grade, although for some educators this definition may come to mind.

Outcomes assessment (in a course or program) is information collected from individual learners as evidence that stated course goals and objectives were achieved. What changes have occurred in what students know and are able to do (learning outcomes) as a result of completing the course, program, or experience? Outcomes can also reflect changes in awareness or behavior.

Program assessment (also termed *evaluation*) is learner cohort information collected in aggregate from a course and reported at the program level in relation to departmental or institutional goals and objectives. For international education, where the focus is often on program assessment, keep in mind that individual learner assessment can be aggregated to inform program or institutional decisions. Often, program assessment in international education may consist of satisfaction surveys, in which participants assess the logistics of the experience (e.g., environment, instructor, materials, lodging) but rarely give information about what they actually learned. However, satisfaction surveys can be modified to include questions related to learning objectives. Program assessment information is used to inform decisions about effectiveness of programs, policies, and so on. See chapter 7 for more on this process.

Another term that serves as more of a principle for assessment (and for this book) is *backward (course) design*. This term refers to choosing goals and objectives before selecting activities and assessments in order to keep them in alignment. Start by asking, "What kinds of change (in knowledge, skills, attitudes) do learners want by the end of this course, program, or experience?"

Goals are broad statements (macro expectations) about what students will know and be able to do upon completion of a course or program. Goals are generally too broad to be measurable.

Objectives are a set of concrete, specific statements (micro expectations) about student learning and performance that lead to the achievement of a stated goal. Objectives are measureable.

Goals and objectives can both be considered *outcomes*, and the terms *objectives* and *outcomes* are often used interchangeably. *Learning outcomes*, for example, are defined as stated expectations of what students will learn (what they know and are able to do as a result of the learning), and those expectations, in turn, guide curriculum, teaching, and especially assessment (Driscoll & Wood, 2007). See chapter 6 for more information on and examples of how goals and objectives fit together into a larger whole.

Assessment Methods Terminology

Formative assessment refers to ongoing assessment efforts over time and throughout a course, program, or experience. The use of the collected information is for *improving* student learning. Formative assessment, which can take the form of learning assignments, often provides more opportunity to give direct feedback to students. Teachers use formative assessment to understand where students are in the learning process, to correct misperceptions, and to understand gaps in student learning that can still be addressed. Students often view formative assessment as "low stakes."

Summative assessment refers to assessment information collected at the end of a course, program, or experience, often used to *prove* what was learned (results). Summative assessment often occurs in the form of a final test or demonstration, and students can consider them more "high stakes." Often, there is little opportunity to provide direct feedback to students, and the purpose is more to see how much students learned at the end of a course or experience and to answer this question: What difference was made? Summative assessment can gauge student achievement.

Formative and summative assessment are both important because they serve different purposes. Too often in international education, however, there is an overreliance on summative assessment only, with little attention given to formative assessment.

Quantitative assessment refers to information that can have a numerical value attached to it. Quantitative information is often considered to provide insights into the *breadth* of the assessment context.

Qualitative assessment refers to information that involves verbal descriptions, either oral or written. Qualitative information often provides richer insights into the *depth* of the assessment context.

Quantitative and qualitative assessments are often thought to be mutually exclusive. However, there are ways to quantify qualitative information through coding and categorizing verbal responses. The merits of each type of assessment can also be combined into a mixed-method approach. (For more, see chapters 6 and 7.)

Direct assessment is actual evidence of student learning, usually collected through student work and performance in a course or experience and can include papers, projects, tests, and observations. Direct assessment is often qualitative in nature.

Indirect assessment refers to *perceptions* of student learning. What do students think they learned as a result of their participation in a course or experience? Indirect assessment is most often collected through self-report surveys, interviews, and focus groups, frequently before and/or after a learning experience. Indirect evidence can be either quantitative (survey scores) or qualitative.

Reliability is an indicator of consistency. A tool or method is reliable if it yields similar results each time it is administered.

Validity is about being "on target." A tool is valid if it measures what it says it measures and aligns with the intended use of the results.

These two terms, *reliability* and *validity*, are crucial to assessment. Please see chapter 8 for more discussion on reliability and validity, as well as the illustrations on p. 9.

Two more specific terms discussed in greater detail later are *rubrics* and *e-portfolios/ portfolios*:

Reliable,
Not Valid

Both Reliable
and Valid

Rubrics represent a predetermined set of criteria, usually at varying levels of achievement, that is used to evaluate learners' work or performance. Rubrics usually contain descriptions of criteria at each level (referred to as *analytic rubrics*, whereas *holistic rubrics* evaluate performance across multiple criteria at a meta level) and may be connected to a point system per level or criterion for the purpose of assigning a grade. A relevant example of an analytic rubric is the Association of American Colleges & Universities' VALUE rubrics. See appendix E for some examples of rubrics developed by the Association of American Colleges & Universities that international educators are adapting. Note that any "borrowed" rubric needs to be adapted to the specific context of one's goals and objectives.

Portfolios/e-portfolios are mechanisms for collecting student work through a course, experience, or even an entire student career, with *e-portfolio* referring to an electronic portfolio, usually consisting of an electronic platform or program where students collect and store their work. The work gathered—such as papers; blog postings; documentaries; photos; videos; projects; and even letters, forms, and rubrics completed by others about the student—demonstrates student learning and is usually evaluated through the use of rubrics (and multiple raters). Students can also engage in self-reflection on the work collected. Without evaluation or reflection, e-portfolios remain merely a collection of work.

Other Assessment Terminology

Pre/post refers to a measure given at the beginning (pre) of a course or experience and then given again at the end (post) of the course or experience to see how much change has occurred, usually in an effort to determine how effective the course or experience was. In international education, *pre/post* usually refers to a self-perspective survey, as opposed to a test, which measures actual knowledge.

Stakeholders refers to any individual, group, or organization that has an interest in or can be affected by an organization or program. In the case of international education, the many stakeholders include students, parents, faculty, administrators, community partners, grant funders, and alumni.

Triangulation is the use of assessment information from a variety of sources and methods to provide a more informed and complete picture of results, specifically the congruence of results from multiple sources, thus providing cross-verification of achieved results. Triangulation helps address the bias and weakness inherent in using a single assessment tool.

This section has covered just a few of the key terms used in educational assessment. (For more on assessment terminology, see Banta & Palomba, 2014.) While a variety of terms are used in international education assessment, many of which can be confusing, practitioners need to be clear and consistent in using assessment terminology.

WHY ASSESS?

What is your reason for assessing outcomes in international education? Is it to improve your students' learning? Is it to show the value of your program? To improve your program? Because of accreditation, or is it mandated or required? (And why is it required?) For many in international education, it may be more about program advocacy—for example, for resources, existence, or justification—than about student learning, although ostensibly the emphasis is on the student. Yet *to what end*? As some assessment experts observe (see Steinke & Fitch, 2011), staff too often push for a selection of easily measurable outcomes or a particular easy-to-use assessment tool without giving thought to why, or even without articulating the goals and objectives. *Don't rush to assessing without first pausing to ask why you are assessing at all.*

The "Why assess" question is critical and must be the focus of any discussion early on, before engaging in assessment. This question must preempt any discussion of how and what to assess, since the purpose determines the direction of any other questions we may ask. So *why* focus on outcomes assessment? That depends on who you ask. For educators, outcomes assessment is about deepening students' learning and improving both teaching and learning. For administrators, outcomes assessment is about evidence for accountability to stakeholders and advocating for program viability and resources. For students, such assessment may be about completion of a credentialing process, as well as about gaining knowledge and skills needed for the future, especially in terms of employability. For employers, outcomes assessment may be about team development or candidate selection. In the end, assessment experts see outcomes assessment as closely linked to student learning, each informing the other. Barbara Walvoord (2004) calls assessment a "powerful instrument for improvement" and "potentially the best lever for change" when done properly. She goes on to add that such "careful attention to students' learning . . . can help create a climate of caring and engagement that supports students' own commitment to their learning" (p. 6). Another assessment expert, Trudy Banta (2005), notes that "learning outcomes assessment has the potential to revamp entire curricula, but only if it's embraced across campuses and not forced to conform to a standardized testing mandate" (p. 35). And while other measures of international education efforts exist, such as faculty research and funding, institutional reputation, and economic impact (see Aerden, 2014, for a full list of elements that can be evaluated in internationalization), focusing on outcomes assessment, and specifically learning outcomes assessment, is at the heart of education: What do our students know and what can they do as a result of their intercultural learning experiences? Student learning outcomes assessment provides the evidence in response to this question. Green (2012) concurs when she states, "An institution that seeks to be comprehensively internationalized, infusing internationalization throughout its many programs and making it a way of accomplishing its central work, must also pay close attention to what students are learning" (p. 8). The importance of learning outcomes in international education was reaffirmed by the 2014 Nelson Mandela Bay Declaration of the Future of Internationalization in Higher Education, written and endorsed by the major international education associations around the world (International Education Association of South Africa, 2014). With proper and careful focus on assessing student learning outcomes, the other reasons for assessment—such as accountability and advocacy—can also be addressed. This book focuses on providing the basic foundation for effectively assessing student learning outcomes in international education, increasingly recognized as being at the core of international education.

Given the wealth of information and knowledge available in the 21st century, stated outcomes help students focus on what really matters, thus deepening their learning experiences. This prioritization not only encourages students to explore what's most important in the learning experience but also sets expectations for achievement by the end of the learning experience. For institutions, learning outcomes inform curriculum, teaching, and even assessment. In the end, teachers and faculty are "the most appropriate source of learning outcomes for their students" (Driscoll & Wood, 2007) and play a central role in assessment efforts (Green, 2013). These observations imply the utmost importance of international educators partnering with instructors in learning outcomes assessment (see chapters 5 and 6 for further discussion).

Let's return to this fundamental question: Why do you want to engage in assessment? Spending adequate time reflecting on the *why* as a fundamental starting point is crucial. Simon Sinek (2009) stresses the importance of starting with the *why* instead of the *what* or *how*. Too often, there is no clear understanding of the purpose of assessment. Is it about the students? The program? The institution? Why? To what end?

Answering these questions is essential before embarking on any assessment endeavor. Otherwise, the question may end up being, "Why bother?" given the amount of time and effort required to invest in effective assessment.

HISTORICAL BACKGROUND: INTERNATIONAL EDUCATION AND ASSESSMENT

The field of international education is a latecomer to assessment. Assessment of education itself has a long history, dating back to Plato and Aristotle, who utilized oral recitation as a method of assessing learning. The University of Bologna in 1063 had juried reviews of student learning. Harvard students during Colonial times engaged in weekly "disputes" as evidence of their learning (Bresciani, Gardner, & Hickmott, 2009). In the 20th century in the United States, outcomes-based assessment developed out of psychology in the 1930s and 1940s. Often noted as the first to introduce backward design, Tyler's classic work (1949) on curriculum development and evaluation outlined key guiding questions, including identification of education purposes (why), selection and organization of educational experiences (how), and evidence of desired results from the educational experiences (what). In the 1970s, Astin's seminal work (1972) focused on longitudinal research and on student talent development through the undergraduate education. His Inputs-Environmental-Outputs (I-E-O) model formed the foundation of "vigorous research methodology" and provides the basis "for outcomes-based assessment programs today" (Bresciani et al., 2009, p. 4). Fast-forward to the end of the 20th century, and the U.S. assessment movement is well developed, partly due to increased external calls for accountability and tighter financial resources. The 1986 report by the National Governors' Association titled *Time for Results* was a bellwether of the times (Bresciani et al., 2009), which called for evidence of student performance that could help inform institutional improvement. In 1999 Alverno College, a gold-standard institution in terms of assessment, published *Student Learning Outcomes in Baccalaureate Education*, which synthesized efforts from 140 institutions (Riordan & Doherty, 1999).

The beginning of the 21st century saw a shift from assessment for accountability to a focus on teaching and learning, meaning an increased emphasis on academic learning standards and curricular alignment (Ewell, 2005). Attention also turned to outside-the-classroom learning, which brought student affairs practitioners into assessment efforts as they now look at assessing outcomes in nonformal settings. One example is the U.S.-based Association of American Colleges & Universities' (AAC&U's) focus on global learning. Working with faculty across the United States, AAC&U initiated a project called Valid Assessment of Learning in Undergraduate Education (VALUE), which involved developing rubrics for 16 learning outcomes in undergraduate education. Final versions of these rubrics were released in 2009, and three—intercultural knowledge and competence, global learning, and civic engagement—are closely connected to international education (see chapter 4 for more discussion on VALUE rubrics). Other surveys, such as the Cooperative Institutional Research Program (CIRP) and the National Survey of Student Engagement (NSSE), "tell a story about institutions, not individual students" (Shulman, 2007, para. 15). For example, NSSE highlights information about opportunities that institutions provide for student learning and includes a global learning module that institutions can use.

A shift in U.S. education has occurred over the past 20 years—from the more traditional "sage-on-the-stage" model of transmitting knowledge, to the learner-centered "guide-on-the-side" model of learning where students are more actively engaged in their learning as facilitated by teachers. The flipped-classroom model is one example, whereby students take initiative in learning materials and then engage with other learners in a face-to-face environment in understanding the materials and concepts. So, too, has assessment moved to incorporate more learner-centered assessment. Huba and Freed (2000) summarize the following implications of this paradigm shift within higher education on learner-centered assessment as follows:

- Promotes high expectations for learning
- Respects diverse talents and learning styles
- Engages students in learning
- Promotes coherence in learning
- Synthesizes experiences, fostering ongoing practice of learned skills, and integrates education and experience
- Provides prompt feedback
- Fosters collaboration
- Depends on increased student-faculty contact

Numerous points in the learner-centered approach align with students' learning in international education, including the integration of learners' education and experience abroad, as well as students' learning in and out of the classroom. In engaging students in learning and in their own assessment of learning through integration of these principles of learner-centered assessment, students are empowered to take more responsibility for their own learning and subsequent outcomes. (For more on a new paradigm shift occurring, see chapter 10.)

While other measures of student success may exist (e.g., through job placement), the focus on student learning outcomes as a key measure is crucial in international education, leading to particular issues for this field. First, there remains a need for documenting student learning more holistically, beyond one course or experience, which is too often the case now in international education. Furthermore, learning outcomes when stated in a measurable way can often be reduced to simplistic statements that are not as meaningful nor capture the deeper complexities around student transformation, which may in the end address the learning process rather than results in international education. Another issue is that the focus on student learning may not address or assess unanticipated outcomes that could occur, particularly in international education experiences.

Ultimately, though, the purpose of postsecondary institutions is to facilitate students' learning. As assessment expert Trudy Banta (2005) concludes, "Outcomes assessment is simply not worth doing unless it is used to enhance the student learning experience by improving instruction in a single class, the structure or sequencing of a curriculum, or the process of offering student services that complement coursework" (p. 38). Thus, administrators and instructors in international education need to move programs and courses beyond surface learning to participants' deeper learning and engagement. Learner-centeredness becomes one approach for achieving this engagement, and evidence-based, learner-centered assessment emerges as a way to document the more complex learning outcomes of international education (see chapters 6 and 7 for more), even though such an approach is not widely used yet in international education.

ASSESSMENT BEYOND THE UNITED STATES

The 21st century has also seen an increased interest in assessment from other countries. Consider the great interest in Tuning Educational Structures in Europe (known commonly as "Tuning"), which was developed in 2000 in the framework of the Life-Long Learning Program. This initiative was connected to the Bologna Process, which brought European institutions more in line with each other, especially in terms of offering three-year undergraduate degrees. Tuning embraces a bottom-up approach in working with faculty to determine each discipline's learning outcomes. The Tuning methodology includes generic and subject-specific competences. The generic competences include three related to international education: (a) ability to communicate in a foreign language, (b) ability to interact constructively with others regardless of background and culture, and (c) ability to work in an international environment (Deardorff & van Gaalen, 2012). Latin American countries have also shown great interest in Tuning, with nearly 200 institutions involved in the Tuning process. Tuning has made considerable progress in Africa (e.g., South Africa uses a National Qualifications Framework [NQF]) and Australasia (where Australia emphasizes Graduate Attributes). How much traction Tuning will gain in the United States remains to be seen.[1] However, with its clear focus on student learning—and stated attainment of what every graduate of a degree program will know and be able to do as a result of a degree in that discipline—Tuning has the potential to greatly transform higher education. This development has implications for international education, given the emphasis on student learning in the classroom, the central role of faculty in assessing student learning, and the establishment of rigorous performance expectations.

Another effort originating from Europe and the Organization of Economic Cooperation and Development (OECD) is PISA—the Programme on International Student Assessment—which looks at student learning (knowledge and skills) at the secondary level; global competence outcomes are being developed as part of PISA, so it behooves university personnel to know what is being done at the secondary level in regard to assessing global learning outcomes.

ASSESSMENT IN INTERNATIONAL EDUCATION

So, where is international education in its assessment efforts? Study abroad has certainly led the way with an increasing plethora of published studies on education-abroad outcomes, many of those utilizing a pre-/post- methodology. Since 2003, NAFSA–Association of International Educators has published an annual report titled *Internationalizing the Campus: Profiles of Success at Colleges and Universities*, featuring institutional recipients of NAFSA's Paul Simon Award. In 2007 the U.S.-based Forum on Education Abroad published *A Guide to Outcomes Assessment in Education Abroad*, edited by Mell C. Bolen, and more recently developed an online resource of assessment tools for study-abroad administrators. In 2009 the European Association of International Educators (EAIE) published *Measuring Success in the Internationalisation of Higher Education* (EAIE Occasional Paper 22), edited by Hans de Wit, which focused primarily on numerical measures of international education. The 2012 *SAGE Handbook of International Higher Education* featured a chapter on "Outcomes Assessment in the Internationalization of Higher Education," co-authored by Darla K. Deardorff and Adinda van Gaalen, which looked at a variety of qualitative outcomes in internationalization. (These and other assessment resources in international education can be found in appendix G.) In Japan, educators have shown great interest in utilizing e-portfolios to document learning in international education (Ashizawa, 2012).

In recent years, assessment efforts have expanded from study-abroad outcomes assessment to assessment of curricular outcomes, as well as co-curricular (outside the classroom) outcomes. For example, accrediting bodies increasingly address relevant learning expectations to international education, particularly around intercultural competence, as noted in the U.S. disciplinary accrediting bodies for engineering, social work, business, education, nursing, and medical schools. Regional accrediting bodies in the United States have also seen an increased focus on intercultural and global-related learning outcomes. Accrediting agencies in other countries are also addressing student learning related to international education, such as a pilot undertaken in 2010 by the Accreditation Organization of the Netherlands and Flanders (NVAO). Beyond accreditation efforts, other organizations, especially in Europe, are also undertaking assessment initiatives. For example, OECD piloted AHELO (Assessment of Higher Education Learning Outcomes), although to limited success. Similar to Tuning, AHELO looked at general and discipline-specific learning, albeit through a series of tests. The Council of Europe has also funded numerous intercultural assessment-related projects in recent years, one of the most recent being an intercultural app (application software) that became available in fall 2013.

SUMMARY

Despite the relatively lengthy existence (over 75 years and counting) of learner-centered approaches as well as outcomes-based approaches, outcomes assessment in international education is in its infancy. Many questions still need answers, and specific areas require further assessment research (see chapter 10). The good news is that more and more international educators are engaging in assessment efforts; within those efforts, though, there's still a long way to go in understanding what makes for effective assessment that adheres to key assessment principles. As a consequence, few examples of best practices in international education assessment are available to date; see appendix F for some examples of good practices. As assessment becomes more established in international education, more examples of good practices—upon which future assessment efforts can build—will hopefully emerge. Much is to be learned from current assessment efforts, and this book helps illuminate some of those lessons.

NOTE

1. The Lumina Foundation in the United States has engaged in an effort related to Tuning (although not the same): In 2011 a Degree Qualifications Profile (DQP) was released in the United States, providing learning expectations and a "common vocabulary" for what students (at associate through master's level) should know and be able to do. Lumina released a revised DQP in 2014. The DQP offers higher education institutions a better understanding of developing specific competencies as well as "reference points for accountability focused on student learning as opposed to job placement rates or test scores of graduates" (Jankowski, Hutchings, Ewell, Kinzie, & Kuh, 2013).

CHAPTER 2

Thirty Frequently Asked Questions on Assessment in International Practice

Following is a list of questions that international educators frequently ask. This list can also serve as an at-a-glance guide for where to find more detailed information in this book regarding these questions.

1. WHAT ASSESSMENT TEST OR TOOL DO I USE? AND CAN'T I JUST DESIGN MY OWN?

The assessment tests or tools (note plural) you should use depend on your clearly stated goals and learning objectives. *Clearly stated learning objectives determine the evidence you need to collect, which in turn determines which tests, tools, or measures you should use.* Please note that in the assessment field, *test* refers to a knowledge or skill test. Surveys and inventories are not considered tests. In international education, surveys and other self-report measures tend to be used more often than actual tests. For more on assessment measures, see chapter 6 and appendix E.

In terms of designing your own tool: that actually involves a lot more time, effort, and resources than it might seem. Designing a reliable and valid assessment tool can take years of research and refinement in order to have a quality tool—it's much more than listing questions on a paper and pilot testing them. (So if you plan to use someone else's tool, be sure to investigate very carefully what kind of research went into the development of the tool.) In the end, designing a quality tool is often an ineffective way to proceed. It is better to spend your time on laying the groundwork for assessment (as outlined in this book) and ensuring that you are collecting evidence of student learning aligned to your stated goals and objectives.

2. WHAT'S THE BEST ASSESSMENT INSTRUMENT OR TOOL TO USE?

There is no one best assessment instrument to use. Certainly, assessment measures vary in quality, and understanding thoroughly how the measure was developed is important, as well as ensuring that the measure is aligned with stated objectives and intended use. Resist thinking that one tool can measure the complexities of international education outcomes. Psychologists Steinke and Fitch (2011) state, "The seduction of a clean measurement, where the measures have unequivocal validity and reliability and the results are unambiguous, is itself an illusion when it comes to assessment" (p. 16). For more on using assessment tools, see chapters 6 and 7, as well as the appendices.

3. WHAT EXACTLY SHOULD WE ASSESS? AREN'T NUMBERS ENOUGH?

While the international education field has traditionally relied on numbers to indicate success (e.g., numbers of students studying abroad, numbers of global courses offered, number of international faculty, amount of research dollars), a growing trend in international education recognizes that numbers alone, while important, are not sufficient (see chapter 1). Thus, attention has turned to looking at the meaning behind the numbers, leading to the focus on outcomes assessment and specifically learning outcomes (see chapter 5). This book is about assessing learning outcomes in international education. Other types of outcomes include retention and graduation rates, alumni employability, improved learning environment, quality teaching and research, and so on (see Aerden, 2014). The more traditional "satisfaction surveys" focus primarily on learners' satisfaction with services or program logistics. Numbers are certainly a starting point for assessment, but beginning to assess the meaning (outcomes) beyond the numbers is important for understanding the impact of international education efforts (see chapter 5 for more).

4. IS LEARNING OUTCOMES ASSESSMENT DONE ONLY IN STUDY-ABROAD PROGRAMS?

No. While more assessment literature and studies are available in the area of study-abroad programming, learning outcomes assessment goes beyond study abroad to include learning outcomes in courses (including general education courses, language courses, and courses in a discipline), in other co-curricular and extracurricular programming (such as orientation and mentor programs), and in experiential learning settings (such as internships and service learning). See chapter 3 for more on the unique context of international education. Given the small percentage of students studying abroad, it becomes crucial that international educators also engage in student learning outcomes for *all* students throughout their higher education careers.

5. WHY CAN'T EVERYONE IN INTERNATIONAL EDUCATION USE THE SAME ASSESSMENT INSTRUMENT?

Not all programs or courses in international education have exactly the same goals and stated objectives, and great variance exists in the actual programs and courses offered, as well as the specific context (e.g., institution type, geographic location, and student population and size). While the overall goals in international education may be similar, specific objectives vary by context and priority. Since assessment instruments need to be aligned to these specific objectives and the results used accordingly, the same instrument should not be used for all situations Furthermore, given the complexities of international education outcomes, a multi-method approach should be used (see question 6), so more than one instrument is generally required. And here's a caution: "What is troublesome is the push towards uniformity, uniformity in aims, uniformity in content, uniformity in assessment, uniformity in expectation. Of course for technocrats uniformity is a blessing; it gets rid of complications—or so it is believed" (Eisner, 2002, para. 14). Further, international educators Hudzik and Stohl (2009) caution, "A limited number of standard measures across institutions minimizes diversity and experimentation. It also tends to ignore valuable niche strengths and outcomes, and homogenizes the outcomes of higher education," leading "individuals and institutions to 'play to the test' rather than develop their own unique goals and programs" (p. 17).

6. WHAT ABOUT COMPARING RESULTS?

International educators are not unique in their desire to want to compare results across programs, even though programs may not be identical and may have different goals and objectives. While the desire to compare results may be natural, it is important to ask yourself, Why? *Why* do you want to compare results? *To what end?* Who benefits? What can be done to improve results if you don't like what you see? What exactly can you change that is under your control? More important, *How do students benefit from such comparisons*? Usually the desire to compare results is to see which programs are doing better or to have a benchmark. While administrators may find this approach useful, in the end such comparisons do not necessarily help the students in their own learning, which is ultimately the main point of assessment. As assessment experts stated, "Benchmarking or any comparative use of performance indicators is not necessarily considered outcomes-based assessment of student learning and development. Likewise, the methods used for benchmarking differ from those used for outcomes-based assessment. Benchmarking is used for comparison purposes and is generally not geared to identifying or informing programmatic outcomes-based improvements of student learning" (Bresciani, Gardner, & Hickmott, 2009, p. 57). If there is a push to compare with other programs, it is important to spend time first discussing *why*. There is a limit to how benchmarking and comparative data can be used, especially in improving student learning, and methods would vary for collecting data.

7. WHY ISN'T A PRE-/POST- SURVEY SUFFICIENT?

While it is a starting point, a pre-/post- survey is insufficient in that it collects indirect and incomplete evidence of student learning. Such a survey is helpful as part of collecting baseline information, but that needs to be combined with information collected as part of formative assessment, which is evidence of ongoing student learning and is used to improve the learning that occurs; this combination tells a more complete story of student learning. A pre-/post- survey also needs to be combined with direct evidence of student learning from outside observers to provide that more complete picture. Also, pre-/post- tools in international education practice seem to be used more for program evaluation and are not as often used to provide feedback to students for their continued learning and development, which is one of the main reasons for assessment. See chapters 3 through 7 for more on this topic.

8. WHY IS IT IMPORTANT TO USE A MULTI-METHOD APPROACH?

As discussed in chapters 6 and 7 of this book, a multi-method approach of both direct and indirect methods is key in providing a more comprehensive picture of student learning, especially with the complex outcomes found in international education. If only one method is used, insufficient information is collected. Furthermore, with complex goals like intercultural competence, evidence must also come from others' perspectives as to the appropriateness of the communication and behavior (see appendix B and Deardorff [2009] for more on this). Through the collection of multiple sources of information, a more complete and accurate picture emerges, resulting in triangulation (see chapter 1 for definitions).

9. WE HAVE ALL THIS ASSESSMENT DATA. NOW WHAT DO WE DO WITH IT?

You need to go back to your stated goals and learning objectives and map the data to those objectives. Given that the data have already been collected without an assessment plan, it's quite possible that you may not be able to use some of the data, which results in wasted resources and efforts. The data must align with stated goals and objectives in order for there to be any utility. Collecting data and then trying to make sense of it is not helpful—a bit like collecting random information and trying to discern patterns without a clear idea of the goal or topic. See chapter 7 for developing an assessment plan. It's not too late to develop such a plan to put a road map in place moving forward.

10. WHY DO WE NEED AN ASSESSMENT PLAN FROM THE OUTSET?

An assessment plan, especially for international education programs, provides a road map for all of the important questions of *who, what, when, where, how,* and especially *why.* An assessment plan ensures not only alignment with goals and learning objectives but also that any information collected will be used. Having such a plan is important; see chapter 7 on how to create it. In the end, investing adequate time in the beginning in developing an assessment plan helps ensure the most effective and efficient use of time, money, and resources, as well as more rigorous, quality assessment efforts that yield desired information. (Even in courses, a professor's syllabus often includes specific details as to how students will be assessed.)

11. I'VE INHERITED AN INTERNATIONAL EDUCATION PROGRAM WHERE ASSESSMENT IS AN AFTERTHOUGHT AND NO ASSESSMENT PLAN EXISTS. WHAT SHOULD I DO?

While engaging in assessment when it's an afterthought is certainly more challenging, developing an assessment plan is still the best approach. Some assessment efforts may not be possible to implement initially if the program is already in place, but hopefully, in subsequent iterations, such assessment will be possible, especially once a plan outlines what is needed and why. See appendix A for some worksheets you can use to help guide your efforts.

12. WHAT ARE SOME BEST PRACTICES OF OUTCOMES ASSESSMENT IN INTERNATIONAL EDUCATION?

International education has so recently come to outcomes assessment (see chapter 1) that there are few best practices to date. There are some examples of assessment practice—some even good practice examples (see appendix F). However, in any examples given, including in conference presentations or publications, the reader needs to examine practices to ensure that they are following principles of good assessment (see chapter 4 and also appendix D). Not all examples shared should be necessarily emulated since they may not follow the principles of good assessment that have existed for over 20 years in the field. The international education field still has a lot of work to do in terms of outcomes assessment (see chapter 10).

13. CAN'T JUST ONE PERSON DO THE ASSESSMENT?

Given the complexities of international education outcomes, identifying all stake-holders (see p. 10) involved is very important, as is putting together an assessment team of stakeholders, including experts—and students!—when possible. Generally, international education outcomes assessment is more than what one person alone can do, unless in a course; however, one person can help coordinate efforts among the assessment team, once identified and in place. For more on this approach, see chapters 6 and 7. The good news is that international education offices (especially study-abroad offices) are more frequently hiring an assessment coordinator to facilitate these efforts and to work with others at an institution to implement outcomes assessment.

14. IT SOUNDS LIKE FACULTY PLAY A KEY ROLE IN ASSESSMENT EFFORTS. HOW CAN WE DEAL WITH FACULTY RESISTANCE?

Yes, faculty do indeed play a key role in assessment efforts since they are often the ones with the most access to direct evidence of student learning. In terms of addressing faculty resistance to assessment, it's important to do several things:

- Work with faculty in utilizing and adapting what they're already doing regarding assessment (e.g., through course assignments), so that assessment is not viewed as an add-on or extra work.
- Seek to understand what would make this assessment most relevant to faculty. What are their needs?
- Be transparent and clear about how assessment information will be used (that is, for improving student learning, and *not* to evaluate faculty effectiveness). Start by identifying champions and allies among the faculty who understand the importance of assessment for student learning and build out from there. It is definitely a team effort!

15. HOW DO WE GET STUDENT BUY-IN TO ASSESSMENT?

Involve students from the outset! Find out from students what their needs are, why they would feel assessment is important, what would make assessment meaningful, and so on. For example, you can use focus groups, student advisory groups on assessment, and student representatives on assessment teams. International educators may also want to consider using assessment tools such as student learning contracts (see appendix E for a template), which actively involve students in their own assessment. Be sure to coordinate with others across the institution so that assessment efforts are more holistic and not ad hoc, and certainly so that such efforts are not redundant.

16. WHAT ARE SOME PITFALLS TO AVOID WHEN ENGAGING IN OUTCOMES ASSESSMENT?

Chapter 8 covers numerous pitfalls to avoid in outcomes assessment, along with some lessons learned. The biggest pitfall is not having clearly stated goals and objectives, given that all assessment efforts flow from them.

17. HOW CAN WE ASSESS INTERCULTURAL COMPETENCE?

Assessing intercultural competence involves more than using one instrument. First, define *intercultural competence* (ICC) based on the literature and within your context. Then prioritize ICC elements based on goals; translate those prioritized elements into stated objectives; and use those objective statements to determine indicators, assessment tools, and methods. Given the complexity of ICC, a multi-method, multi-perspective assessment approach must be used. For more detail, see appendix B.

18. WHAT ABOUT ASSESSING LANGUAGE IN INTERNATIONAL EDUCATION?

Assessing students' language ability can indeed be an important outcome to assess within international education. Language assessments are quite well-developed and often focus on knowledge as well as performance. Books about assessing language ability include Cohen's *Assessing Language Ability in the Classroom* and Hughes's *Testing for Language Teachers*. Because such resources already exist, this volume focuses primarily on how to approach and prepare for assessing other nonlanguage outcomes of international education, such as intercultural competence (see appendix B), which is also critical to assess in language classrooms. For more on languages within international education, see *Languages in a Global World: Learning for Better Cultural Understanding*, edited by Della Chiesa, Scott, and Hinton (2012).

19. WHY DOES VALIDITY MATTER?

Both reliability and validity matter when it comes to assessment measures and tools. In some ways, validity matters even more. Many indicators of validity are available (see chapter 8), and when a measure purports to be valid, you need to ask the developer for more details about how that validity was determined. (If you don't feel like you understand sufficiently, ask an assessment colleague for assistance.) Further, if a measure—even a valid measure—is not aligned with your stated objectives, then the measure is *not valid in that particular context*. So, alignment of goals and objectives with the selected measure(s) becomes absolutely crucial in order to be valid in your context. *Caution*: Do not use a tool and what it measures to change and restate an objective for the sole purpose of aligning the two. This then becomes a matter of ethics. (See chapter 3 for more.)

20. WHAT IS THE DIFFERENCE BETWEEN OBJECTIVES, OUTCOMES, AND GOALS?

Even in the assessment field, a variety of terms discuss assessment efforts, and the discussion can get confusing. Regardless of the terms employed, use them consistently within your context. Generally, a *goal* is a broader, nonmeasurable statement of where you hope participants will be (e.g., "develop global citizens"), which then must be broken down into more concrete, measurable steps (stepping-stones, if you will) to reach that goal. Those objectives are sometimes are referred to as *outcomes*. See chapter 1 for more on terminology, and pages 45–47 and chapters 6 and 7 for more concrete how-tos. Here is a brief example:

> *Goal:* Develop interculturally competent students

> *Objective (outcome):* By the end of this course, students will be able to articulate the issue of global climate change from three different cultural perspectives.

21. HOW DO OBJECTIVES ACHIEVE GOALS?

Objectives are the measurable, concrete steps that move learners closer to the broader goals—the destination. Since goals are often too broad to measure (yet they still set the direction of the course or program), the objectives further define the goals. There can be different sets of objectives toward the same goals; much depends on the specific context of learning. See chapter 5 for further discussion.

22. HOW DO WE KNOW IF OUR OBJECTIVES ACTUALLY ALIGN WITH OUR GOALS?

Aligning objectives to goals is crucial in assessment to ensure valid assessment results. How do you know if they're aligned? Work with content experts to map not only objectives to the goals but also the learning interventions and the assessment tools.

You can then also bring in external experts to gauge alignment of learning objectives to goals. For more, see chapter 7.

23. HOW WILL WE KNOW IF THE EVIDENCE WE'RE COLLECTING ALIGNS WITH OUR GOALS AND OBJECTIVES?

An assessment plan is quite useful in mapping alignment between goals, objectives, learning interventions, and evidence collected. Having assessment experts as well as content experts (in this case, international educators) regularly review the assessment plan helps ensure that collected evidence demonstrates achievement of stated objectives.

24. WHAT'S THE DIFFERENCE BETWEEN RESEARCH AND ASSESSMENT?

This question goes back to the issue of *why* (see chapter 1). Research is typically done for the purpose of testing a hypothesis or adding to the theoretical base of knowledge, while assessment is ultimately intended to improve student learning. The biggest difference between research and assessment, then, is in the initial question that is explored. Research requires a specific focused question or questions you are hoping to answer, and you'll align your research methodologies with the research question(s). (For example, research studies usually use a control group, whereas assessment may involve the collection of baseline data only, with no control group.) In learning outcomes assessment, you are assessing the degree of change in learners' knowledge, skills, attitudes, or awareness, and usually within an institution or course. It is sometimes possible for the two to be the same (which is known as *action research*), but not always. Note that if individuals at higher education institutions (at least within a U.S. context) are conducting research of any kind involving humans, the researchers first need to apply for and receive Institutional Review Board (IRB) approval through their institution before continuing with their work.

25. IS PUBLISHING ASSESSMENT RESULTS POSSIBLE?

While assessment studies can be published in journals, rigorous research studies are more likely to be published, depending on alignment with a journal's purpose, mission, and focus. Of course, there are other ways to publish results aside from journals, including practitioner-oriented publications and university publications, and through social media outlets. Regardless, communicating assessment results with relevant stakeholders is extremely important (see Bolen, 2007).

26. WHAT'S THE DIFFERENCE BETWEEN ASSESSMENT AND EVALUATION?

While assessment is the systematic process of collecting, analyzing, and using information from multiple sources about student learning, evaluation is the systematic process of collecting, analyzing, and using information from multiple sources to inform decisions about a program, course, or project (Rossi, Lipsey, & Freeman, 2004; Chen, 2005; Jason, 2008; Knowlton & Phillips, 2013). Assessment information can be aggregated to the program level (see question 27) and also used to make decisions about a program. In the end, evaluation helps provide vital information about what works and what does not—which is different from assessment, which provides feedback to students on their own learning.

27. HOW CAN STUDENT LEARNING ASSESSMENT BE USED TO IMPROVE PROGRAMS?

While student learning assessments' focus is at the individual level, the information collected from students through courses or programs can be aggregated at the course, program, or even departmental level—through coding and categorizing qualitative information—so that patterns and themes in student learning outcomes can be identified and reported, based on meta-goals. (Through this process, you can quantify the qualitative information and report on percentages and trends that emerge through this aggregation.) Based on these patterns, decisions can emerge on implementing changes to improve courses and programs. Ultimately, individual student learning assessment is useful for individual student feedback as well as helping improve overall courses and programs.

28. WHEN SHOULD ASSESSMENT BE DONE?

Ideally, a needs assessment would occur in the beginning of (or even before) a program or course to determine learners' needs, how much they already know, and what they want to learn within the context of the course or program (see appendix E for a tool you can use). Then, pre-measures can be given, information can be collected *throughout* the course or program, and post-measures can also be administered, so that assessment is actually done *throughout* a course or program and includes both formative and summative assessment, as well as direct and indirect evidence (see chapter 1 for definitions). Depending on goals and objectives, longitudinal assessment would also be addressed, especially since it's often difficult for students to articulate precisely what they learned immediately after a transformational international education experience.

29. THIS WHOLE PROCESS STILL SEEMS TOO COMPLICATED. WHAT'S THE EASY WAY? WHERE CAN WE START?

Assessment is indeed hard work and takes time, resources, flexibility, and patience. However, if you seek the easy way out (e.g., using just one pre-/post- measure—see question 7), your efforts may be in vain since using one measure only would be insufficient for assessment and potentially end up wasting the time and resources invested, especially if the tool is not closely aligned to your stated learning objective(s). (Remember, misalignment means invalid results!) Make sure you're effective in your assessment efforts by setting the groundwork through ensuring the articulation of the right goals, clearly stated objectives, and an assessment plan. As assessment experts observe,

> While the time, effort, and resources required to engage in effective outcomes-based assessment may seem daunting to already overtaxed higher education professionals, it is nevertheless important that . . . professionals become well-versed in the assessment of student learning to ensure that the true value of co-curricular experience is not lost or misunderstood by external stakeholders, particularly in a time where available resources are growing even scarcer. (Bresciani et al., 2009, pp. 12–13)

Reframe your thinking about assessment—from "What's the easy way to assess?" to "How can we best support our students in their learning, both in and out of the classroom?"—thus recognizing assessment as a powerful tool for student learning that must be built into all of what we do, not as an add-on or a pre-/post- exercise done primarily for program evaluation. See chapters 1 through 8 for more. By focusing on student learning we are, in fact, also focusing on program improvement (see question 27).

In terms of getting started, certainly you can start with collecting numbers (see chapters 5 and 6), but it's important to then put together a team and follow the other steps outlined in this book so that you can begin assessing the meaningful outcomes of international education, beyond the numbers. Don't try to assess too much at once (see chapter 8 on pitfalls), and examine how current efforts can be adapted and tweaked to collect the evidence needed to demonstrate achievement of the stated learning objectives. In that way, the process is not necessarily about finding assessment tools. Start with what's currently being done in assessing student learning. In other words, ask: What are academics and administrators already collecting in terms of evidence that would help indicate achievement of student learning outcomes? And what methods and assessment measures can be adapted to collect such evidence of learning?

30. I STILL HAVE SO MANY QUESTIONS. WHERE SHOULD I GO FOR ANSWERS?

Given the complexities around outcomes assessment, readers will surely have many more questions than those listed here. There exists a wealth of assessment literature that contains many of the answers to other questions. See appendix G for some of the key resources available that can help answer further questions you may have. You may also want to consult with assessment experts at your institution or in the assessment and international education fields.

CHAPTER 3

The Unique Assessment Context of International Education

Given the unique context of international education, it is helpful to gain an overview of the nature of international education, including five aspects that affect assessment efforts in this field. *International education* broadly refers to efforts that address the integration of international, intercultural, or global dimensions into education—more specifically, postsecondary education. Within international education, the predominantly used term *internationalization* is defined by Knight (2004) as the *process* of integrating these dimensions "into the purpose, functions or delivery of post-secondary education" (p. 11).

Why internationalize? The numerous rationales for international education include academic (e.g., student learning, research), economic (e.g., revenue generation, labor market), political (e.g., foreign policy, national security), and social (e.g., citizenship development, intercultural understanding). A 2014 survey of the International Association of Universities (IAU) found that the top rationales for universities to internationalize were related to human resource development and academics. Stepping back to examine why an institution or program wishes to internationalize is important because of its effect on the assessment process. If the main rationale is economic, for example, then the emphasis on student learning outcomes could be misaligned with the overall purpose. An emphasis on economic rationales would point to the collection of economic data to determine whether economic outcomes were achieved. Given the increased focus worldwide on student learning as part of the trend toward greater accountability, this book focuses on the academic and social rationales for international education. (For more on rationales, see Knight, 2012. For more on the topics discussed here, see Deardorff, de Wit, Heyl, & Adams, 2012.)

Internationalization efforts have been broadly characterized as "cross-border" (involving mobility) and "at home," discussed further in the following sections.

CROSS-BORDER EFFORTS

Cross-border efforts primarily refer to mobility—of people, programs, providers, and projects, including efforts such as branch campuses, development projects, and so on. (For more, see the work of Philip Altbach, Jane Knight, and Hans de Wit.) In terms of assessment, much work has already been done in assessing outcomes of study-abroad programs, efforts that typically involve pre- and post-assessments, along with a program satisfaction survey, all of which are insufficient for assessing learning outcomes. Recently, though, an increasing number of education-abroad programs are more intentionally addressing intercultural learning and incorporating assessment throughout the program (Vande Berg & Paige, 2009). Beyond the typical pre-/post- surveys, other more integrated assessment efforts may include a self-perspective inventory, along with direct evidence of student learning such as critical reflection papers, others' observations of students' interactions, and final projects. Given that education-abroad programs, from traditional study-abroad programs to internships and volunteer programs, are more experiential and nonformal in this context, assessment should go beyond traditional efforts when possible to include authentic, performance-based methods.

AT-HOME EFFORTS: WITHIN THE INSTITUTION

Given the small percentage of students who study overseas, institutions need to examine ways in which curricula, co-curricular, and extracurricular opportunities can be assessed in terms of international education outcomes: What international and intercultural learning occurs for *all* students? Such opportunities include meaningful interactions with international students and scholars, international faculty, and service-learning opportunities in the community. Collectively these efforts are referred to as "internationalization at home" (Nilsson, 2003) or "comprehensive internationalization" (Green & Olson, 2008; Hudzik, 2012).

Curricular assessment is arguably at the heart of international education assessment. This book details much of the formal assessment efforts that can occur through courses, starting with the statement of learning goals and objectives. Instructors become key in assessing student learning that occurs throughout a course, and can implement formative and summative assessment measures, as well as methods for collecting direct and indirect evidence (see chapters 5–7 for more). Members of academic departments and programs should engage in reflection and collaboration around questions such as: What intercultural skills and knowledge are needed in this major? How does globalization affect this major, and what global learning should be required of graduates of this major? How can departmental and course assessments of students' intercultural competence go beyond one aspect, such as knowledge or language, to ensure that students have actually attained a degree of intercultural competence, and what evidence will show this? How can students be prepared through the curriculum to comprehend the multitude of countries and cultures that may affect their lives and careers? How are students being taught to think interculturally (see Bok, 2006)? More broadly, what knowledge, skills, and attitudes do students need to be successful in the 21st century? These questions are not only the purview of language, general education, and international studies courses but are cross-cutting throughout courses within higher education institutions, from chemistry to engineering to music, to physical education, to sociology, and so on.

One trend that combines both formal and informal learning in the curriculum is service learning, which involves application of in-course concepts in the local community through volunteering within a course context. (For more on assessment in service learning settings, see Camacho, 2004; Fitch, 2004, 2005; Kiely, 2004; Merrill & Pusch, 2007; Parker & Dautoff, 2007; Slimbach,1996; Urraca, Ledoux, & Harris, 2009).

Co-curricular and *extracurricular* efforts occur outside the formal classroom and can be useful in developing more holistic learning for students and can contribute to the achievement of specific learning outcomes within international education. Co-curricular efforts contributing to such outcomes include guest speakers, seminars, and intercultural training. Extracurricular activities include student clubs and campus events celebrating or highlighting different cultural traditions (such as India Night, musical concerts, or a foreign film series) that bring students from different backgrounds together in meaningful ways (such as mentor programs, conversational partner programs, community volunteer projects, etc.), as well as residential programming.

Bok (2006) notes, "The best way for undergraduates to learn from one another is not through taking classes but in the dorm room discussions, mealtime conversations, and other group activities" on campus (p. 248). However, intercultural learning unfortunately does not just happen because persons from different backgrounds are in each other's vicinity or are even interacting with each other (Allport, 1954). The contact hypothesis theory (Allport, 1954) provides a helpful foundation upon which to implement intercultural experiences successfully. "Contact theory . . . was introduced and developed by social psychologists to examine and evaluate the various conditions under which face-to-face contact would promote greater personal and social understanding between members of different ethnic and racial groups" (Erickson & O'Connor, 2000, p. 63). Those conditions for optimal learning interactions include common goals, intergroup cooperation, equal status of those in the interaction, and mutual support for rules, laws, customs, and authorities.

In assessing the results of outside-the-classroom activities and programming, one must recognize the limits of learning that can occur unless sufficient parameters are in place or, at a minimum, be realistic about the outcomes that can be achieved through nonformal experiences. Nonetheless, given the "value added" of co-curricular and extracurricular programs in terms of the international education context, assessing the outcomes from such programming is important. Such assessment is understandably more complicated given the informal nature and context of the learning that occurs. Appendix F contains some examples of informal assessment.

WHO'S INVOLVED IN INTERNATIONAL EDUCATION?

Given that international education includes many different facets—from study abroad to courses—many different offices and persons are involved in programs that impact student learning in this area. First and foremost are the students themselves—domestic and international students, undergraduates and graduate students. When talking about international education outcomes assessment, we should be thinking about *all* students and *including* them as the key stakeholders. Too often, the focus has been primarily on undergraduate domestic students. Faculty are core to international education, and some, such as language faculty, are even involved in leading study-abroad programs for students. Other faculty, particularly those engaged in research, may be involved in international projects, too.

Beyond faculty, many administrators and professional staff are involved in international education offices. Most higher education institutions have at least one person or office in charge of student mobility, often known as study abroad, international exchange, or global education abroad. Within such an office, the trend is to hire someone with expertise in assessment to coordinate assessment efforts. In U.S. institutions, other individuals or an office are tasked with ensuring institutional and student compliance regarding immigration policies and regulations. Staff are also involved in recruiting and enrolling international and exchange students, and others administer and teach in language programs for international students (such as English as a Second Language).

Increasingly, higher education institutions have senior administrators (known generally as senior international officers or, in Europe, international relations managers) or an office tasked with internationalizing the institution overall, addressing many of these different aspects of international education. Chapter 9 presents information for individuals leading international efforts at their institutions, who face increasing interest and pressure regarding learning outcomes assessment.

The actual structure and titles of these university offices and positions in international education vary widely by institution, with some being more centralized and others more decentralized, meaning that they may report to different units. For example, some international education offices may be housed in student affairs, while others are under academic affairs. Communication within and beyond international education offices becomes crucial, especially in regard to assessment.

Many other people at a higher education institution are involved with and support international education efforts—from those in housing, religious life, and dining to financial services, transportation, student life, the registrar, and beyond. International education touches so many facets of the institution that people closely involved in international education need to partner with others both at the institution and in the local community to create and facilitate meaningful learning experiences. A key part of this facilitation is supporting and providing professional development opportunities for all members of a higher education institution to enhance their intercultural skills (see appendix B).

WHAT'S UNIQUE ABOUT INTERNATIONAL EDUCATION AND ASSESSMENT?

Much of this book highlights basic assessment principles and concepts that can be used in any educational setting, including contexts inside and outside the classroom (formal and nonformal, respectively). However, in assessing outcomes within international education learning experiences, it's important to ask: What's unique about assessing outcomes in international education? International education is about so much more than simply sending students abroad. It's about the learning that occurs from cross-border as well as on-campus experiences. Given that many of the outcomes in international education, such as those related to intercultural competence and global citizenship, are considered more complex in nature, this chapter outlines eight aspects that are important for international educators and assessment experts to understand when assessing learning outcomes in this field. (See also appendix C for a published article on this topic.) These aspects make international education unique and apply to any international education context:

1. Going beyond knowledge
2. Experiential learning
3. Critical reflection
4. Complex outcomes
5. The developmental and lifelong nature of the learning
6. The importance of intentional learning interventions
7. The involvement of interactive elements
8. A more holistic perspective

Beyond these aspects, specific ethical considerations that should be taken into account are highlighted at the end of this chapter.

More Than Knowledge

Higher education, over its long history, has primarily been concerned with knowledge transmission and creation. Within international education, the focus is not only on knowledge acquisition but also on knowledge application through performance. It's not enough for student to engage cognitively in an international experience. More traditional assessment measures—survey instruments, blogs, journals, and papers—are insufficient in capturing the performance and behavioral goals (e.g., communication goals) that are often part of international education courses and programs. Further, traditional assessment measures are suited to particular learning styles, while more authentic assessments (e.g., project-based, visual arts, performing arts) could be a better fit for more visual, concrete learners. Moreover, in numerous employer surveys in recent years (British Council, 2013; House, Dorfman, Javidan, Hanges, & Sully de Luque, 2014; House, Hanges, Javidan, Dorfman, & Gupta, 2004), authentic *skills*, such as communication, adaptability, and teamwork, are often cited as extremely important in the hiring process (Kyllonen, 2013). In fact, one recent study by economists showed that "cognitive skills accounted for only 20 percent of the educational-attainment efforts on labor-market outcomes such as higher employment and wages" (Levin, 2012). Given the more experiential nature of learning in international education, performance-based approaches become incredibly relevant, with outcomes focused on some of the authentic skills that employers value—such as teamwork and successful communication across different backgrounds and cultures. The implication is that assessment should focus more on real-world contexts and include performance-based methods such as observation and 360-degree assessment (i.e., assessments from others on the team or in the interaction). Institutions and organizations ultimately need to ask themselves what students should not only know but be able *to do* as a result of international education experiences. Focusing on outcomes beyond knowledge and using relevant, authentic assessments, such as performance-based assessments, can add value to assessment efforts.

Experiential

While international education occurs both within and beyond the classroom, international education can broadly be characterized as falling under experiential learning, where the learning occurs through hands-on experiences. Obviously in study-abroad programs, and even in the "at-home" context, such hands-on experiences are crucial to learning—whether through interactions with those from different backgrounds (e.g., international students), through service learning in the community, or through role plays or classroom simulations. The experiential nature of the learning means that assessment can be more performance-based, such as through observation.

Reflective

Given the experiential nature of international education, the participants' critical reflection on their hands-on experience plays a key role in processing the learning that occurs. Critical reflection goes beyond the *what* of what was learned to include the *so what*—why was that learning important?—and the *now what*—what actions will be undertaken because of that learning? (For more on critical reflection, see Kiely, 2004.) With awareness being an oft-cited outcome in international education, critical reflection can lead to the realization of how much more one needs to learn about the other—and self—which can often impact self-report measures. If self-report instruments (depending on what is actually measured) are administered as a pre-/post- tool, the post results could potentially be lower as a result of this heightened awareness, which emphasizes the importance of using direct and indirect measures (see chapters 6 and 7) to provide a more complete understanding of the learning.

Complex

Learning outcomes in international education tend to be more complex and include *intercultural competence* and *global citizenship*, terms rarely defined in the institutional context; and if they are defined, they are not typically grounded in the literature and research (de Wit, 2009; Lewin, 2009; Penn, 2011; Deardorff, 2011). Definitions grounded in the literature are imperative because educators need to know exactly what is being assessed before they can engage in assessment. The focus of international education outcomes needs to move from what is easy to measure (e.g., numbers of participants) to what is meaningful to measure, outcomes that are often more transformational. According to Kiely (2004), citing Mezirow, "The main goal of transformational learning is for learners to develop more valid meaning perspectives for interpreting experience and guiding action" (p. 7), with long-term outcomes potentially resulting in a change in lifestyle habits, increased ability to question and resist cultural norms, and engagement in social action. (For more on measuring intercultural competence, see appendix B; for examples of how some of these complex outcomes are being assessed, see appendix F.)

Developmental and Lifelong

One unique aspect of international education is the developmental nature of the learning (see M. Bennett, 1993; Kegan, 1994; King & Baxter Magolda, 2005; Perry, 1970). This developmental nature has numerous implications for assessment.

First, students are at different stages developmentally, especially given increasing numbers of "nontraditional" students, so any assessment needs to take this fact into account. Understanding the students—especially their needs, perspectives, backgrounds, and developmental stage—is crucial in assessment efforts; a "one-size-fits-all" assessment or intervention is not going to be as effective. Tailored student feedback, ideally through coaching, will become more important in helping students' personal and intellectual development. Second, lifelong learning is increasingly becoming a key theme running through international education outcomes. Thus, the limitations of assessments need to be acknowledged—particularly in regard to outcomes around intercultural competence, which is a lifelong process, meaning that there is not a point at which one becomes interculturally competent, as some assessment tools purport to measure. (For more, see appendix B.) Moreover, international education outcomes may need to be more process-oriented and practice-focused, concentrating on developmental aspects and applied real-life contexts, than results- or achievement-focused. Assessments need to incorporate longitudinal elements to gain a picture of what happens over time.

Intentional

A fundamental aspect of international education courses and programs is the adequate preparation of students in intercultural learning so that they are better able to articulate the learning that occurs, beyond a vague notion of "It changed my life." Such adequate preparation means providing students with an understanding of intercultural and global frameworks, vocabulary, and concepts so that they can apply them to the learning that occurs before, during, and after the experience. Instructors must have adequate intercultural knowledge and competency as well. Intentional interventions include prerequisite foundational work relevant to learners' needs (through readings, videos, discussions, simulations, etc.) combined with critical reflection on one's identity development and so on. Key intercultural theories should be covered and applied, if appropriate, providing learners with frameworks, concepts, and vocabulary to apply to real-life and hands-on experiences. Keep in mind that teaching these foundational pieces requires more than international experience alone; instructors also need a background in intercultural theories. Further, adequate preparation needs to go beyond a one-time training or course and be interwoven throughout a learner's educational experience. (See R. Bennett, 2009; Deardorff, 2009; Vande Berg, Paige, & Lou, 2012, for more.)

Interactional

Many international education outcomes ultimately have a practical application of preparing learners to engage in interactions with others, whether in social relationships or the workplace. This interaction aspect involves communication, which is seldom actually assessed, and can occur in face-to-face settings as well as virtually. In fact, other cultural perspectives on possible intercultural outcomes are often more relational in nature (see Deardorff, 2009). Moving forward, assessment may need to include these interactional outcomes, which would be more performance-based in nature and involve authentic assessment when possible.

Holistic

International education outcomes—such as intercultural competence and global learning—are often parsed out as separate from other key areas of learning and development even within international education. However, in reality, international education outcomes are more than the ones generated through global learning but rather encompass the range of educational outcomes that need to be integrated more holistically, including emotional intelligence, personal development, critical thinking, academic outcomes, language outcomes, career development, and so on. (Much has been written separately about each of these topics, and you are encouraged to delve further into the literature on these various outcomes and to think about how they relate to international education.) Such a holistic approach, of course, has implications for many international education outcomes assessments—particularly those in education abroad—that have, up to this point, often occurred in isolation.

* * *

This list of eight unique characteristics can also serve as a checklist of sorts that assessment experts can use in guiding further development of appropriate goals, learning objectives, and assessment measures.

OTHER CONSIDERATIONS FOR INTERNATIONAL EDUCATION ASSESSMENT

Impact on Community

Beyond the learning outcomes, what are other possible outcomes and considerations? Assessment can include other types of outcomes, such as for host families, parents, instructors, community organizations, the campus climate, and so on. While such assessment may be beyond the scope of a program or course, the impact on other stakeholders beyond the learners is an important consideration, since others are being affected—either positively or negatively—by interactions generated through international education. One example of such outcomes assessment is a current study at the University of Coventry that is working on developing an index of social integration.

As mentioned earlier, simply bringing people together does not necessarily result in positive and desired outcomes, which leads to further questions that need to be explored in the process of outcomes assessment (Allport, 1954; Putnam, 2007).

Ethical Considerations

Ethical considerations unique to international education that should be taken into account throughout assessment efforts include the following:

- *Adequate preparation* (discussed already in this chapter). What are the ethical responsibilities of supporting learners in achieving intercultural outcomes? How have learners been prepared for their international education experiences? This kind of preparation, or lack thereof, impacts assessment results.

- *Power dynamics.* In international education, a huge emphasis is placed on partnerships, yet within the partnerships and mobility of students, staff, and faculty, power dynamics inevitably arise. Underresourced partners may not be able to assess in the same ways, for example. Thus, universities with more resources may assume an advantage in dictating what can be done or in assessing only their own constituencies. How will these power imbalances, often based on access to resources, be addressed in assessment? How will *all* learners be given access to the learning that can occur through assessment, especially feedback on assessment results?

- *Intercultural competence/sensitivity.* What are the cultural aspects at play in assessment? Are cultural considerations taken into account? For example, if assessments are focused on the individual, what are the implications for learners coming from a more "we," or collective, culture? How will this impact results? Do instructors exhibit intercultural competence as they work with learners? How does this affect assessment? To what extent should intercultural aspects be taken into consideration?

- *Knowledge.* For the last several centuries, knowledge has been dominated by so-called Western knowledge. In international education, we need to question assumptions around knowledge, especially if it is tested. Whose knowledge? Have other forms and sources of knowledge been taken into consideration? Are all sources of knowledge valued equally? What is still not known? In assessing multiple sources of knowledge, what's beyond "the West" is an important ethical consideration.

- *Perspective/bias.* Throughout any assessment in international education, the perennial questions can be asked: According to whom? Who is setting the standards and benchmarks? Who is defining the terms? What is the impact of the perspective and cultural bias of the assessment tool or method? It is crucial to acknowledge and address the perspectives and bias in any assessments being used.

CONCLUSION

Assessment experts must understand that assessing international education outcomes is quite a bit more complex than assessing other learning outcomes, given the more experiential nature of the learning (which leads to performance-based assessment as well as elevating the role of critical reflection), the developmental and lifelong dimensions of intercultural learning, the holistic nature of the learning, the importance of learning interventions, and the complexity of the outcomes themselves. Thus, some of the more traditional means of assessment (such as self-report measures or surveys) may not be as appropriate within the complexity of international education outcomes, as outlined in this chapter. For these reasons, it is very helpful for assessment experts and international educators to partner together in order to form a more robust team with unique expertise in assessing holistic learning outcomes in international education.

Chapter 4

Principles for Effective Assessment in International Education

One frequently raised question in the field of international education revolves around whether the same assessment tools could be used by many programs since international education and intercultural efforts generally have similar goals and even missions. While this way of thinking seems plausible, not all programs are identical. No "silver bullet" or perfect measure is available as an assessment tool in international education. In fact, each program, course, department, institution, and organization is unique in terms of priorities; they all have specific goals and concrete, measurable objectives unique to their context. No "one-size-fits-all" assessment approach is adequate for measuring intended outcomes. Rather than pursuing the one best assessment tool or standardized tests to use across the board, a more useful approach is exploring principles of effective assessment that can serve as a foundation—even a checklist—for intercultural assessment efforts. Since there are different ways to approach assessment, underlying principles become all the more valuable in ensuring quality results.

This chapter provides an overview of some classic assessment principles and hallmarks as well as an outline of some of those key assessment principles. These principles are not only based on lessons learned within international education assessment but also based in the assessment literature and applications to intercultural and international education assessment efforts. Such principles help move beyond a *measuring-what's-easy* approach, which may not yield meaningful results, to *measuring what matters* as aligned with goals and objectives. These principles also help move beyond the pressure from within international education to standardize assessment in the field, which would be a disservice to the unique strengths of international education.

One of the classic lists of assessment principles is the 1992 American Association of Higher Education (AAHE)'s nine "Principles of Good Practice for Assessing Student Learning":

1. The assessment of student learning begins with educational values.
2. Assessment is most effective when it reflects an understanding of learning as multidimensional, integrated, and revealed in performance over time.

3. Assessment works best when the programs it seeks to improve have clear, explicitly stated purposes.
4. Assessment requires attention to outcomes but also and equally to the experiences that lead to those outcomes.
5. Assessment works best when it is ongoing, not episodic.
6. Assessment fosters wide improvement when representatives from across the educational community are involved.
7. Assessment makes a difference when it begins with issues of use and illuminates questions that people really care about.
8. Assessment is most likely to lead to improvement when it is part of a larger set of conditions that promote change.
9. Through assessment, educators meet responsibilities to students and to the public. (Gardiner, Anderson, & Cambridge, 1997, pp. 11–12)

As these principles are applied to international education, outcomes are emphasized, within the context of experiences that lead to those outcomes. These principles also raise the following questions: Are student learning outcomes in international education grounded in educational values? Is there an understanding of multidimensional learning? Is assessment ongoing, or is it done only at the beginning and end of a program, as is the case frequently in international education?

Another principle within this list that is quite relevant is the need for internationalization efforts to have clear, explicitly stated purposes (see chapter 1 for a discussion on why to assess). In addition, these principles also raise other issues for administrators of internationalization strategies, such as the importance of involving many members of the academic community in the ongoing assessment of student outcomes and experiences as well as viewing assessment as one piece of a larger picture ("larger set of conditions that promotes change"). To that end, how are our institutions being changed by international education? Assessment use and relevancy are also emphasized in these principles, meaning that international educators need to begin assessment efforts with use in mind: How will results be used? This approach can ensure the ongoing relevancy of outcomes assessment efforts in international education, as well as exploration of the pivotal question of *why* to engage in assessment (see chapter 1). These principles also suggest to administrators that effective assessment of students' intercultural, global, and international learning outcomes should take the form of observing students' performance over time as part of an integrated, multidimensional context; this perspective seems to fit especially well with discussions on the complexity of the concept of intercultural competence and the inadequacy of one single method for assessing competence (see appendix B).

From these broad-based assessment principles, we can delve more specifically into assessment efforts. Assessment expert Trudy Banta (2004) writes about hallmarks of assessment, categorized under planning, implementing, and improving, as paraphrased and summarized here:

HALLMARKS OF EFFECTIVE ASSESSMENT PLANNING

- Involves stakeholders (faculty, administrators, students, student affairs professionals, employers, community representatives) from the outset.
- Begins when the need is recognized and allow sufficient time for development.
- Has a written plan with clear purposes related to goals that people value.
- Bases assessment approaches on clearly stated objectives.

HALLMARKS OF EFFECTIVE ASSESSMENT IMPLEMENTATION

- Has knowledgeable, effective leadership.
- Recognizes assessment as essential to learning (and therefore is everyone's responsibility).
- Includes faculty and staff development in assessment.
- Devolves responsibility for assessment to the unit level.
- Recognizes learning as multidimensional and developmental and thus uses multiple measures, maximizing reliability and validity.
- Assesses processes as well as outcomes.

HALLMARKS OF EFFECTIVE IMPROVEMENT AND SUSTAINABILITY

- Produces credible evidence of learning.
- Is undertaken in an environment that is receptive, supportive, and enabling.
- Incorporates continuous communication with constituents.
- Produces data that guides improvement on a continuing basis.
- Demonstrates accountability to stakeholders within and outside the institution.
- Maintains expectation of ongoing outcomes assessment (not episodic).
- Incorporates ongoing evaluation and improvement of the assessment process itself.

By applying these hallmarks within each of the assessment areas, international educators can benchmark their efforts at each phase of the process.

As you'll see, these principles are interconnected, and readers already familiar with the topic will recognize them as general assessment principles that apply in any context. Here are some of the key principles again, with further elaboration, including action steps (for more on assessment principles, please see Banta & Palomba, 2014). These steps have emerged through the literature as well as through a decade of working with international educators. The steps are crucial in ensuring quality outcomes assessment efforts in international education:

- **Effective assessment requires a clear understanding of the purpose of assessment.**

Action: Understand why it is necessary to engage in assessment, and to go beyond program improvement to focus on the learner.

Assessment involves a lot of time and resources. Engaging in effective assessment means no shortcuts, and measuring only what's easy may result in somewhat useless data or information not aligned with goals and objectives. So, why engage in assessment? This is a key issue to explore before moving further down the assessment route. Who benefits from the information collected? More specifically, how do our students benefit from our assessment efforts, and how do assessments help deepen students' learning and intercultural development? Assessment literature pairs assessment and learning together. Often in international education, the focus of assessment efforts tends to be more on program advocacy and improvement and not so much on the learner. This tendency leads to a predominant focus on pre-/post- surveying of program participants with little focus on *improving* individuals' learning and personal development. Thus, there is little benefit to the learners from the information collected. Understandably, administrators want evidence to show that their programs are effective. However, instead of focusing primarily on improving (or justifying) the program, the *why* can go deeper, to the level of the student—accomplishing both purposes at the same time. Here's how.

Effective assessment efforts can target both program-level assessment (via pre-/post- efforts and aggregated learning outcome data) as well as the individual level (via ongoing, integrating efforts that provide feedback to individuals) by focusing on the learner. Assessment at the individual level can be analyzed for common themes and patterns and aggregated to departmental and institutional levels. Focusing on the learner brings assessment into a different paradigm. In fact, assessment literature often stresses the connection between assessment and student learning; according to one author, the "main purpose of both instruction and assessment is to improve student learning" (Gronlund, 2006, p. 19). In going deeper on the *why* by focusing primarily on the learner (and the benefit to the learner), assessment efforts in the end can also aid in program and course improvement.

- **Effective assessment requires well-defined goals, learning objectives, and terms.**

Action: Clearly articulate goals and learning objectives based on mission/purpose.

Schools or programs embarking on assessment efforts often ask, "Where do we begin?" or "What do we measure?" or even "Which tool should we use?" While these questions seem logical, they are actually not the best ones to ask. Quality assessment begins with a clear mission statement, well-articulated and well-defined goals aligned with that mission, and detailed objectives on how to achieve those goals. As part of this articulation, defining ambiguous terms—*intercultural competence* (see Deardorff, 2009), *global citizenship*, and *global learning*, to name a few—becomes necessary. In order to assess outcomes effectively, any ambiguous terms must be clearly, thoughtfully, and thoroughly defined, preferably based on previous research and scholarship, so that definitions are grounded and valid. This crucial alignment of mission, goals, and objectives will naturally point to which tools and methods are needed to collect evidence that these outcomes have been achieved. For example, a course that has a goal of "developing different perspectives" in learners may have a related objective that states, "By the end of this course, learners will be able to articulate the issue of climate change from three different cultural perspectives," which points to the use of an essay, documentary, or some other assignment that collects direct evidence of a learner's ability to achieve this learning objective. In this case, a survey or inventory would not be as helpful in collecting such evidence. See appendices B and C for more detail, including a research-based framework on defining and assessing intercultural competence as a stated goal. See also Exhibit 4.1 for more detail on articulating goals and learning objectives.

Exhibit 4.1
Developing Learning Objectives and Outcomes

As Green (2012) states, "Because the development of clear and measurable learning outcomes is so central to the assessment process, it is important that the process be credible and take into account the views of many people" (p. 12). She goes on to caution that this process can indeed take a lot of time. In fact, the development of the AAC&U VALUE rubrics (see appendix E) took many months, with faculty from across the United States. The goal usually states a broader result that may not be measurable (as discussed in chapter 5); the goal flows from the mission statement and provides direction for the course or program. The objectives and outcomes, in turn, flow from the stated goal and are measurable because they are more specific in nature. In thinking about outcomes, first explore what changes should occur in the learner by the end of the course, program, or experience. What should the learner know or be able to do as a result of the learning? You can think about this assessment in regard to the initial (short-term) outcomes, as well as the intermediate- and longer-term outcomes. So, within a certain time frame, what change should occur for the learner, and what will be the evidence of this change?

In the case of more complex international education outcomes, these changes in learners can be categorized under *content* (change in knowledge), *practice* (change in skill or ability), or *process* (change in attitude). To articulate these changes, Bloom's taxonomy of learning outcomes (1956; more recently updated by Anderson & Krathwohl, 2001) can be consulted as a classic reference in developing outcome statements. According to the revised taxonomy, the higher-order thinking skills are analyzing, evaluating, and creating, while the more basic-level skills involve remembering, understanding, and applying. (For more on assessing higher-order thinking skills, see Brookhart, 2010.) Well-written outcomes statements often start with an action verb, include a time frame, are relevant, and are realistic within the given parameters. Some action verbs aligned to the levels of learning are as follows:

- Remembering: recognize, list, describe, identify, retrieve, name.
- Understanding: interpret, exemplify, summarize, infer, paraphrase, compare, explain.
- Applying: implement, carry out, use.
- Analyzing: compare, attribute, organize, deconstruct.
- Evaluating: check, critique, judge, hypothesize.
- Creating: design, construct, plan, produce. (Green, 2012, p. 12)

Drafts of stated learning outcomes within international education (see appendices F and G for resources) can be a helpful place to start since such drafts may provide a platform for discussion with stakeholders and then involve editing or tweaking outcomes instead of starting with a blank page. An example of a stated outcome from the Association of American Colleges & Universities includes the following (with the goal in parentheses): "Students can describe a social problem requiring collective remedies that transcend national boundaries." (Goal: To spur greater civic engagement and social responsibility.) One way to assess the achievement of this outcome is to provide students with a writing assignment and then evaluate their descriptions based on a predetermined rubric.

According to Kettner, Moroney, and Martin (2013), a good outcome statement is "clear, specific, measurable, time-limited, and realistic, and represents a commitment" (p. 134). In other words, the SMART format is used: **s**pecific, **m**easurable, **a**chievable, **r**elevant, and **t**ime-based. An example of a SMART outcome is as follows: *First-year students who complete three intercultural skill seminars will be able to identify at least three out of five communication styles in a video of an intercultural team working on a project.* Regarding SMART outcomes, relevancy is key. International educators need to make sure that the stated outcomes are indeed relevant to the learners. The best way to ensure relevancy is to either involve the learners or engage in a needs assessment of the learners *before* developing the outcome statements. Relevancy ensures that what matters gets measured.

Musil (2006) notes that beyond individual course learning goals, there can also be divisional and departmental learning goals and institutional goals, as well as campus life goals and general education goals. The important takeaway is to think through what changes realistically need to occur at each of these levels within certain timeframes (short-term, intermediate, and long-term) in regard to international education outcomes.

- **Effective assessment aligns tools and methods with stated goals and objectives, which requires that a variety of assessment procedures be used.**

Action: Align assessment tools and methods with clearly stated goals and learning objectives.

Effective assessment ensures that assessment tools are aligned with the desired objectives and are not being used merely because another school is using that tool or because the tool is easy or accessible. Too often, institutions or programs seek the one "perfect tool," which simply does not exist. In fact, when assessing something as complex as global learning or intercultural competence development, quality assessment involves the use of a multi-method, multi-perspective approach; use of one instrument points to lack of rigor in assessment and provides a very limited snapshot of what is being accomplished. With complex outcomes, a variety of assessment procedures must be employed to collect the evidence needed to determine if the objectives have been adequately achieved. Furthermore, administrators need to thoroughly explore existing tools in terms of exactly what the tools measure (not just what the tools *say* they measure), the reliability and validity of the tools (see chapters 3 and 4 for more on these concepts), the theoretical basis of the tools, and so on—including how well the tools align with the specific outcomes to be assessed. (See appendix A for a worksheet on selecting assessment measures.) The prioritized outcomes vary by institution and program, so no one-size-fits-all approach applies to assessment tools. Regarding the pre-/post- use of assessment, effective assessment incorporates and integrates assessment on an ongoing basis throughout a program or course, not just snapshots at the beginning and end. In fact, in a well-designed assessment program, assessment activities may be barely distinguishable from the learning activities. For example, a minute paper at the end of a class or intercultural training can capture student insights and burning questions, allowing an instructor to know what the students are learning as well as further questions they have that future class sessions or learning interventions can address. (See appendix E for an example of this and other similar tools.) Furthermore, international educators need to continue to address longitudinal assessment when possible to determine long-term impact, understanding that longitudinal assessment can be quite challenging, given inherent limitations.

- **Effective assessment starts with an assessment plan.**

Action: Develop an assessment plan from the outset.

Another key principle of quality assessment is that efforts need to be holistically developed and documented through a well-designed assessment plan. An assessment plan not only outlines what will be measured and how the information will be collected but also details who will be involved (which needs to be more than one person or office unless this is a course), the timeline, implementation details, and how the information will be used and communicated. This last point is crucial. The collected information must have a use (e.g., student feedback, program improvement, advocacy), or collecting it serves no purpose. In particular, offices should not be collecting information randomly and then trying to determine what to do with it. Spending 10% of the time in the beginning to develop an assessment plan and thinking through these issues is time well invested during the later 90% of the effort that goes into assessment, particularly since a well-designed assessment plan increases the validity of the results. An assessment plan would ideally be developed from the outset, before the program or course is implemented. In this way, assessment is not an afterthought but rather helps inform the program or course design from the beginning. (See chapter 7 for more detail on developing an assessment plan.)

- **Effective assessment involves others in the planning, preparation, implementation, and evaluation of the process.**

Action: Identify and include in the assessment process relevant stakeholders and experts.

Assessment can often seem quite overwhelming, especially if only one person or office is tasked with doing it. Thus, quality assessment involves a team of stakeholders comprising not only international education experts but also assessment experts, students, instructors, and others involved in international education outcomes. Leadership and support play a critical role in the success of assessment efforts (see chapter 9 for more). Once assembled, this team prioritizes outcomes to be assessed, conducts an audit of assessment efforts already under way, and adapts current assessment efforts to align with stated goals and objectives (no need to reinvent assessment efforts!) before seeking additional assessment tools and methods. The initial prioritization of objectives and desired outcomes is very important in ensuring that the assessment plan is feasible and realistic. One pitfall for numerous schools is trying to assess too much at once. (See chapter 8 for more on pitfalls in assessment.)

- **Effective assessment must be transparent in outlining expectations and specifications of criteria for evaluating successful achievement.**

Action: Communicate clearly the expectations and specifications of criteria for evaluating successful achievement, by delineating what specifically constitutes success.

What will learners need to know and be able to do as a result of completing a course, program, or experience? Expectations and ways in which learners will be evaluated should not be ambiguous or defined by judgmental or subjective categories such as "low, moderate, high," which do nothing to *describe* what learners should know and be able to do. Communicate clearly what is expected of students, including level of performance. Degrees of success can be expressed through clear descriptors on rubrics, rating scales, and other measures used to describe student achievement. Establishing specific criteria for more complex outcomes may be difficult; stated goals and objectives might need more attention and refinement to elicit concrete and clear descriptive criteria. It may even be appropriate to involve learners in defining criteria for evaluation, as well as in peer evaluation, depending on the context.

Assessment must not be used to accomplish hidden agendas, and the learners themselves should view the content and experiences as well as the assessments as relevant. Learner involvement and transparency are keys in learner buy-in regarding assessment efforts. Otherwise, learners may not invest adequate time and effort, thus reducing the effectiveness and quality of the results.

- **Effective assessment must be supported by aligned learning activities and interventions.**

Action: Ensure that intercultural learning is intentionally addressed and supported.

Intercultural learning does not automatically happen, especially not just because a program takes place in an international setting. Data show that less than 10% of U.S. undergraduates take a course in international relations, less than 20% of four-year colleges even require more than two years of foreign language study (Bok, 2006), and less than 5% of U.S. students study abroad (IIE, 2013). Regardless, intercultural learning must go beyond one course or experience. It becomes incumbent on postsecondary institutions, then, to ensure that intercultural competence is integrated throughout undergraduates' coursework. Mapping stated goals and objectives to specific learning interventions (i.e., programs or courses) helps ensure that intercultural learning is intentionally addressed. For example, infusing intercultural competence development and global learning into courses could include

- Finding multiple ways throughout a course to bring in diverse perspectives on issues (beyond one or two readings or assignments).
- Helping students begin to see from multiple cultural perspectives.
- Building on students' own life experiences within a course.

- Requiring students to apply their intercultural learning through a local cultural immersion or education-abroad experience (possibly through research, service-learning, or an internship). Such a requirement would include adequate intercultural preparation before the experience as well as a thorough debriefing and processing upon completion of the experience (and, depending on the length of the experience, intentional learning intervention during the time may be required).

- **Effective assessment requires use of collected information.**

Action: Use the collected assessment information for learner improvement as well as program improvement.

This point comes back to the first principle of understanding why. Using the collected assessment information (data) is crucial in a number of ways: to provide direct feedback to students on their continued intercultural learning, to improve the program, to communicate results to stakeholders, and for accreditation purposes. In the assessment field, this process is known as "closing the loop," and any collected information must be used. For example, if survey questions are used, ensure a use for information collected from the questions. Otherwise, some questions may not be needed and may waste time for the learner and the administrator. Consider beginning assessment efforts with these questions: How will we use the information collected? Will this information be meaningful to the learner? Ultimately, how will this benefit the learner?

- **Effective assessment requires regular evaluation and revision of the assessment plan and process.**

Action: Evaluate the assessment plan and process.

One area that is easy to overlook is evaluating how well the assessment plan worked and what could be improved in the future. Within that review, evaluate how well the tools or methods worked in collecting the evidence needed and whether the same set of priorities (as indicated by goals and objectives) should be continued in the future or reset to include other priorities. Assessment is always a work in progress, so regularly review how to improve the process. Other areas to consider include a cost/benefit analysis, the degree of change detected by the outcome measures, the adequacy of resources and infrastructure for implementing the assessment plan, and the adequacy of the learning interventions for yielding the desired outcomes (Banta & Palomba, 2014; Palomba & Banta, 2001). Critical reflection on the assessment program and system is important not only for making changes in the assessment process but more importantly for making necessary changes in courses and programs.

* * *

Other principles of quality assessment include utilizing a control group (if appropriate), best practices in terms of sampling, the use of longitudinal studies, and so on. There is certainly need for further reflection and discussion on what truly makes for effective assessment in international education. Questions for further reflection and discussion include

- How well are assessment tools and methods aligned with mission and goals? (Exactly what do those tools measure, and why are they being used?)
- Is there more than one tool being used?
- Is there an assessment plan in place?
- How are assessment efforts integrated throughout a course or program, beyond pre-/post- efforts? How is the collected information being used?
- Is more than one person or office involved in assessment efforts?
- Is the assessment plan itself being reviewed regularly for improvement?

For a checklist based on the principles discussed in this chapter, see page 78. For a more in-depth list of assessment principles adapted to international educators, see appendix D.

If institutions are serious about assessment and about student learning, such efforts must result in quality work so that the results are actually meaningful for all involved, including our students. The principles and hallmarks highlighted in this chapter help ensure effective assessment that goes beyond the futile search for the best assessment tool. As the adage goes, it's time we measure what we value and not value what we measure.

CHAPTER 5

Approaching International Education Assessment Holistically

The Logic Model

How should you approach assessment so that it is not an ad hoc activity disconnected from the larger whole? This chapter discusses a holistic framework for approaching assessment efforts, one that helps move beyond seeing assessment as a discrete activity to viewing assessment as an ongoing process that is part of a larger picture of educating learners. This holistic approach helps make your assessment more effective, meaning that your time and resources are used in a better way than if you simply engaged in ad hoc efforts without a comprehensive framework. And in the larger picture, the use of this framework will lead to lasting change, both individually and programmatically.

MAKING ASSESSMENT PART OF A BIGGER PICTURE: AN ASSESSMENT FRAMEWORK

From the outset, an assessment team needs to use a holistic framework for assessment efforts and to think of assessment as an ongoing process that is integrated into student learning (see chapter 6 for setting up an assessment team). This approach may result in a paradigm shift for international educators from the more traditional view of assessment as a separate activity that is added on to an international or intercultural experience to thinking of assessment as part of a larger picture (see chapter 10 for more on this paradigm shift). One concise framework that's been used in numerous organizations for nearly the last 50 years is known as the *program logic model* (N. Bennett, 1976; Knowlton & Phillips, 2013; Rogers, 2000). Use of logic models began in the 1970s, grew in popularity in the 1990s, and is now widely found in the private, public, and nonprofit sectors.

This logic framework, which can address student learning outcomes as well as program outcomes, takes into account the inputs as well as the overall impact. By applying a framework such as the logic model to either a course, a student orientation, specific study-abroad or international program, a non-formal or co-curricular program, or a broader international education program (even a collection of study-abroad programs, for example), outcomes assessment can be placed within a more holistic context, thus ensuring a more systematic and rigorous approach to assessment efforts. Additionally, the framework created by this logic model is useful not only for providing a road map for clarifying intended outcomes but also serving as an analytical tool that leads to lasting change within the program or organization. Other benefits of the logic model include developing a common language among stakeholders, documenting explicit outcomes, clarifying what works and why, and the model's influence on an organization's overall effectiveness (Knowlton & Phillips, 2013). These benefits might, in turn, account for why the model is widely employed by entities such as the U.S. Department of State, the Kellogg Foundation, and United Way.

In the end, the program logic model addresses three essential questions that underlie learning, and in this case, learning that occurs through international education:

- Where are we going? (Goals)
- How will we get there? (Outcomes)
- How will we know when we've arrived? (Assessment)

These three questions focus efforts on the end result of learning within international education programs, similar to the backward design approach noted in chapter 1. These questions also help individuals focus on the evidence that the goals have been achieved. For example, what exactly should students be able to know and do by the end of the course or program? In the international education context, the answer to that question is often stated as "graduating global citizens," having "global-ready" graduates, or "developing interculturally competent students." These general goals (macro expectations), however, are too broad to assess. That's where objectives come in; think of the objectives (micro expectations) as the stepping-stones or mile markers toward the destination (goal). The specific objectives themselves are assessed. While there can be a few goals or destinations—perhaps even across an institution or across programs—the methods for reaching that destination can vary, which means the assessment methods can vary accordingly. The emphasis, particularly within international education, is on demonstration and performance (ideally in real-life settings), not just on knowledge alone, which has implications for assessment tools and methods, that is, beyond the use of a single inventory. Beginning with the end in mind is a well-tested adage that can yield great benefits in terms of international education learning outcomes (see reference to backward design in chapter 1).

For changes to occur in knowledge and performance, factors such as resources and learning interventions affect the results. To better understand how such factors influence assessment, let's examine in more detail how the specific components of the program logic framework operate.

Inputs

What is needed to support the learning activities to achieve the stated goals? Inputs are the resources required to develop and implement activities that will achieve stated outcomes. Inputs can include staff, faculty, administrators, time, money, partners, facilities, or other resources available to the institution or program. Inputs can also include employer surveys, focus group results, and alumni surveys. These inputs can be mapped and assessed in terms of how they might affect the other four components of this model.

Activities

What are the specific learning actions undertaken to achieve change? In the case of learning within international education, activities can involve learning opportunities that occur through curriculum, education-abroad experiences, research abroad or in virtual global teams, involvement of faculty abroad, co-curricular and extracurricular activities, and so on. Activities can also include process mechanisms such as technology.

Outputs

Who is involved in the activities and who are the activities affecting? Outputs often include participation numbers, such as the number of students in an education-abroad program, number of international students at an institution, number of students enrolled in language courses, or number of students benefitting from a joint program. A prime example of outputs is the participation numbers appearing in the annual *Open Doors* report published by the Institute of International Education. While numbers can be a starting point for assessment, we need to go beyond numbers to outcomes (changes) if we want to know the results of international education efforts.

Outcomes

What are the results of the learning activity for individuals, programs, departments, and the institution? The results are the expected or actual effects of the outputs of an intervention (activities). In other words, what *change* will occur? Outcomes can look at change in the next one to three years (short-term), four to six years (intermediate-term) and seven to 10 years (long-term). Outcomes are directly related to the set goals and therefore often identified on a deeper level than outputs—as in the meaning (outcomes) behind the numbers (outputs). Intercultural learning outcomes are often stated in terms of specific knowledge, skills, and attitudes that students should acquire. An example of a measurable outcome statement in an international education program includes the following (see chapter 6 for more on developing measurable learning objectives):

> By the end of the course, students will be able to articulate three different cultural perspectives on climate change. [Aligned to overall goal of being able to see from different perspectives.]

Given that international education courses and experiences often lead to complex, transformational outcomes (see chapter 3), one should also anticipate potential unstated outcomes—transformational changes not stated from the outset in the learning objectives. Identifying these changes requires clear, ongoing communication with the learners throughout and beyond the course or experience, and empowering learners to identify other changes that occurred beyond the ones stated. Examples include change related to personal growth and development, such as becoming more independent, confident, or mature. In one case, an online course led to a deep friendship between two individuals from different cultures that later resulted in marriage. Uncovering unanticipated outcomes can also be ascertained through post-experience interviews and longitudinal studies.

Impact

What is the long-term impact (consequences/results) of the learning and change on the institution, educational program, and students or alumni, as well as on stakeholders such as staff, business, industry, the local community, and international partners? Longitudinal studies are often necessary to assess long-term impact. One example of such a study is the Dwyer and Peters (2004) survey among participants of the Institute for the International Education of Students (IES Abroad) study-abroad programs. This study is valuable for its use of data over a considerable time period (alumni who participated in these programs between 1950 and 1999) to assess mid- and long-term (50 years) impact on the participants' career and personal development. Another example of gauging impact is the Study Abroad for Global Engagement (SAGE) project, which ran from 2006 to 2009. In this case, data were collected to document the long-term personal, professional, and global engagement outcomes of study-abroad experiences. Beyond impact on individuals, one question at the institutional level is *how the institution has changed* as a result of its study-abroad programs, international research partnerships, international studies major, teaching of Chinese and Arabic, or its English as a Second Language program, and so on.

Internationalization ultimately needs to result in institutional change, and if such change is not occurring, then international educators need to examine more closely what is happening. Exhibit 5.1 illustrates the program logic model adapted to the internationalization of higher education.

Exhibit 5.1
Logic Model: Internationalization at Higher Education Institutions

Inputs and Resources for Internationalization

Needed for development and implementation of activities and components of internationalization (resources include time, funding, staff and faculty expertise, leadership, international resources on campus, physical space, participants, sponsors, materials, etc.)

↓

Activities/Components of Internationalization

Specific actions designed to yield changes in the learners: can be tools, events, programs, processes, and other learning interventions (curriculum, education abroad, co-curricular programs, guest speakers, orientation, volunteering, service learning, international week, virtual mobility, baseline needs assessments)

↓

Outputs of Internationalization

Deliverable targets measured most often through numbers (e.g., number of international students, number of study-abroad programs, percentage of students studying abroad, number of students studying foreign languages, number of foreign-born faculty)

↓

Outcomes of Internationalization

Changes that occur in learners and in programs (could be short-, medium-, and long-term outcomes), usually focused on changes in skills, knowledge, attitudes, and behavior (e.g., language ability, intercultural competence development, civic engagement, adaptability, emotional resilience, global knowledge, communication skills, critical thinking skills)

↓

Long-Term Impact of Internationalization

Ultimate intended and desired change in the institution, community, and beyond (measured longitudinally)

General program logic model applied to internationalization. (Adapted from Deardorff, 2005)

A framework such as the program logic model helps reframe assessment more holistically. Based on this theory of change, the focus is on specific strategies (intentional actions) leading to concrete results (effects of strategies). The logic model in turn helps to move institutions, programs, and courses beyond simply counting numbers by *shifting the focus* to the meaning behind the numbers, such as the achievement of intercultural learning outcomes. Of course, no model is perfect. A limitation of the program logic model includes the challenge of causal attribution since a variety of factors (e.g., students' backgrounds and prior experiences, self-selection of individuals in study-abroad or language programs) might influence outcomes, especially in education-abroad experiences. Other limitations include the lack of documenting unanticipated outcomes and the perceived static nature of the model, although in reality it should always be considered a work in progress with every model considered a draft and not a fait accompli. Logic model experts Knowlton and Phillips (2013) state, "We believe the greatest value of logic models is their use in an iterative, intentional process aimed at improving the thinking they illustrate" (p. 11), "and better thinking always yields better results" (p. 4). They suggest working with stakeholders in developing a visual representation that makes evaluation more accessible. In the end, it's about effectiveness and results. As Knowlton and Phillips observe, "Effectiveness is not limited to, but certainly depends on, a clear vision, capable implementation, and the means to monitor both processes and results" (p. 4), and the logic model makes that possible. (For a more thorough background on the program logic model, see Knowlton & Phillips, 2013; for more on this model in relation to international education, see Deardorff, 2005.)

PUTTING A LOGIC MODEL TO WORK: STARTING WITH THE END IN MIND

Begin with the end in mind. What results are to be achieved through a course, event, or program? Categorize these results into short-, middle-, and long-term. In using the logic model, you actually start at the end and work backward (cf. backward design, noted in chapter 1). Engaging multiple stakeholders (e.g., students, faculty, administrators, parents) through informal meetings, interviews, and conversations is crucial in this process of delineating results. Dialogue with multiple stakeholders—including students—should be explicit about the assumptions made since stakeholders will hold diverse assumptions about strategies and impact. Dialogue is essential, because different stakeholders may have very different expectations around their desired results of a course or program.

Once the results (goals) have been identified, then your team can use backward design to identify the series of outcomes that will show progress toward achievement of the goals. Note that the focus should be on *expected changes in the learner*, not on activities; that step comes next. Identify what learning interventions and activities will help learners achieve the stated outcomes that will lead to change in participants, or later the program or organization. Once you have specified activities and learning interventions, you can map the resources and inputs, which will highlight what you may still need to make the activities happen. Here is a plan of action in developing a logic model (as adapted from Knowlton & Phillips, 2013), and you can find a worksheet on p. 120 to help you with developing your logic model, which in the end can be placed into a visual representation (see example in appendix A on p. 121):

Logic Model Plan of Action

1. Engage multiple stakeholders in determining desired, realistic results (both short- and long-term results) = goal setting.
2. Acknowledge the underlying assumptions and beliefs of stakeholders in achieving results.
3. Outline a series of outcomes (changes) that will show progress toward achieving results (impact).
4. Identify all activities (learning experiences and interventions) that are needed to reach the stated outcomes.
5. Define the resources and inputs that link directly to the stated activities.
6. Identify the outputs (numbers) that reflect accomplishment of the activities.

Remember that this process is iterative and co-created—a model that will continue to be modified. *The resulting model should never be considered a finished product.* Other common pitfalls in the modeling process include unrealistic goals, equating outcomes with actions, equating knowledge with action, and developing the model without actually using it to make change. Make sure your outcome statements do not embody actions—such as an objective stating, "Give a presentation on a study-abroad experience." This is an activity and not a learning outcome. (See pp. 45–47, chapter 7, and appendix B for more on developing learning outcome statements.)

ENSURING QUALITY IN PROGRAM LOGIC MODELS

Modeling experts have posed the following questions to determine the quality of a program logic model.

- Are the results specified with shared meaning among all stakeholders?
- Are target audiences clearly defined?
- Did we identify and question our assumptions and carefully examine research, practice, and theory as grounding for our choices in activities?
- Does the program have enough depth that results are likely? Do the program (course) parameters match the stated goals in terms of being realistic and feasible?

- Do the outcomes logically contribute to intended results?
- Did we challenge the recipe of activities and outcomes to ensure feasibility, especially given identified challenges and the expected changes in learners? In other words, are activities mapped to outcomes, and are they realistic?
- What activities have worked under similar conditions? What current conditions might influence selection of activities? Is there evidence that these activities are best?
- Does the interaction among activities contribute to intended stated outcomes or objectives? To what extent?
- Do we have adequate resources and time to accomplish the intended results?
- Have we received feedback from internal stakeholders as well as external sources on alignment of inputs, activities, outputs, outcomes, and results, as well as ways to improve the model? (adapted from Knowlton & Phillips, 2013)

Investing time and energy in the co-creation of a program logic model is very important for effective assessment and in placing assessment within the larger context of design, implementation, evaluation, and adaptation. As Knowlton and Phillips stated, "Evaluation in isolation will not improve effectiveness—it is just an activity" (2013, p. 65). They go on to add, "The logic model serves as the focal point for discussion about evaluation because it displays when, where, and how to look for the information most needed to manage the program and determine its effectiveness. . . . When the model of your program is used to guide evaluation, it then becomes . . . a navigational aid (informs direction) and a dashboard (informs data collection and gauges progress)" (p. 65). Regardless of the modeling used, investing careful thought in thinking through a road map at the beginning is key to making sure that the destination is clearly noted so that you are headed in the right direction.

Chapter 6

Getting Started

Assessment can seem quite daunting. What is the best way to get started so that it is manageable? This chapter explores the foundational pieces that need to be put in place, including putting together an assessment team, understanding the evidence of learner success, and mapping the context. Before any of this is done, you need to understand *why* assessment is being done (see chapter 1).

WHO TO INVOLVE? PARTNERING TOGETHER FOR INTERNATIONAL EDUCATION ASSESSMENT: PUTTING TOGETHER AN ASSESSMENT TEAM

As mentioned, assessment of international education learning outcomes is too complex for one person to implement alone. Understand the context for assessment within your institution (see the worksheet on p. 119 to identify others in the organization who could aid in this assessment process. Think about assessment more in terms of a dialogue. Who do you need to be in dialogue with about learning outcomes assessment? Such persons may include external and internal stakeholders (including the learners themselves); any persons with whom you collaborate on this program (including those you may have consulted in developing the initial goals and objectives); persons with particular expertise in technical, content, or assessment areas; and so on, along with faculty and others who may have access to direct evidence of student learning or performance. This group can comprise supervisors, community organizers, and even host families. Faculty are an important group to involve in an assessment team. Palomba and Banta (2001) write, "Faculty need to participate in all aspects of the assessment process, including the development of objectives, the selection of assessment techniques, and the review of assessment results" (p. 23). Once faculty and other persons have been identified, then an assessment team can be formed (American Council on Education, 2008); see p. 119 for a worksheet on putting together an assessment team. This team may change and evolve over time, depending on the assessment needs, and would meet periodically to undertake a number of key tasks, including conducting an initial assessment audit, developing an assessment plan, overseeing the implementation of the plan, and reviewing the plan regularly to ensure that evidence is aligned with goals and objectives.

WHAT DO YOU WANT TO MEASURE?

The first step to do together as an assessment team is to determine not only why assessment is important but also exactly what needs to be measured. Often, international educators, when embarking on assessment, may start with the frequently asked question, "Which assessment test/tool should we use?" The answer is, "That depends on what you're trying to measure, and why." In order to know what you need to measure, you need to first start with your overall goals, which should be aligned with your program, course, or organizational purpose. Overall goals should be "the destination": Where do you want students to be at the end of the course or program? Usually in international education, general goals often include statements about "developing global citizens," "developing students' intercultural competence," or "preparing students for the 21st-century career," or some variation thereof. These broad goals cannot be fully measured as stated. The next question is, "What are the stepping-stones—the markers—toward achievement of these broader goals?" There should be a series of at least two or three statements that are very specific, meaningful, and measurable; these statements become the learning objectives. These objectives may take time and effort to get right, so work on them should not be rushed. Walvoord (2004) also cautions, "Do not let assessment become an exercise in reduction" (p. 30). Make sure that the learning objectives are not trivializing the learning (or reducing learning to "what's easy to measure") and are indeed meaningful markers along the journey to achieving the broader goals.

What do measurable objectives or outcomes look like? In the assessment arena, a common way of thinking about measurable objectives is through the acronym SMART: **s**pecific (what, why, how), **m**easurable, **a**ction-oriented, **r**ealistic, and **t**ime-based. (An alternative is **s**pecific, **m**easurable, **a**chievable, **r**elevant, and **t**ime-based; there are others, too.) A key part of this statement is that the objective is realistic or achievable; it needs to fit what can realistically be accomplished with the parameters of the course or program. For example, an unrealistic objective for a participant in a beginning-level language course would be to speak that language fluently after only two or three weeks in another country. For short-term study-abroad programs in postsecondary institutions, outcomes must realistically match the program length. For example, if the program exposes participants to another culture for six weeks, what can participants realistically be expected to achieve regarding intercultural competence development within that six-week period, given the level and quality of cultural preparation, the program parameters, and the way in which the intercultural experience has been set up? Even in a semester-long course on intercultural competence, one wouldn't realistically expect students to be interculturally competent upon completion. Furthermore, relevancy is key: the objectives must be relevant to the learner. Prioritizing specific desired changes in knowledge, skills, or attitudes, based on what is relevant to learners, is key in this process of developing SMART learning objectives.

In writing a learning objective, usually only one action verb is used per outcome statement. These can be based on Bloom's classic learning taxonomy (1956), later revised by Anderson and Krathwohl (2001). See Exhibit 6.1 for sample action verbs based on this revised taxonomy. Outcome statements (objectives) are focused on *changes* in learning itself, not on infrastructure, instructor, or activity. When appropriate, work with participants to have them develop their own learning objectives related to the overall intercultural competence goals. This approach ensures a more effective and relevant learning process for the learner. In some cases, learning contracts are negotiated between the learner and instructor (see the work of Malcolm Knowles [1986] for further details on learning contracts) in which learners take responsibility for their own learning. (Appendix E shows a learning contract template.) Given the learner-centered approach introduced in chapter 1, learning contracts fit well with students who desire to have a more active role in co-creating their learning experiences.

International education goals and related learning outcomes can occur at five levels (Musil, 2006): institutional, divisional or departmental, general education, individual course or program, and campus life (outside the classroom). The logic model (discussed in chapter 5) can be used to frame holistic assessment with any of these levels. As Musil notes, "Each level is vitally important, and each must be linked to the others. All must function synergistically in order to have the most dynamic impact" (p. 5). Examples of measurable outcomes at the course level under the general goal of "Understanding others' perspectives" are

---

Exhibit 6.1
Action Verbs Based on Bloom's Revised Taxonomy

Remembering: Recognize, list, describe, identify, retrieve, name
Understanding: Interpret, exemplify, summarize, infer, paraphrase, compare, explain
Applying: Implement, carry out, use
Analyzing: Compare, attribute, organize, deconstruct
Evaluating: Check, critique, judge, hypothesize
Creating: Design, construct, plan, produce
Source: Green, 2012, p. 12.

- "By the end of the course, learners can articulate two different cultural perspectives on climate change."
- "By the end of this class, learners can define what a *worldview* is and three ways in which it impacts one's behavior."

Even more specific,

- "First-year students who complete three intercultural skill seminars will be able to identify at least three out of five communication styles in a video of an intercultural team working on a project" (with the broader goal of "Developing intercultural communication skills").

Other considerations when developing goals and objectives:

- **Time frame.** Consider what changes can be made in the short term, intermediate term, and long term; you may want to have objectives that address these different time frames.
- **Audience.** Clearly identify the audience of your goals and objectives and the reasons you are creating goals and objectives for them. Do objectives address specific changes that should occur in the learners' knowledge, skills, or attitudes? Do the goals and objectives seem realistic and achievable for the audience? In the case of international education outcomes, do the stated objectives take into account the audience's different developmental levels? (See chapter 3 for more.)
- **Context and level of influence.** Goals and objectives can be applied within formal contexts (classroom) or informal contexts (events, programs). However, within these contexts, be realistic about what can be accomplished based on depth of experience and content, frequency of contact with learners, and duration of the event. For example, what realistically can be achieved (changed) through participating in a Chinese New Year's celebration (a onetime, short-term event) is quite different from a 20-week service learning project in the community. Also recognize the level of influence one has on learners; for example, faculty in a classroom setting have much more direct influence than an administrator who sends students on an exchange program. Within your realm of influence, look also at the level at which you want change to occur—individual, course, program, or institution.
- **Level of commitment.** What is the level of commitment (from the instructor, administrator, other stakeholders, etc.) in helping learners achieve these objectives? Commitment may be expressed in a variety of ways, including intentionality, level of interest, degree of designated resources, degree of follow-through, and level of engagement.

This exercise of goal setting and developing learning outcomes cannot be done in a vacuum by one person, unless it's a faculty member writing goals and learning outcomes for a course. Instead, dialogue and discussion need to occur through a process that involves stakeholders as well as the assessment team. This process of discerning and determining goals and objectives can take a while—in some cases, more than a year. The identification and involvement of stakeholders and allies throughout the process are crucial for assessment success later, which brings us to the question about who should be involved more formally in this process.

FOCUS ON EVIDENCE

After the team has determined goals and learning objectives (which may take longer than you may think), it's time to explore the following question: "What evidence is there of student success in this course or program?" (There may be a push to start assessing by discussing which assessment tools to use, but refrain from going there quite yet.)

To begin the discussion on evidence, you may want to use the Student Success worksheet on p. 118 for discussion with key stakeholders, including students and faculty. Beyond the initial question, explore other variations of the questions found on the worksheet, such as, "How will students know they've been successful?" and "How will others know students have been successful?" Chances are that this response necessitates going beyond simply citing a score on a test or survey. What's the actual evidence of student success in the program or course? Evidence can be categorized as either direct or indirect. *Direct evidence* is actual student performance or immediate evidence of learning, whereas *indirect evidence* is the perception of student learning that often occurs outside of the student learning experience. Direct evidence is considered to be authentic assessment through student-generated opportunities to demonstrate learning that is directly aligned with the learning context or experience. The downside of direct evidence is that it is not very easily quantifiable and is often more time-consuming to evaluate. On the other hand, indirect evidence helps explain the context around the student learning that occurred but does not actually represent student learning. Maki (2004) notes, "Indirect methods function to complement direct methods rather than substitute for them" (p. 118). (See chapter 5 for more, along with Table 6.1 for examples of direct and indirect evidence. See also chapter 8 for more on validity and reliability regarding assessment methods.) Often, assignments in courses are means of collecting direct evidence, which would then be evaluated using rubrics (see appendix E for sample rubrics). In international education as well as in higher education in general, the trend is to collect direct evidence through the use of an e-portfolio, which can even span a student's entire academic career. (See Exhibit 7.1, p. 74, for more on e-portfolios.) Utilizing both direct and indirect evidence is crucial in international education in order to provide a more complete view

Table 6.1
Sources of Evidence

Direct Evidence (actual student learning)	Indirect Evidence (self- and other reflections/perceptions of student learning)
Course assignments Student projects (including final projects) Team-based projects E-portfolios Performance assessment (internships, service projects, research) Observation (of performance) Knowledge tests and oral examinations Presentations Visual representations (e.g., photos, documentaries, concept mapping, dance)	Surveys Questionnaires Inventories Student evaluations Self-evaluation Interviews Focus groups

of student learning. Thus, a mixed-methods assessment approach should mean direct and indirect evidence, not just multiple measures under one or the other categories. Using multiple *indirect* measures, for example, still only collects information pertaining to reflections and perceptions of learning. Frequently, international educators rely solely on indirect evidence (i.e., one pre-/post- inventory), which provides only a partial picture of what is happening in regard to student learning and development.

When combined with direct evidence, an entirely different picture can sometimes emerge. For example, a pre-/post- survey may show regression, whereas looking at direct evidence over that same time frame can show student growth. Since international educators may not have direct access to students in courses, partnering with others, especially faculty, becomes very important in collecting evidence of holistic, ongoing student learning.

WHAT'S ALREADY BEING DONE? CONDUCTING AN ASSESSMENT AUDIT

After identifying an assessment team, developing goals and learning objectives, and discussing evidence needed to demonstrate achievement of the stated objectives, the next step is to engage in an assessment audit within the context of international education outcomes to find out what's already being done and where gaps exist in assessment efforts and collecting needed evidence. Conducting a thorough assessment audit from the outset can potentially save lots of money and time in the long term, identify assessment expertise on campus, and prevent duplication of efforts.

Conducting an assessment audit is also crucial and, according to one assessment expert, can take from one to six months, again depending on context and how quickly the information can be collected (Walvoord, 2004). During an assessment audit, the goal is to find out the kinds of evidence already being collected that show how stated learning goals and objectives are being met, as well as how that information is already being used, both for program improvement as well as for continued learner development. During this audit, look for ways in which information is being collected that could be adapted as further needed evidence. For example, many education abroad programs use satisfaction surveys at the end of a program. How can a satisfaction survey be adapted to also collect evidence of student learning, perhaps by adding one or two questions related to the intended objectives of the program and evidence the student would cite regarding how well she achieved those objectives? If an instructor is already collecting various assignments from learners, how can those assignments be adapted to yield further evidence of learning in regard to the stated objectives? Seeking ways to adapt and embed assessment into already existing assessment mechanisms is an excellent starting strategy, especially when working with faculty, since faculty are doing assessment already. The assessment audit can collect the goals and learning objectives of a course or program that are related to international education goals and objectives. Then, determine what evidence (direct and indirect) is being collected that aligns with those objectives. Document the assessment history to include what is already being collected, including in-class assignments such as journals/blogs, reflection papers, projects, and so on. Recognizing and building on (adapting) assessment that is already taking place offers one way to counteract faculty (and others') resistance to assessment efforts. Assessment doesn't have be an add-on that is extra work. In fact, adapting what's already being done to collect the needed evidence is an optimal way to proceed with assessment.

Another part of the assessment audit is thinking broadly at different levels of the institution about which units may be involved in collecting evidence of student learning. Here again, looking at how to adapt or use what's already being collected is useful: For example, how can exit surveys that the institution uses be modified to collect needed evidence? How can a survey like the National Survey of Student Engagement (NSSE) be used in other ways? (NSSE is the most comprehensive survey of U.S. undergraduate students, gauging students' responses in regard to their institution's level of academic challenge, collaborative learning, student-faculty interaction, educational experiences, and campus environment.) Schools and departments may be likely units to engage, as well as looking at the course level (see appendix B for questions that departments can explore related to intercultural competence in the major or degree). Some professional accrediting associations (e.g., business, engineering, education, social work, medicine, nursing) explicitly address standards related to global competence. (See appendix F for a list of universities addressing aspects of international, global, or intercultural learning as part of their re-accreditation process.)

Beyond curricular units, there are co-curricular and extracurricular units to consider, including student affairs and residence halls. Other structural units may also be collecting information that could be of use in international education assessment, including alumni affairs, career placement, academic advising, office of institutional research and advancement, counseling services, teaching and learning centers, and so on. Units vary by institutional context, but you can still think broadly about who to involve when doing the assessment audit. Thoroughly exploring what is already being done and thinking carefully through how existing efforts can be adapted can save time and resources, as well as help uncover gaps and provide insights into lessons learned.

In addition to documenting who's already doing assessment at the various levels, what evidence is being collected, and how the evidence is being used, you can interview key stakeholders and heads of various strategic units to gain in-depth insights into what has worked in terms of assessment and, equally important, what hasn't worked; what the assessment challenges have been; and what changes have occurred recently to improve student learning within the institution in regard to international education objectives. Be sure to document the information collected from these interviews and conversations, which can provide more in-depth insights into the current assessment landscape at your institution as well as build relationships for future assessment efforts. An assessment audit should yield documentation on who is collecting evidence of student learning around international education goals and objectives, how the information is being collected, and what is being done with it. In addition, helpful details include who is available to aid in collecting assessment information, any financial resources available, and assessment expertise available within the institution. Documenting assessment efforts to date also highlights particular methods or tools that could be adapted in collecting the evidence needed to demonstrate achievement of learning outcomes. The information collected from this audit can then be analyzed to determine existing gaps at the various levels (institution, department, program or course), as well as ways in which current assessments can be adapted.

Conducting a thorough assessment audit is a key part of the assessment process, before determining the additional assessment tests, tools, or methods needed to collect the remaining evidence. Assessment expert Barbara Walvoord (2004) states, "The audit is time consuming, but do not skip it! You need it whether you have a previous assessment plan in place or whether you are just beginning formal assessment. The knowledge of current campus assessment practices, dreams and plans must inform everything you do from here on. Without that knowledge, you run the risk of costly mistakes" (p. 34). An assessment audit becomes a crucial part of the foundation that ensures effective assessment.

CONCLUSION

Similar to following a recipe, where certain preparations must be undertaken before actually making the dish of food, it is necessary to prepare for assessment endeavors. Several steps culminate in the development of an actual assessment strategy (discussed in chapter 7). The first is to put together your assessment team. Second, as a team, explore and understand the context and purposes (the "why") of assessment. Third, articulate the learning goals and objectives. Fourth, discuss and explore what evidence is needed to demonstrate the extent to which the objectives have been achieved. The fifth step in this preparation process is to conduct an assessment audit (Walvoord, 2004). Once these steps have taken place, you are ready to develop your assessment strategy (which is described more fully in the next chapter).

Preparing to Develop an Assessment Plan

1. Put together an assessment team.
2. Understand context and purpose of assessment.
3. Articulate learning goals and measurable outcomes/objectives (aligned with purpose of course/program).
4. Explore evidence needed to indicate achievement of stated outcomes.
5. Conduct an assessment audit to determine what evidence is already being collected and possible gaps.

This initial preparation process can take time, since the assessment team and stakeholders need to be involved throughout—particularly in articulating learning goals and measurable objectives/outcomes. An inclusive process of developing these statements can help strengthen the support for assessment and increase buy-in, especially from faculty, and even from students. The preparation work outlined in this chapter is crucial to effective assessment and getting it right.

***

Once all the preparation work has been done, what's next? You and your assessment team develop and implement an assessment plan, as discussed in chapter 7. See also appendix A for worksheets that you and your team can use as you go through some of these steps on the way to developing an assessment plan for outcomes related to international education.

Developing an Assessment Strategy

The Assessment Process

Chapter 5 provided a holistic framework for approaching outcomes assessment more comprehensively. Chapter 6 discussed key steps for getting started on outcomes assessment. This leads us to a critical question: What is your assessment strategy for ensuring that efforts are effective and yield meaningful results to stakeholders? This chapter delves further into the assessment process by providing the blueprints for developing an effective assessment strategy. Specifically, after a brief overview of the assessment process, this chapter highlights key aspects of developing an actual assessment plan, which is crucial for ensuring that outcomes assessment in international education is not an ad hoc, disconnected exercise, but rather part of and connected to the institution.

INTRODUCING THE ASSESSMENT PROCESS AND PLAN

Assessment can be quite manageable if a process and plan are in place. Let's look at three main steps for assessment:

1. Articulate goals and objectives for student learning.
2. Gather evidence about how well students are meeting the objectives.
3. Use the information for improvement (in learners and in the program or course). (See Driscoll & Wood, 2007; Walvoord, 2004)

An assessment plan provides more information around these three main steps as to the who, what, when, where, and how details, as well as ensuring alignment of goals, objectives, methods, and interventions. Page 122 shows a worksheet for answering questions that can guide the development of an assessment plan; page 123 includes an assessment plan template that the assessment team can complete. Spending the time from the outset in thinking through the specifics of an assessment plan not only ensures that the information and evidence collected will be used, but that the assessment efforts will be more effective, maximizing the time and resources used in the assessment process. More importantly, the time spent in developing an assessment plan increases the chances for validity of such efforts, since goals, objectives, and methods will be better aligned.

An assessment plan is formed simultaneously with the steps outlined in the previous chapter. Included in such formation are putting together an assessment team, the team identifying goals and objectives, and conducting an assessment audit of what's already being collected in terms of evidence.

WRITING THE ASSESSMENT PLAN

The assessment team's first task is to develop an assessment plan, taking into account the results of the initial review of what's already being done in terms of assessment (the assessment audit) and ways in which to adapt currently used assessment methods (see chapter 6). Key components of the assessment plan begin with the overall mission, goals, and specific measurable learning objectives, which must align with each other; objectives flow from goals, which in turn flow from the mission or purpose. The assessment team then explores what evidence is needed to show achievement of the objectives, keeping in mind that learning objectives in international education often have more to do with actual behavior or performance than on cognitive skills. Once the types of evidence have been identified (see chapter 6), then the team determines the best ways to collect this evidence, leading to a discussion on assessment tools or methods. One tool or method alone is not sufficient to measure the complexity of international education outcomes, nor is use of a single tool recommended if the assessment efforts are to be considered effective. The team needs to put together a comprehensive package of a variety of tools and methods to use in the assessment plan, which, at a minimum, triangulates the information collected, meaning that at least three different sources are used to ensure the validity and reliability of the information. As assessment expert Peggy Maki (2004) reiterates, "Relying on one method to assess the learning described in outcome statements restricts interpretations of . . . achievement within the parameters of that method" (p. 86).

ASSESSMENT TOOLS AND METHODS IN INTERNATIONAL EDUCATION

As international educators become more sophisticated in their assessment knowledge, they move from asking, "What tool should we use?" to "What evidence do we need, and what are the best ways to collect that evidence?" Evidence can be collected in many ways, including adapting already existing efforts, as discussed earlier in this book. Let's review a few of the primary methods for collecting evidence of learning outcomes in international education. In reviewing methods, we need to return to the discussion of direct and indirect evidence (see chapter 1), with direct evidence consisting of evidence of *actual learning* (collected through course assignments, journals, projects, etc.) while indirect evidence is related to *perceptions* of learning (collected through surveys, inventories, focus groups, interviews, etc.). International education assessment needs to involve evidence from both categories in order to gain a more complete understanding of the student learning that is occurring (see chapter 6 for more on this). Relying on only one method or tool is insufficient and incomplete. (For more detail on direct and indirect assessment methods for learning outcomes, see Banta & Palomba, 2014.)

Direct Methods

E-Portfolios

Many institutions are turning to e-portfolios as a means by which to collect direct evidence of students' intercultural or global learning; as a result, e-portfolios are not so much an actual method as they are a platform for collecting direct (and indirect) evidence. Artifacts that students place in the portfolios include reflection papers, term papers, photos, and other documentation of student learning. Software programs exist to support e-portfolio development and track specific learning outcomes. Rubrics become a key way of evaluating these portfolios. To that end, the Association of American Colleges & Universities (AAC&U) worked with faculty across the United States over an 18-month period to develop rubrics in specific areas, including intercultural learning, global learning, and civic engagement—three rubrics that various universities have adapted to assess international education outcomes. See appendix F for examples from the AAC&U Intercultural Rubric, based on M. Bennett's Developmental Model of Intercultural Sensitivity (1993) and Deardorff's Intercultural Competence Framework (2006, 2009). Learners can also include in their e-portfolios indirect evidence, such as an inventory score, or evidence from others' perspectives, such as a recommendation letter. For more resources on e-portfolios, see Exhibit 7.1 and appendix G.

Critical Reflection

Reflection is key in developing learners' intercultural competence (Deardorff, 2006). Thus, journaling, blogging, and reflection papers become tools through which to collect information on student learning. One tool to use in pushing students to go beyond descriptive reflection is to use the following "what" questions: What? So What? Now What? You can even simply ask students, "As a result of this learning, what will you do now?" (Kneffelcamp, 1989). Writing prompts can also be used, such as "I learned that. . . . This is important because. . . . As a result of this learning, I will. . . ." (Clayton, Ash, & Jameson, 2009). Reflection should be thought of as a critical and legitimate process for promoting and assessing learning. Well-designed

Exhibit 7.1
E-Portfolios

International education programs are increasingly turning to e-portfolios as a means of collecting direct evidence of student learning. Books written on the use of portfolios include those by Cambridge (2010); Light, Chen, and Ittelson (2011); and Stefani, Mason, and Pegler (2007). E-portfolios are structured in terms of organization and content. Planning for e-portfolios involves determining the electronic platform, the purpose of the e-portfolio, guidelines for selection and evaluation of entries, procedures for maintaining and using the portfolio (some platforms allow students access even after graduation), and criteria for evaluating the overall portfolio. The key points to understand about e-portfolio usage are that (a) they provide assessment of students' learning over time, (b) students play an active role in maintaining their portfolio (taking more responsibility for their learning), and (c) feedback on student work in the e-portfolio is crucial. Simply having a place for students to deposit samples of their work is not considered to be an e-portfolio. Rather, portfolios require teacher-student collaboration in terms of selecting appropriate work and periodic review and feedback on students' learning progress (Gronlund, 2006). To that end, rubrics (rating scales) and evaluation criteria need to be articulated for use by self, peers, and instructors. In addition to feedback on individual samples of student work, holistic evaluation of the overall portfolio should occur in terms of student improvement over time. Portfolios can be maintained within one course or program, or more comprehensively throughout a student's career at an educational institution.

reflection goes beyond descriptive journal writing, although that may be an aspect of it; reflection is an "intentional, structured, and directed process that facilitates exploration for deeper, contextualized meaning linked to learning outcomes" (Rice & Pollack, 2000, p. 124). Through effective critical reflection, students can engage in an examination of their personal opinions, attitudes, and positionalities; their relation to the community members; their learning context/location; and the work in which they are engaged. With that information they can bridge their day-to-day interactions with individuals to broader social and cultural issues (O'Grady, 2000; Rice & Pollack, 2000). Such reflection can provide a rich source of data for research on students' intercultural learning development within the curricular context and, when combined with other information sources and methods, can help inform a more rigorous assessment plan.

Performance (Practice)

Increasingly, observations of students' performance in real-world intercultural situations are offering a way in which to obtain others' perspectives on the appropriateness of students' behavior and communication in intercultural interactions. For example, host families may be asked to complete a reflection on students' homestays. Supervising teachers may be asked to complete an observation of classroom interactions with teachers. Supervisors may be asked to do the same for interns and so on. Such performance assessment provides the opportunity for students to apply intercultural knowledge and skills in relevant contexts. Project-based learning and team-based learning can also provide situations for performance evaluation by peers, "clients," and instructors.

Learning Contracts

When appropriate, work with learners in having them develop their own learning objectives related to the overall intercultural competence goals. This approach not only ensures a more effective and relevant learning process but also allows the learner to indicate the evidence for successful learning. Learning contracts consist of the learner negotiating with the instructor on the following items:

- What specifically will be learned
- How it will be learned
- Timeline for learning to occur
- Evidence of learning
- Action taken as a result of the learning

(See the work of Malcolm Knowles [1986] for further details on learning contracts. See appendix E for a template to use for learning contracts.) While not employed as frequently yet in international education, this method holds great promise, especially given the trend toward increased learner customization and personalization of learning experiences.

Indirect Methods

Indirect evidence of student learning around intercultural competence is collected primarily through surveys or inventories from the learner's perspective. More than 100 such instruments are currently available, some more reliable and valid than others. (For a list, see Fantini, 2009.) In using these instruments, it is absolutely critical that administrators understand exactly what the instrument measures and how that aligns with the stated learning outcomes. Use of any these indirect measures must be coupled with direct measures of student learning as discussed earlier in order to provide a more complete picture. For example, some administrators have found regression in post inventory scores for some learners, yet when combined with direct evidence of student learning, they discover that students are indeed experiencing positive changes in their learning that are not reflected on a post survey.

As assessment tools are being reviewed and identified for collecting needed information (evidence), one should ask, "What are the criteria for determining which assessment tools or methods can best be used to collect evidence of learning aligned with specific objectives?" Some key questions to aid in selecting the most appropriate tools are as follows: What are the goals and objectives to be assessed? What evidence is needed to indicate success in achieving these objectives? What does the tool measure? How well does the tool align with the stated objectives? What are the limitations and cultural biases of the tool? Is the tool valid (accurate) and reliable (consistent)? Have other validity issues been considered? Is there a theoretical foundation for the tool? Are the administrative and logistical issues involved manageable? How will the collected information be used to provide feedback to students on their own intercultural learning? See the worksheets on pages 126 and 127, which can help determine the assessment tools to use.

Many of the international education goals are related to intercultural or global competence, and an increasing proliferation of primarily self-report instruments (indirect evidence) purport to measure various aspects of this concept in individuals. These tools are not listed here since numerous lists already exist; readers are encouraged to see appendix E for specific references to these resources. Using specific criteria in selecting these tools is important, rather than simply choosing a tool because it's accessible, inexpensive, recommended, or used by a peer institution. Be sure you understand exactly why a tool is selected, based on what, and how it is aligned with goals and objectives to collect the needed evidence, so that the evidence is valid (accurate).

Regardless of the tools or methods selected for collecting the needed evidence, two key issues are associated with assessment tools and methodologies to ensure assessment effectiveness: reliability and validity. As defined in chapter 1, *reliability* refers to the consistency of results, while *validity* broadly refers to the accuracy of the results, although validity is more complex. Chapter 8 discusses more on the importance and complexity of validity within assessment efforts. Bottom line: Remember that a combination of direct and indirect evidence (see chapter 6 for more) provides a more complete understanding of the learning that is taking place.

COMPLETING THE ASSESSMENT PLAN

With the complexity of international education outcomes, especially intercultural competence, an assessment plan involving a multi-method, multi-perspective assessment approach is desired. Advocating the use of multiple measures in assessing competence, Pottinger (1979) stresses that "how one defines the domain of competence will greatly affect one's choice of measurement procedures" (p. 30). Pottinger (1979) also notes that pen-and-paper assessment tests have been widely criticized, due in part to the effect of the test format and also due to the limits a paper test places on the complex phenomena being measured.

Because learning varies by setting, context, and individual, using a variety of assessment methods and tools ensures a stronger measurement and more rigorous assessment. The key question to ask is, "What is the *evidence* of student learning regarding the stated outcomes, beyond students' self-perspectives?" (For more, see chapter 6.) Another key question to explore in international education outcomes is, "Through what process did the student learn this?" Given the transformational nature of international education, assessing the process may be as important, or more so, than assessing the actual achievement of learning outcomes.

Once the assessment team has determined which tools and methods best fit the learning objectives (outcome statements), the team can complete the assessment plan, including determining a timeline and then assigning roles and responsibilities for implementing the plan. The assessment plan can then be implemented by collecting the information, which administrators can then analyze for trends, consistency over time, anomalies, or gaps. A key question in the analysis process is, "What does the information tell us?" See appendix A for an outline of an assessment plan template.

USING THE ASSESSMENT INFORMATION

The assessment plan ensures a specific use for the information collected, including information from specific questions. If no use has been determined, then the question or tool should be reconsidered and possibly eliminated. Investing time and resources is unnecessary if the information collected will not be used. Too often, international education offices collect information—thinking, "There may be something there"—and try to determine the use later. In those cases, feedback is very rarely given back to students for their continued learning and development. Make sure you have determined specific use of all information collected through assessment efforts (which goes back to the key principles discussed in chapter 4).

The collected information can be applied in numerous ways: First and foremost, the information should be used to provide feedback to the learners in improving and honing their learning and development. Learner feedback involves going beyond a pre-/post- assessment to giving feedback throughout an experience or course. Dialogue with the learner is crucial in this process, if possible. To that end, a current trend is to use collected assessment information to coach students in their continued intercultural development. (See appendix A, p. 128, for feedback questions and guidelines.)

The information can also be used in aggregate to determine gaps in the learning program and to recommend program changes; ultimately those recommendations would be implemented by making changes that continue to improve participants' learning. The information can even be employed at broader levels to map entire curricula to overarching goals and learning objectives.

Regardless of how the information is used, the collected information needs to be interpreted and communicated to other stakeholders who could benefit from the assessment results. For that reason, answering the question, "Who needs to know what and why?" is often helpful in telling the story to stakeholders (students, faculty, administrators, parents, funders, the general public, etc.). The key is to focus on telling a story using the information collected through assessment efforts. Advocacy also becomes a key use of the information collected, particularly advocating for the value of international education programs (for more, see chapters 3–9).

COMPLETING THE ASSESSMENT PROCESS: REVIEWING THE PLAN AND PROCESS

In sum, the assessment plan includes details on how the information from each tool or method will be analyzed, interpreted, communicated, and used. Once the assessment plan has been fully implemented, the final step is to evaluate its effectiveness to determine what is working well in the assessment process and what needs to be improved to ensure continued effective assessment. The checklist in figure 7.1 can be used to evaluate this process.

Figure 7.1
Outcomes Assessment Checklist

☐ Aligned and Articulated: Are goals, objectives, and assessment measures aligned and articulated?

☐ Intentional: Is assessment intentionally addressed?

☐ Developed: Have assessment issues been carefully analyzed before a plan is implemented?

☐ Integrated: Is assessment integrated throughout the program and not viewed as an add-on—that is, implemented only as a pre-/post- phenomenon?

☐ Focused: Is assessment realistic, with two to three outcomes being assessed per program per year?

☐ Shared: Is assessment shared with others on campus through partnerships?

☐ Supported: Does the senior leadership support assessment efforts?

☐ Resourced: Is there adequate time and funding for assessment efforts, and have administrators received sufficient training and knowledge in assessment, with ongoing professional development?

☐ Analyzed: Have the assessment tools, results, and process been analyzed and evaluated (from multiple perspectives, when possible)?

☐ Communicated: Have the results been communicated to all stakeholders?

☐ Used: Have the results been used for program improvement and for learner feedback?

☐ Reviewed: Have the assessment process and strategy been reviewed on a regular basis and improved upon?

Source: Deardorff, 2008

KEY POINTS IN DEVELOPING AN ASSESSMENT STRATEGY

In developing a comprehensive assessment strategy, here are some key points to remember (adapted from Lewin, 2009). A comprehensive assessment strategy is one that is

- **Aligned and articulated.** Are mission, goals, objectives, and assessment measures aligned and articulated? As discussed earlier in this chapter, the assessment measures must fit with the stated goals and objectives. In using such tools, you need to understand what the tool measures. In the case of global citizenship or intercultural competence, one single tool does not measure the entire whole of these complex concepts. Thus, what is the specific focus or purpose of the tools under consideration? How does this fit with the goals and objectives?

- **Intentional.** Is assessment intentionally addressed? If assessment is not intentionally addressed through the creation of an assessment team and through the articulation of a comprehensive assessment strategy or plan that is reviewed at regular intervals, then assessment may occur more randomly without becoming integral to student learning and program improvement.

- **Developed.** Have assessment issues been carefully analyzed before a plan is implemented? (See Figure 7.1 for specific questions.) For example, have assessment measures been examined for inherent bias?

- **Integrated.** Is assessment integrated throughout the program and not viewed as an add-on—that is, implemented only as a pre-/post- exercise? While pre-/post- surveys are popular among administrators, assessment needs to be implemented comprehensively throughout a program. Faculty are key in integrating assessment into the curriculum.

- **Focused.** Is assessment realistic, with two to three outcomes being assessed per program per year? An assessment plan can help prioritize specific goals and objectives that can vary annually.

- **Shared.** Is assessment shared with others on campus through partnerships or as an assessment team? Assessment is a complex process, so partnering with others on campus, including faculty, assessment specialists, senior administrators and so on, thus becomes important.

- **Supported.** Is the senior leadership supportive of assessment efforts? Senior administrative support is crucial to the success of assessment efforts; without such support, assessment efforts can be less than successful. (See chapter 9 for more.)

- **Resourced.** Is there adequate time and funding for assessment efforts, and have administrators received sufficient training and knowledge in assessment, with ongoing professional development? Successful assessment efforts require adequate financial resources as well as trained staff and faculty to undertake such efforts.

- **Analyzed.** Have the assessment tools, results, and process been analyzed and evaluated from multiple perspectives? This can include taking into account the limitations of the assessment tools and the process. Think through who will do this analysis.
- **Communicated.** Have the results been communicated to all stakeholders? In the case of education abroad, for example, stakeholders include students, parents, faculty, program directors, academic advisors, administrators, advisory groups, alumni, and possibly funders or funding agencies. Communication mechanisms include direct student feedback, summaries and reports on websites, and alumni magazines.
- **Used.** Have the results been used for improving student learning? For program improvement? Use the information collected through assessment and only collect what will actually be used. In providing feedback to students, consider such questions as how the feedback can promote their learning instead of merely providing an indication of the monitoring of their learning, particularly in regard to students' continued intercultural development. Further, how can the feedback help students redirect their learning to achieve intended goals, such as global citizenship development? Is feedback mutual, allowing students opportunities for sharing information and reflecting on the experience in the classroom, abroad, or other international or intercultural learning opportunity? How and how often is the feedback communicated to students? Rubrics (rated scales) are often a more precise way to document student learning and provide specific feedback (see appendix E for sample rubrics). In regard to program improvement, what do assessment results indicate about changes that the program may need, including issues relating to procedures and personnel, to improve the learning experience itself? Consider how the assessment information can be used to revise the current goals and objectives of the program or course, and explore what students are doing well and what areas need to be strengthened to improve their learning in those areas. Note: Of the points listed here, this one is the most important; use of assessment results is absolutely crucial to an effective assessment strategy.
- **Reviewed.** Have the assessment process and strategy been reviewed on a regular basis and improved upon? Regular, planned review of the assessment team, process, and strategy is important in improving the overall assessment efforts.

Figure 7.1 shows a checklist on outcomes assessment that you can couple with the program logic model (see chapter 5) to provide a solid framework within which to develop and implement effective assessment strategies that are connected within the institution.

CONCLUSION

Assessment takes time, effort, and money—so it's tempting to look for the easy way out. However, the easy way out often means wasted time, effort, and money given the ineffectiveness of such efforts (see pitfalls, chapter 8). How can you make sure you're getting a reasonable return on your investment? It comes down to the kind of process and framework you put in place from the beginning (chapter 5). If you invest time engaging stakeholders in developing an assessment strategy through the lens of a logic model, your assessment efforts are far less likely to be in vain. Instead, this kind of preparation (assessment strategy) will yield effective assessment results that will not only improve students' learning but also lead to improvement of programs and courses.

CHAPTER 8

Pitfalls to Avoid, Strategies, and Lessons Learned

International educators who engage in outcomes assessment may want to explore some common pitfalls that can impact the effectiveness of assessment efforts. Use this list to gauge assessment efforts within your program or institution.

1. *Not clearly defining or prioritizing what is being measured, and not consulting the literature when developing a working definition.* Any terms such as *intercultural competence* or *global citizenship* need to be defined, ideally based on theoretical principles and frameworks found in the literature. See appendix B for more on defining *intercultural competence*, since this common term (or variation thereof, such as *global competence*) appears in many goal statements.

2. *Not planning intentionally for assessment, or simply not having an assessment plan.* Not having a developed assessment plan means that implementation logistics have not been thoroughly examined. Without a plan, outcomes assessment occurs randomly and may or may not actually measure the stated goals and learning objectives. Note: For those teaching courses, a syllabus documents much of the information that would be in an assessment plan.

3. *Borrowing assessment plans, tools, and methods from others.* Just because another organization is using a particular assessment tool doesn't mean that the tool will match your stated goals and learning objectives. The measurable objectives should point exactly to which evidence needs to be collected. Tests and tools thus vary by program and course. The assessment plan needs to be tailored to your specific mission, goals, objectives, and program parameters, which means others' plans and methods may not work in your particular assessment context. In fact, using tools without ensuring alignment with your goals and objectives will lead to invalid results. (For more on validity, see the discussion later in this chapter.)

4. *Making assessment the responsibility of one individual.* Assessment involves teamwork, collaboration, and the support of many, as discussed in earlier chapters. To garner that needed support and expertise, more than one person

needs to be involved in the assessment process, although one person can coordinate efforts with others. Thus, delegating assessment to one person or office alone is generally not a good idea, since assessment is not a solitary effort. Even in a classroom setting, assessment is an endeavor between the instructor and student to improve student learning.

5. *Leaving assessment to the end.* Dialogue about learner success and learning outcomes should take place among all relevant persons at the beginning of the process (see chapters 6 and 7). Too often, programs may bring in "an assessment person" or mistakenly think assessment can be addressed as an afterthought toward the end of the process, when it's already much too late to properly develop and implement an assessment plan and team. Backtracking then becomes quite difficult, if not impossible (see chapter 2). Beginning a course or program design with the end in mind is necessary for assessment to be integrated throughout a course, program, or experience. When possible, do not leave assessment to the end, but rather start with assessment, as outlined in this book.

6. *Not aligning assessment tools or methods with stated goals and objectives.* Understand the purpose(s) of each tool and method to make sure it fits in collecting the evidence needed to determine whether the learning objectives have been achieved. If assessment tools and methods are not aligned with stated objectives, the results will be invalid, regardless of the validity of the tools used.

7. *Using only one tool or method to assess outcomes.* Outcomes in international education tend to be complex (see chapter 3). One tool or method does not provide a comprehensive measurement of the complexity of outcomes. Moreover, there are numerous elements to intercultural competence (see appendix B), and tools and methods should include a multiple-perspective approach. For example, part of intercultural competence can only be determined by "the other" as to how appropriate an individual has been in the intercultural interaction. A multi-method, multi-perspective assessment package needs to be developed as part of the assessment plan to provide a more comprehensive picture of student learning in international education. Remember, outcomes assessment needs to be both formative (ongoing) and summative (final), meaning that it is woven into the entire process as well as assessed at the end. See chapter 4 for more on this.

8. *Trying to assess too much at once.* Given the amount of effort and resources needed in using a multi-method, multi-perspective approach in assessing concepts such as intercultural competence, you need to prioritize specific objectives that are aligned with overall goals. Keep it simple by evaluating a limited number of objectives per year, instead of assessing everything.

9. *Collecting information and then stopping.* Too often, programs may engage in assessment and collect information but not follow through by using this information effectively. Instead, collected information may reside in a spreadsheet or on a shelf until eventually discarded. It is incredibly important for data gatherers to effectively use information that is collected—providing feedback to the learners, improving the program, and communicating results to stakeholders. Thus, one adage in the assessment process is to collect only what will actually be used. If it's not going to be used, then don't collect it. To ensure proper usage of assessment information, the assessment plan (see chapter 7) needs to include specific details about how information collected from each tool and method will be used. For example, carefully scrutinize questions on surveys to ensure that each question is important enough to keep. Any unnecessary questions should be deleted.

10. *Analyzing the information from only one or two perspectives.* When possible, engage with colleagues, especially from other disciplines, in reviewing and analyzing the information collected from the assessment. This approach ensures a less biased interpretation and opens up the information to greater possibilities of analysis. Viewing the collected assessment information from only one perspective introduces the possibility of a narrower, and possibly erroneous, interpretation.

11. *Not evaluating the assessment plan and process.* One area that is easy to overlook is evaluating how well the assessment plan worked and what could be improved in the future, including how well the tools and methods worked in collecting the evidence needed and whether the same set of priorities (as illustrated through the goals and outcomes statements) should be continued in the future or reset to include other priorities. Learners should also assess the learning process—to be able to reflect on the overall process and progress of their intercultural learning. This reflection is key to a learner's development, and learners need to be made aware of their own role in this assessment process.

12. *Not using a control group or collecting baseline data.* Depending on the purpose of the assessment (beyond providing feedback to students), a control group or baseline information may be desired to ascertain whether a certain intervention or learning experience was successful in contributing to a learner's development. Control groups and baseline information are some of the best ways to demonstrate the success of such interventions. Using control groups, though, can sometimes be a challenge since administrators or faculty may not have access to information from a similar group of students not going through the course or experience abroad.

ASSESSMENT CHALLENGES IN INTERNATIONAL EDUCATION

Several challenges in assessing international education outcomes are considered in this section. Many are not unique to international education but are inherent in general assessment efforts.

Learner Articulation of Outcomes

Too often, without adequate preparation as well as a balance of intervention and support in the cultural learning processes, learners are not able to articulate clearly and specifically what they have learned. When asked to respond about a particular cultural learning experience, such as an overseas internship or education-abroad program, learners may only be able to allude to a "life-changing event." The question becomes, Have learners been prepared adequately for intercultural experiences and interacting appropriately with those from different cultural backgrounds, thus intentionally developing learners' intercultural competence to at least some degree? This perspective goes beyond "objective" cultural knowledge of literature, history, and so on to include "subjective" cultural knowledge such as communication styles and underlying cultural values so that learners better understand some of what is beneath the tip of the "cultural iceberg" of what influences others' behaviors and communication patterns. Through adequate preparation and in-depth cultural learning, as well as ongoing intervention and support, learners are able to more sufficiently articulate the change that occurs.

Integration of Assessment Tools and Methods on an Ongoing Basis

Have assessment tools and methods been integrated into the program or course on an ongoing basis instead of being proctored as a pre-/post- assessment only? Integration of such assessment and tools remains a challenge in some contexts when assessment is viewed as an add-on—something done only as a pre-/post- exercise. However, to be truly effective, such assessment—and thus learner feedback—is integrated as much as possible throughout the duration of the course or program, and ideally even beyond the end of the program. This approach allows for more guided feedback to be provided to the learner. Examples of integrated assessment include more direct and qualitative measures such as journals or blogs and e-portfolio assessment (see chapters 6 and 7). Thinking about how to collect evidence throughout an experience or course is the first step in integrating assessment efforts.

Validity

There's more to validity than whether a test or assessment measure is "valid." Validity has less to do with the actual instrument and more with the consequences of using the instrument and the interpretation and use of results (Gronlund, 2006). *Validity,* defined broadly as accuracy, has many layers: Does the test or instrument measure what it says it measures? More important is whether the instrument measures what *you're* trying to measure (learning objectives). *If you're not using the instrument for its intended purpose and it's not aligned with your learning objectives, the results will be invalid!* As assessment expert Robert Thorndike (2005) states, "The worthiness of a test cannot be separated from its use and the inferences that result," which he terms "unified validity" (p. 428). Furthermore, other factors weaken the validity of the assessment results:

- Inadequate sample of the achievement to be assessed
- Use of improper or misaligned types of tasks/assessments
- Unclear directions
- Improper inferences based on limited data or on too few tasks
- Improper administration—including inadequate time allowed, poorly controlled conditions, poorly trained administrators or raters, or lack of multiple raters
- Biased ratings or interpretations based on lack of adequate rubrics (adapted from Gronlund, 2006, p. 205)

Other types of validity to consider include *curricular validity*, which refers to the match between the measure and the content/curriculum (Thorndike, 2005), as well as *instructional validity*, which refers to the match between what is assessed in the measurement tool and what actually happens in the classroom or experience (Thorndike, 2005). For example, if students are not accustomed to or experienced in using a particular measure, then this can impact validity. External validity is yet another layer to consider, with the greatest challenge being "developing effective ways to communicate the results of . . . assessments to multiple audiences both on and off campus, including parents, policy-makers, employers and legislators" (Rhodes, 2010, p. 6).

Validity is also an issue in regard to the instrument itself. *Content validity* refers to the degree to which the instrument measures what it says it measures. *Face validity* relates to participants' perceptions of what the instrument measures. *Predictive validity* involves the degree to which behavior can be predicted, and *differential validity* gauges the degree of cultural bias. See chapter 9 for more on leaders' role in validity.

Validity is a huge issue and challenge in assessment, especially in international education assessment, when it seems that assessment measures are often used with little thought given to how closely such measures align with stated objectives or how specifically the results will be used for the measure's intended purpose. As mentioned numerous times throughout this book, a particular instrument may be valid and reliable, but misalignment between the instrument and the goals and objectives to measure reduces the validity of the results (more on this in chapters 2 and 4). To address validity issues, build in validity during the preparation and planning stages of assessment (which is why two chapters of this book focus on those crucial foundational steps in assessment).

Professional Development, Training, and Leadership

Given that there is no "quick fix" or easy way to assess international education outcomes, resources can become quite a challenge to implementing such assessment. Not only does this assessment take time and money, it also requires leadership support for efforts to be successful (see chapter 9). In addition, those involved in the assessment need to be trained in content and process, given that lack of training can lead to weakening of the results, as discussed in the validity section. Someone may have assessment expertise but lack in-depth knowledge of intercultural competence, for example; conversely, someone may be an intercultural expert but lack assessment knowledge. The importance of the assessment team can be highlighted here, with team members leveraging needed resources—money, time, or expertise (see chapter 6). Sometimes an organization needs to hire a consultant who has expertise in intercultural learning and assessment to guide a team through the international education assessment process.

STRATEGIES FOR ADDRESSING CHALLENGES

Based on an assessment study conducted by Bresciani, Gardner, and Hickmott (2009), the following strategies emerged as ways professionals dealt with inherent assessment barriers and challenges:

- *Educate colleagues* through workshops and one-on-one meetings, bringing in consultants, and sharing what works and what doesn't.
- *Define and clarify common terms* (like assessment, outcomes, intercultural competence, global citizenship, assessment plan, templates and rubrics, and especially expectations; see chapter 1).
- *Collaborate with others across the institution*, including students when appropriate.
- *Coordinate assessment efforts* through an assessment plan, utilize committees for coordination, and organize planning and review meetings and retreats.
- *Celebrate engagement* in assessment efforts, collaborations, and progress made on collecting evidence of student success, communicating results to all stakeholders.

Within these strategies, recognize that communication and transparency underlie all assessment efforts.

LESSONS LEARNED

What are some lessons learned from international educators who have engaged with learning outcomes assessment?

- **Keep it simple.** Prioritization of goals and objectives is the main way to keep the assessment process manageable. Don't try to assess everything at once. Focusing on one to two goals with two to three clearly stated measurable objectives under each goal is more than sufficient within a given year. The assessment plan and priorities can be revisited with a different order of priorities to assess in the following year.

- **Focus on what you can control.** Given that assessment is a collaborative effort, international educators may only have direct influence or control over limited aspects of student learning and assessment. Focus on what you can deliver in terms of evidence of student learning. International educators can also focus on the *process* of learning through international education experiences, including ensuring adequate preparation of students *before* they engage in an experience that may be outside their comfort zone (see Vande Berg, Paige, & Lou, 2012).

- **Align assessment measures/activities with outcomes.** Alignment is the primary key to success in effective international education outcomes assessment. Are measureable objectives aligned with goals? Are assessment measures aligned with objectives? Do activities align and support those goals and objectives? To ensure alignment, work with assessment and content specialists at your institution or beyond, given how crucial alignment is to assessment efforts.

- **Use direct and indirect measures.** Direct and indirect assessment measures are both needed to provide a more thorough picture of student learning. (See chapter 6 for examples of direct and indirect measures.)

- **Adapt.** Build on what's already there. Assessment is not just about what tool to use. It's about collecting evidence of student learning. How can existing courses, surveys, and other mechanisms be used to collect direct and indirect evidence of student learning? It could be as simple as adding an item on a satisfaction survey about listing "two to three insights you feel you learned through this experience." See chapter 6 for more on conducting an assessment audit to help you know what can be adapted.

- **Utilize well-developed rubrics.** Books have been written on how to develop rubrics (see the resources in appendix G) or either criteria for evaluating student work. Well-developed rubrics—which go beyond criteria such as "excellent, good, average, poor" or "met, didn't meet" certain expectations, but rather describe the change in learning or behavior occurring at different levels—takes time and work through discussions with a variety of stakeholders. Time spent reviewing, adapting, or developing rubrics is time well invested.

- **Incorporate multi-method, multi-perspective assessment methods.** Given the complexities of international education outcomes, especially those around intercultural competence development, a multi-method (direct and indirect), multi-perspective (beyond a self-perspective) approach to assessment must be used to collect evidence of student learning. See chapters 5 through 7 for more.

- **Ensure ongoing and integrated assessment.** Effective assessment in international education is recognizing that a pre-/post- survey is insufficient in telling the full story of student learning. Rather, assessment efforts must be ongoing and integrated as much as possible in order to provide a more complete picture of student learning in international education. See chapters 6 and 7 for more on this topic.

- **Use assessment information, especially for student feedback and coaching.** As emphasized at several places in this book, actually using assessment information that has been collected is very important, and an assessment plan developed from the outset will ensure that a plan is in place for using the information collected. Most importantly, using the information to provide feedback to students for their continued learning and development is crucial. A growing trend is to provide personal coaching for students, using the information collected.

- **Have a team and a plan.** In the end, assessment is a team effort and involves collaboration across the institution, especially with those engaged most closely in the classroom: the faculty. Start by identifying allies throughout the institution and get them involved in international education assessment. An assessment plan *from the outset* will help identify stakeholders and collaborators, and highlight next steps on how to get started with assessment so that efforts are coordinated, integrated, and utilized, and so that stakeholders "buy in" to the process. When developed early on and implemented properly, an assessment plan should yield quality information on student learning and ensure an effective, rigorous process.

CONCLUSION

There are pitfalls and challenges to be overcome through the intentional implementation of international education outcomes assessment, and too often, not enough attention is given to these issues. Those engaged in assessment efforts must explore carefully the numerous pitfalls inherent in the assessment process, many of which can be addressed through laying the appropriate foundation for assessment and engaging in the necessary preparation before jumping into actual data collection. As Palomba and Banta (2001) state, "The ultimate goal of assessment is to . . . improve . . . learning. Whether or not assessment will be successful in this regard is not determined at the time evidence is generated; it is determined early in the process when the groundwork for assessment is put in place" (p. 21). This book outlines some key ways to ensure that the groundwork is indeed in place for meaningful international education outcomes assessment, and in so doing, helps proactively address some of the pitfalls and challenges along the way.

CHAPTER 9

The Leadership Role in International Education Assessment

While leaders in international education may not be actively engaged in assessment efforts, leaders should still understand what is needed to support and facilitate such assessment, as well as how to leverage assessment results. What do leaders need to know and be able to do in order to lead assessment efforts effectively? This chapter outlines key competencies that leaders need for engaging successfully in assessment efforts and also discuss crucial questions that leaders should ask regarding internal assessment efforts. It also outlines strategies for leveraging assessment results to achieve larger institutional goals.

Effective leaders must pay attention to assessment. As Hudzik and Stohl (2009) note, "Lack of attention to assessment weakens the priority which the institution gives to internationalization" (p. 9). Heyl and Tullbane (2012) add that "being proactive in the assessment arena . . . helps make the university a true learning organization" and that leaders can "contribute to the continuous assessment and renewal of the university's human capital, a key to the future of institutional vitality in the 21st century" (p. 125). Focusing on assessing internationalization efforts can help leaders play a critical role in not only elevating the profile of internationalization within an institution but also linking assessment to "diverse units on campus, from academics to student affairs and institutional research" (Heyl & Tullbane, 2012, p. 125) so that internationalization becomes increasingly institutionalized and integral. As internationalization becomes integrated within an institution, assessment becomes even more crucial in bringing together various constituencies and stakeholders.

LEADER COMPETENCIES IN INTERNATIONAL EDUCATION ASSESSMENT

While leaders may not need to understand the intricacies of assessment (although assessment basics are outlined in this book), leaders should still have a common frame of knowledge and competence in terms of being able to support and lead assessment efforts more effectively. Here is a list of basic competencies for leaders; this list is by no means comprehensive, but it represents the essence of the competencies that leaders should have.

- Understand the necessity of clear goals and objectives as the starting point of assessment efforts, and provide leadership in developing clearly stated goals and objectives aligned with mission.
- Understand that learning outcomes assessment is the foundation to effective assessment in international education.
- Understand that assessment is more than a pre-/post- measure.
- Understand the necessity of a multi-measure approach to assessment, given the complexity of international education outcomes.
- Understand that assessment is more than numbers (outputs).
- Understand the role of effective assessment in internationalization efforts and stay current on published outcome studies in international education, reviewing them carefully to determine the quality of the studies and corresponding results and conclusions. (Note: There are varying degrees of quality in such research studies and conference presentations on assessment.)
- Develop sound assessment policies that support and reinforce assessment efforts.
- Ensure that the assessment plan is well-designed (see checklist provided on p. 78 and p. 129) and that assessments are of high quality, analyzed appropriately, and used effectively.
- Ensure that a productive, balanced assessment system is in place that serves the needs of a wide variety of stakeholders, especially the learners, in terms of what decisions need to be made.
- Understand that those engaged in implementing assessment need support, which means promoting the benefits of assessment, utilizing assessment results, and providing professional development opportunities to ensure that staff are prepared and equipped to develop assessment teams, plans, and practices.
- Understand that implementing assessment goes beyond delegating it to the "assessment people or office" and making sure that adequate infrastructure is in place to support assessment efforts.
- Ensure effective use of assessment results at the program and institutional levels, thereby turning assessment information into action.
- Communicate assessment results effectively and appropriately to a wide range of stakeholders.
- Understand the importance of reviewing and revising the assessment plan and practice on a regular basis.
- Understand issues related to unethical and inappropriate use of assessment practices and information, and protect learners and staff from such misuse (adapted from Stiggins, 2008).

In addition, leaders should keep in mind the learners and their holistic learning experience, beyond just the outcomes associated with an international or intercultural experience. To that end, leaders should take into account the personal development and holistic learning across a student's educational career at an institution, and how international education outcomes fit within this larger picture. (See chapter 5 for a way to view assessment more holistically, beyond the numbers.)

ASKING THE RIGHT QUESTIONS

Leaders should also know which questions to ask to ensure that quality assessment is being done, given the time and resources invested in such efforts. Here are some questions to ask in order to evaluate the quality of the assessment work:

- Who is on the assessment team? Does the team include learners themselves, as well as assessment experts?
- How was the assessment plan developed? What are the strengths of this plan? What do you see as the weaknesses of the plan? What are the procedures for reviewing and revising this plan? Has an external expert reviewed the assessment plan?
- Have all the terms in the goals and objectives been thoroughly defined based on the literature and in dialogue with others across the organization?
- How do these assessments map to the stated goals and objectives, as well as to learning activities and interventions?
- Why were these assessments chosen over all others?
- What do the assessments actually measure? What are the reliability and validity statistics of each assessment to be used?
- What specific evidence, direct and indirect, will these assessments yield that fit with the stated goals and objectives?
- What are the limitations of the selected assessments, and how will you account for them?
- Where do these assessments fit in Bloom's taxonomy? Are higher-level thinking skills emphasized?
- How will collected assessment information be used and communicated? With whom? By whom?
- What else is important for you to know about the assessment work to date?
- What about costs—human and financial resources that must be devoted to the assessment process? Is the cost worth the potential benefit to the student? To the course or program? To the institution?
- How meaningful and relevant are the assessment results? To whom?
- How do these assessment efforts align with institutional mission and goals?

HOW TO LEVERAGE ASSESSMENT EFFORTS AND RESULTS

One of the most crucial roles a leader can play in assessment is leveraging the results effectively. Here are some strategies for utilizing assessment efforts within the institution.

Mapping current international education efforts to the assessment plan and collected information (coordinating an assessment audit—see chapter 6 for more). Mapping is extremely beneficial—to be able to see what's being done already and where the gaps are, which can result in development of additional programs, partnerships, and courses. This is sometimes also known as an *assessment audit,* which is valuable to conduct at the institutional-level (what institution-wide data are being collected that can help inform achievement of international education outcomes), departmental level, program level, and course level. Include information on who reviews the data and how data are currently being used. As part of the mapping exercise, leaders can review how international education assessment relates to broader institutional learning outcomes.

Connecting and aligning international education assessment to accreditation processes. Leaders have found it helpful to align international education outcomes assessment with broader institutional efforts around accreditation. For example, see appendix F for a list of higher education institutions in the southeastern United States that have focused their accreditation Quality Enhancement Plans (QEPs) on some aspect of international, global, or intercultural learning. Leveraging international education assessment to bring value to institutional accreditation enhances the role of international education within the institution.

Connecting with others on campus, especially stakeholders, and involving others in international education efforts. Given that stakeholder identification is a key step in the assessment process (see chapters 6 and 7), assessment efforts provide an opportunity to connect stakeholders, which then allows for strengthening of overall international education efforts.

Identifying other allies on and off campus. Assessment is not an effort for one sole person or office. Thus, leaders are in a position to identify others across and beyond the campus who are allies in either international education, assessment, or both. Leaders can leverage assessment efforts to build greater support for international education efforts.

Begin to create not only a culture of assessment but also more of an intercultural and global culture at the institution. In the end, a desired overarching goal is the creation of a culture of assessment in which learning and assessment are viewed as core to everything else. Once a culture of assessment is in place, assessment is no longer viewed as an add-on or as a necessary evil but rather as an integral part of the teaching and learning process. Once intercultural and global outcomes are incorporated into the curriculum as well as the co-curricular and extracurricular efforts, internationalization becomes more institutionalized, and an intercultural and global culture is able to develop. Leaders can emphasize the importance of integrating assessment into all international education efforts, which in the end improves the quality of the institution itself. The culture of a discipline often drives the assessment process (Muffo, 2001).

Advocating for additional resources, including staffing. A common way to leverage assessment efforts is in advocating for more resources to enhance student learning in international education. This could also include strengthening the infrastructure to support student learning, including the hiring of additional staff, the development of additional partnerships, and so on.

Implementing change. Assessment should and can lead to actual change. Leaders play a significant role in implementing and supporting such changes, some of which may be structural as well as programmatic. To facilitate change, a key question leaders can ask here is, "As a result of what we've learned from the assessment results, what will we do now?" Changes may affect programs, and even curriculum, which is arguably at the core of international education. Changes in curriculum can result in more coherence across courses, as well as deeper integration of international education outcomes across degrees and programs.

Communicating results. One of the major roles a leader can play in assessment efforts is in communicating the results widely to all stakeholders and, in so doing, telling a vital story about international education efforts and the impact it has on all involved. Walvoord (2004) says that a good starting point on communication is to ask, "Who needs to know what, for what?" Successful communication needs to be facilitated by a leader—someone who can encourage communication externally as well as internally, within departments and programs. Such facilitation may occur through planned events like brown-bag lunches, faculty retreats, and student exhibits and showcases, as well as through written communication online and more creative communication such as video or other displays.

SOME ISSUES FOR LEADERS

While leaders could address many issues related to assessment, five highlighted here pertain directly to international education.

Quality and Effectiveness of Assessment Efforts

Leaders want to make sure that resources, including staff and finances, are being used effectively. Given the amount of resources invested in assessment, such efforts should meet certain basic standards (see chapter 4, p. 129, and appendix D) and produce desired results.

Certificates

Numerous higher education institutions offer some variation on a global or intercultural certificate. Leaders need to be aware of some of the issues inherent within offering such certificates—namely, that caution must be used when developing and offering such a certificate. For example, is an institution certifying that students are globally proficient? If so, according to whom? To what degree? Based on what evidence? What exactly is the certificate certifying? What are students able to *do* with such a certificate (beyond claiming it as part of their transcript)? Offering certificate programs even has legal and ethical ramifications sometimes. Often questions such as the ones noted here have not been thoroughly explored. In fact, too often, such certificates or variations thereof are given based simply on the completion of requirements, such as designated courses, a language requirement, and completion of a learning-abroad experience. Yet beyond a checklist of requirement completions, what is the evidence of actual student learning achievement? Leaders need to be careful about not falling into the trap of an empty certificate without meaningful and rigorous learning assessment to support certification.

Resistance

Resistance to assessment efforts is normal and common. How do leaders counteract such resistance? They can play an important role in ways that others may not be able to do. For example, leaders can reach out to people who are more reticent, including faculty members, and listen to their concerns, to discover and address underlying issues. Usually those revolve around lack of time, concern about how assessment results will be used, and perceived lack of benefit. Ideas for addressing resistance include organizing and hosting a roundtable discussion or forum, bringing in an expert to serve as a keynote speaker, identifying and using allies and inviting others to join in a working group, holding a showcase or celebration honoring those already engaged in assessment efforts, and of course, offering incentives (financial or otherwise) to help limit resistance—in other words, helping others see the benefits of involvement in assessment. In terms of faculty concern about use of assessment results, leaders should stress ethical use of results, meaning that use of results must align with the purpose(s) for which they are collected. Evaluation of faculty is generally not a stated purpose of international education assessment. Resistance to assessment efforts, regardless of the reasons, can certainly hamper such endeavors. In the end, leaders may need to move forward with those who are on board; eventually, people who are more resistant will see how doable assessment can be.

Staffing

Many people involved in international education are not necessarily trained in assessment, which goes far beyond being able to administer a pre- and post- measure.

Thus, in addition to using principles of effective assessment, reviewing a checklist is also important for assessment administrators—meaning those who are involved in coordinating and implementing assessment efforts. Leaders can ensure that those implementing assessment have the background and training necessary to be effective in assessment endeavors.

Competencies for staff involved in assessment efforts include the following:

- Can put together and facilitate a team of stakeholders in developing an assessment plan.
- Can guide the development of clear goals, defined terms, and objectives.
- Can understand validity and reliability issues related to assessment tools and methods (see chapter 8).
- Can understand the unique context of international education (see chapter 3), including implications of the developmental and lifelong learning aspects of intercultural learning.
- Can differentiate good tools from bad tools, as well as quality assessment studies from poorly done studies.
- Can guide selection of assessment methods and tools aligned to stated goals and objectives that are appropriate for learners' developmental levels.
- Can develop and adapt rubrics and other measures as needed (using descriptive vs. judgmental criteria).
- Can administer, score, interpret, and apply results in a competent, professional manner.
- Can provide professional and useful feedback in dialogue with learners.
- Can guide the review and revision of the assessment plan and process.
- Can recognize unethical, illegal, and otherwise inappropriate assessment methods and practices, as well as inappropriate and unethical uses of assessment information.

If staff are not equipped with the necessary competencies as outlined here, leaders should support professional development opportunities to help staff acquire needed assessment skills, through attending assessment conferences, workshops, or courses (see appendix G for more). In addition, leaders should consider hiring practices as an opportunity to find suitable staff with assessment skills as well as to reward staff for assessment efforts implemented through programming.

Changes in the Institution

Given that most of the learning outcomes assessment focuses on the individual level, how can leaders use such assessment for institutional improvement? Outcomes information can be aggregated (often through coding and categorizing the information) to discern overall patterns within and across courses, programs, and departments.

Careful analysis of these patterns can not only be reported quantitatively in aggregate, but in turn lead to broader changes that impact and improve student learning.

Beyond this, an often-overlooked area of international education outcomes assessment is the overall impact that such efforts are having on the institution itself. If internationalizing the institution is so vital for a 21st-century education, then it should not be business as usual for the institution. Rather, the institution itself should be changing as a result. Thus, it behooves leaders to spend time examining the questions, "How is my institution being changed by international education efforts? By the partnerships we have? By the returning study-abroad students? By technology that is connecting my institution with the rest of the world? By the international students, scholars, and instructors here at the institution? Within the leadership of the institution?" If real change is not occurring within the institution as a whole as a result of international education efforts, then leaders need to rethink the internationalization process to determine ways to be more effective (see Heyl, 2007, for more).

CONCLUSION

What's the bottom line for leaders in assessing outcomes of international education? Leaders ignore assessment at their peril. Furthermore, leaders must be knowledgeable about assessment in the ways outlined in this chapter, including knowing what questions to ask, what competencies they themselves need, and what assessment competencies staff need. Leaders can utilize and leverage assessment as a powerful tool to accomplish the goals and outcomes of international education. Yet, for assessment to succeed, it needs to be tied to actual student learning. Active learning and feedback for students must be reflected in the assessment process itself. Flexibility and patience are required throughout the assessment process, which must be sustained through leadership support and oversight by pan-institution committees. Given the focus on student learning, faculty become key partners in this process. Leaders thus need to "create opportunities for faculty discussion and foster a sense of shared purpose" (Palomba & Banta, 2001, p. 261), so that they can see the important role assessment plays in student learning. A leader, working together with others, can leverage the power of assessment not only to improve and enhance international education efforts but also to increase the overall quality of the institution.

CHAPTER 10

The Future of International Education Assessment

This book has synthesized some of the key points in assessment literature in an attempt to demystify the assessment process in international education, especially focusing on how to prepare and set up assessment so that efforts are effective and meaningful, yielding desired results. In looking to the future of international education assessment, some issues remain, as does a recognition of the changing paradigm in assessing international education outcomes. A compelling research agenda as outlined here will contribute to the growing maturity of this relatively new area of international education.

ISSUES

This book has raised numerous issues that need to be addressed in international education assessment. Summarized here are some related directly to assessment, others related to the infrastructure, and some to the international education field. (See also chapter 3.)

Assessment Issues

Validity. Many issues are related to validity, besides whether the measure itself is "valid" (see chapter 8 for more). One of the most pressing validity issues is whether the *results* are valid, which depends on how closely the purpose of the measure is aligned with stated goals and objectives.

   Traditional assessments not aligned with reality. Traditional assessments, such as inventories and surveys, often do not reflect diverse real-life situations. International education learning outcomes assessment needs to focus more on assessing behaviors in realistic contexts.

   Developmental and longitudinal issues not being addressed. International educators need to consider to what degree current outcomes assessment reflects students' developmental growth (with the need to tailor assessments to the students), and focus more on students' needs (regarding learning) instead of educators' needs (regarding program evaluation). In addition, international educators need to address the dearth of longitudinal assessment, meaning the long-term impact on student learning and development.

Lack of multi-measure, multi-perspective approach to outcomes assessment. International educators need to move beyond the use of one assessment tool (see chapters 5 through 7 in this book) in order to gain a more complete picture of what and how students are learning from their international education experiences.

Infrastructure Issues

Need for further professional development around assessment. Many international educators do not have a background in assessment nor have they been formally trained in this area. Thus, international educators should gain more knowledge in assessment through professional development opportunities and assessment resources (see appendix G).

Need for more collaboration within an organization or institution. To avoid assessment being an isolated activity, international educators need to collaborate with others within their institution, including students, so that assessment efforts are part of the overall mission of the institution, are part of students' holistic learning (see chapter 3), and can be leveraged strategically to institutionalize international education within the institution, as well as to bring greater value to higher education.

International Education Assessment Issues

Myths are being perpetuated, even at conferences and in published studies. Given the lack of formal training in assessment prevalent among international educators, misinformation and myths (such as some of those reported in chapter 1) get transmitted—via conference presentations and even in published studies. International educators need to question what they hear and read about international education assessment and go beyond a tendency to think, "That sounds good so it must be right." Learn as much as you can beyond those presenting or publishing on outcomes assessment so that you can determine for yourself what makes for effective, quality assessment.

Proliferation of assessment instruments in international education. Given how new the international education field is to assessment, measurement tools within the field are proliferating, many of them for-profit in nature—and others are developed in-house, often with little attention paid to such issues as reliability and validity and the recognition that it can literally take years to develop a sound, reliable, and valid instrument.

Lack of quality assessment in international education. International educators need to take assessment to the next level by developing and using actual assessment plans, using assessment information for student learning, and so on. It's time to move beyond the use of one pre-/post- measure in international education, which is quite an inadequate approach, as discussed throughout this book.

LOOKING TO THE FUTURE

Global Efforts

Tuning and other qualification frameworks are elevating the level of discussion around the meaning of degrees. This continued discussion and proliferation of qualification frameworks around the world will undoubtedly affect international education. Specifically, international educators may want to take an active role in such discussions by looking at what students should know and be able to do in regard to international education outcomes within a particular degree.

Accrediting bodies are increasingly operating beyond national borders, and many of those include international education–related outcomes, as discussed in chapter 1. For example, ABET Inc. and AACSB International (Association to Advance Collegiate Schools of Business) are most active in this arena (Green, Marmolejo, & Egron-Polak, 2012). In Europe, the European Quality Assurance Register for Higher Education (EQAR) provides a list of "recognized accrediting or quality assurance agencies," but "It is possible to envision EQAR or a similar agency becoming a world-wide registry" of such accrediting bodies (Green et al., 2012, p. 452). How will international education–related outcomes be reflected in accrediting standards as they continue to develop around the world?

Questions for the future in regard to global efforts on outcomes assessment include how such efforts will affect institutions and teaching staff or faculty, as well as the degree to which such efforts will take into account the more holistic, developmental nature of outcomes within international education.

Technology

In looking to the future, technology will play an increased role in the assessment of international education outcomes. In particular, e-portfolios seem to be a mechanism that not only allow for collection of primarily direct evidence of student learning but also a way to track student learning over time, beyond one course or experience. E-portfolios and other technologies facilitate more collaborative assessments. With clear instructions and guidelines, students provide feedback to each other as modeled by the instructor. Well-designed rubrics are used for online work and discussions, and students are invited to provide input on other online assessments (Palloff & Pratt, 2009). Class response systems (with clickers or mobile phones, for example) are increasingly being used to collect real-time evidence of student learning. And employing mobile phones (e.g., using apps) in assessment carries the possibility of more innovative assessment techniques in the future. For example, the Council of Europe recently developed a mobile app for intercultural competence self-reflection. Other potential areas for assessment in the future include online games and simulations.

With the rise of massive open online courses (MOOCs), and the realities of 24/7 access to information, the concept of *digital badges* earned for completing online courses or acquiring skills emerges as a potential way of credentialing learning in international education. Badges are symbols or visual indicators of the acquisition of an accomplishment, skill, quality, or interest. Badges have significant implications for assessment of international education learning outcomes, in that these indicators could be developed to document the knowledge, skills, and behaviors gained through international education courses and experiences from across a wide variety of providers. In this way, badges accommodate numerous and more personalized pathways in the acquisition of such knowledge and skills. For example, learners may be able to document significant learning experiences that occurred prior to their matriculation into a university (a high school exchange program, for example, or time spent living overseas, or an internationally oriented curriculum such as offered through the International Baccalaureate Organization). Badges can be used for formative and summative assessment, as well as for formal and nonformal learning, and work quite well within competency-based learning. As in the already existing world of physical badges (e.g., the Boy Scouts), a digital badge would need to indicate how it was earned, who issued it, the date of issue, and, ideally, a link back to some form of actual evidence relating to the work used in earning the badge. Badging systems have been developed to aggregate badges earned from a wide variety of experiences—beyond one university, for example. The use of digital badging is expected to increase and is already gaining prominence. For example, in 2012, the MacArthur Foundation, with additional support from the Gates Foundation, funded a Badges for Lifelong Learning Competition.

Questions related to using technology for assessment include some of the following, raised by assessment experts Bresciani, Gardner, and Hickmott (2009): How does the use of this technology promote formative as well as summative assessment? How does the technology enable us to better use results to improve student learning and development? Who benefits from the use of this technology? How does this technology promote meaningful learning and deep engagement with international education content and processes? How can you ensure that the technology does not drive assessment but that the need for evidence is driving the use of technology?

With the rapid evolution of technology, other tools may emerge that could work well for collecting evidence of student learning and performance (behavior), and international educators should stay abreast of technology developments that could be used in assessment efforts.

A Changing Assessment Paradigm in International Education

As international education assessment continues to develop and mature, a changing paradigm is emerging. While continuing to proliferate, self-reporting tools are insufficient in measuring the complexity of the learning that occurs through international education. Thus, the more traditional evidence paradigm is shifting to one that goes beyond individual knowledge and written surveys to that of authentic evidence. Given the realities of a 21st-century society, the needs of today's learners, and the possibilities afforded through technology, assessment will shift to a performance-based, learner-centered paradigm that is relevant, collaborative, integrated, and more meaningful to the learner. What are the implications of this changing paradigm? Educators need to change their thinking about assessment from something that is "done to" learners that ultimately benefits the educators and administrators more than the learners. Instead, educators and administrators need to explore thoroughly questions such as: Do the learners view these assessments as relevant in their contexts? How can assessment be more collaborative by engaging the learners? How will learners benefit from these assessment efforts? If self-perspective instruments continue to be used, *is it always about obtaining the higher score?* Given the complexities of international education outcomes, though, perhaps a lower score is desired on post surveys, which may indicate more of a willingness to learn, a sense of cultural humility, and an awareness of the scope of personal development still needed (depending on the parameters of the actual tool used). How will assessment approaches encourage and recognize lifelong learning in a more holistic manner?

And ultimately, to return to chapter 1 of this book, *why* engage in assessment efforts? Is it about finding the easy way out (i.e., the one tool—which doesn't actually exist [see chapter 2]) in terms of "doing assessment," or is it about "assessment as a powerful tool for learning"? This changing paradigm necessitates moving beyond traditional self-report surveys to more observable behavior assessment, including the ability to work as a team and subsequent relationship development. A more tailored assessment approach takes into account individuals' *different pathways* for acquiring global, international, and intercultural learning outcomes, addressing different personal development levels within a more holistic framework of lifelong learning. With this new paradigm, the results of assessment efforts will shift from program improvement to individual coaching for further personal development. See Figure 10.1 for a summation of the changing paradigm of assessment within international education.

A RESEARCH AGENDA FOR INTERNATIONAL EDUCATION ASSESSMENT

A robust research agenda is emerging to aid in this paradigm shift. Some of these issues remain at the assessment level, while others are broader and more far-reaching.

Figure 10.1
The Changing Paradigm of Outcomes Assessment in International Education

From . . .	To . . .
Program/course centered	Learner centered
Traditional evidence	Authentic evidence
Self-perspective	Multiple perspectives (including self)
Universal/standardized	Tailored/customized
One approach	Multiple pathways
Participant	Citizen-activist
Separate	Holistic
Results	Process

- What are the implications of different cultural perspectives on outcomes assessment? What can be learned from these different perspectives to enhance assessment efforts and make them more relevant?
- How do cultural biases inherent in assessment practices impact learners and the resulting assessment information that is collected? How can these cultural biases be better mitigated?
- What are concrete examples of institutions and programs engaging in solid, quality assessment efforts that are based on principles of good assessment (see chapter 4) and adhere to assessment standards (see appendix D)?
- What makes for quality research studies in outcomes assessment in international education? As Deardorff and van Gaalen (2012) note, "Studies obviously vary by quality, and it is important to examine the research methodologies, data, and data analyses to determine the strength and quality of each study, including use of control groups" (p. 174). All too frequently, published studies or conference presentations may present the findings of a small group (e.g., a case study) with no control group, misaligned research methodologies, and lack of theoretical underpinnings, particularly regarding assessment.
- Given the plethora of existing assessments, what are the most effective assessment measures, methods, and tools to use when assessing students' intercultural, international, and global learning outcomes? This question

involves necessary research on the various tools, methods, and measures themselves, in a variety of settings under various conditions with diverse populations and parameters.

- Following on the previous question, what are the current limitations of any existing measures, and what are the gaps in measurement tools in collecting evidence of stated objectives in international education (e.g., behavior-based objectives may spur the need for more performance-based measures)? Outside-the-box thinking is needed on developing and evolving assessment measures to align with current and future realities and needs (see, for example, the discussion in this chapter on digital badging).

- What are the most effective means to collect direct evidence so as to move beyond—or at least augment—the predominant use of self-perspective tools, given the insufficient story that such tools tell?

- What are effective ways and methods to measure students' development more holistically, including the role of emotional intelligence in international education outcomes?

- What are the most effective ways to document unanticipated outcomes in international education?

- How do international education experiences "interrogate issues of power, racism, oppression, or social injustice" (O'Grady, 2000, p. 14), and how can learning from such experiences be documented?

- What is the impact of international education on higher education institutions? How has international education changed institutions? Many would argue that, to date, there has been little noticeable change in institutions as a whole, in the curriculum and beyond.

- What are the long-term results of international education outcomes? Answering this question means engaging in more longitudinal studies that examine students' lifestyle choices, careers, degree of civic engagement, and so on (see Paige & Goode [2009] as an example for how to set up such a longitudinal study). This also means undertaking longitudinal studies that look at institutional change over time, as well as the social impact on the local community, beyond economic impact, as a result of international education efforts.

- Given the changing migration patterns in today's world, to what extent does prior significant intercultural or international experience affect students' learning, intercultural interactions, and subsequent assessment results? How can the learning from those prior experiences be assessed and documented?

- What can be learned from other areas of higher education, such as student affairs, in regard to outcomes related to intersections of multi-cultural competence and international education? For example, how do multi-cultural outcomes in student affairs compare with those intercultural outcomes in service learning? What are the comparisons between methodologies used and effectiveness thereof?

- What can be learned from those in secondary education, including organizations facilitating high school exchanges, in assessing students' global learning so that postsecondary efforts build on, rather than duplicate, such efforts?
- How can international educators and administrators collaborate with others at the institution (e.g., academic staff, education-abroad colleagues, international education administrators, multi-cultural professionals, student affairs colleagues) to more holistically address students' intercultural development, so that such development does not occur within a vacuum but is connected to participants' postsecondary education and lifelong learning as a whole?

These are only some of the research questions that need further exploration as international educators move forward in developing more robust assessments to collect evidence of student learning and transformation. Other questions will continue to emerge as the international education field matures in regard to outcomes assessment, fueled by research results and further debates around student learning and the quality of international education efforts.

CONCLUDING THOUGHTS

The trend in measuring learning outcomes in education is here to stay. Outcomes assessment in international education is indeed doable within a holistic framework and a collaborative approach. Effective outcomes assessment begins with a clear purpose, aligned goals, clearly stated objectives, and an integrated collection of evidence that objectives have been achieved. There are numerous pitfalls to avoid and issues to be addressed within assessment efforts, as outlined in this book. The chapters have illustrated why calls for the "one best tool" that "everyone" can use in international education will not lead to meaningful results or effective assessment of what students actually learn and are able to do as a result of international education efforts, both on and off campus. Assessment is hard work but well worth the investment when placed within the larger vision of preparing students for a lifetime of learning in a rapidly changing and increasingly diverse world.

Appendix A

Handouts and Worksheets

PRACTICAL APPLICATION: ENGAGING IN ASSESSMENT DIALOGUE

Getting others engaged in thinking about assessment in international education assessment is a great place to start. On the following pages, you will find some handouts and worksheets you can use for discussion, including one on assessment myths and another on responses to assessment. (These may also be adapted with proper citation.) Many of these worksheets correspond to and support the chapters in this book.

Handouts and worksheets in this section:

HANDOUT: MYTHS IN INTERNATIONAL EDUCATION ASSESSMENT

Discuss your reactions to the following assessment myths.

1. Pre-/post- surveys are sufficient for assessment.
2. It's fine to collect the information and then figure out what to do with the results later.
3. There's one best tool to assess outcomes in international education programs.
4. It's best to develop the program first and add the assessment in later.
5. One person or office can do the assessment.
6. International educators should agree on one standardized tool that everyone can use.
7. The starting point is asking: Which assessment tool should we use?
8. The main reason to assess is for program improvement.
9. Assessment is too expensive, takes too long, and is a waste of time.
10. Anyone can do assessment—no special training or background needed.

Reproduced from: Deardorff, D. K. (2015). *Demystifying outcomes assessment for international educators*. Sterling, VA: Stylus.

MYTHS IN INTERNATIONAL EDUCATION ASSESSMENT

Facilitator's Guide

Note: This guide contains the responses to the myths sheet and is meant for facilitator use only (not as a handout).

1. Pre-/post- surveys are sufficient for assessment.
   - Pre-/post- surveys can be part of the assessment efforts, but they provide an incomplete picture of student learning.
2. It's fine to collect the information and then figure out what to do with the results later.
   - It's important to actually *use* the information collected; otherwise, it can be a waste of time and effort if the data are not used. An assessment plan ensures use of data.
3. There's one best tool to assess outcomes in international education programs.
   - There is no one best tool. The best tools and methods to use are the ones that most closely align with stated goals and learning objectives. Multiple tools and methods need to be used to provide a more complete picture of student learning.
4. It's best to develop the program first and add the assessment in later.
   - It's best to "start with the end in mind" and develop a program with clearly stated goals and objectives. An assessment plan developed from the beginning can be very useful for program development, too. (And that is the purpose of this book—to help administrators and educators better prepare for outcomes assessment so that it is not an afterthought, but rather is addressed in the beginning of program and course development so that efficient use of resources results in effective, usable assessment efforts.)
5. One person or office can do the assessment.
   - If possible, it's best to identify an assessment team that can plan and implement assessment, including the involvement of students. Assessment can quickly become overwhelming for one person. Use the expertise around you, including faculty.
6. International educators should agree on one standardized tool that everyone can use.
   - International education programs are not all identical. There are different missions, purposes, priorities, goals, objectives, needs, contexts, strengths, and so on. Assessment tools must align with goals and objectives in order for results to be valid. Given the many variances, no one tool will align with all the varied differences and circumstances.

Reproduced from: Deardorff, D. K. (2015). *Demystifying outcomes assessment for international educators*. Sterling, VA: Stylus.

7. The starting point is asking: Which assessment tool should we use?
   - The starting point is in asking, What are our goals and objectives? What do we want our students to know and be able to do? What evidence is needed to show that the objectives have been achieved? Clearly stated goals and objectives determine which assessment methods and tools to use.
8. The main reason to assess is for program improvement.
   - The main reason to assess is to improve student learning—to provide feedback to students. Program improvement, advocacy, and other reasons become secondary.
9. Assessment is too expensive, takes too long, and is a waste of time.
   - With appropriate planning, assessment can be manageable, affordable (especially when adapting what's already being done instead of trying to do something "extra"), and efficient.
10. Anyone can do assessment—no special training or background needed.
    - Many incorrect notions are perpetuated about assessment, even presented at international education conferences, so it is important for people engaged in assessment to receive professional training and knowledge in the foundations of assessment. It's more than doing a pre-/post- measure.

HANDOUT: RESPONSES TO ASSESSMENT

1. What is your experience with assessment?

2. Which response below most closely aligns with how you are feeling about assessment?
    a. Assessment? What's that?
    b. Assessment? I don't know how.
    c. Ignoring it
    d. Negotiating with someone else to do it
    e. Complaining about it
    f. Losing sleep over it
    g. Looking for the easy way out (one pre/post will take care of it, right?)
    h. Doing it

3. What would be helpful for you to know more about in regard to assessment?

ASSESSMENT QUIZ/DISCUSSION SHEET

To what extent do you agree with the following statements? (Some of these are meant to be provocative!) Please rate them according to the following:

1 = Don't agree; 2 = Somewhat agree; 3 = Agree

1. ____ All faculty and administrators need to be **actively engaged** in assessment for a department or program to really be "doing assessment."
2. ____ The best way to build a campus culture of assessment is for top administration to be prescriptive in student learning outcomes as well as assessment measures and methods.
3. ____ All departments and programs should be moving ahead on assessment at the same pace, meeting specific goals within specified time frames.
4. ____ Assessment is a time-intensive add-on that will be a huge burden to faculty and staff who are already overburdened.
5. ____ The most effective assessment programs are ones in which the students are not aware they are being assessed.
6. ____ Assessment is mainly about pre-/post- surveys.
7. ____ Good assessment practice is integrated throughout the program and is not something done at just one point in time.
8. ____ It's sufficient for one office to primarily implement assessment.
9. ____ Assessment is mostly a waste of time and is not very helpful.
10. ____ Assessment is primarily about student learning.

Adapted from S. Hatfield (2005)

Reproduced from: Deardorff, D. K. (2015). *Demystifying outcomes assessment for international educators*. Sterling, VA: Stylus.

ASSESSMENT QUIZ/DISCUSSION SHEET

Facilitator's Guide
(Note: This is not meant to be used as a handout)

Facilitator: Below are the instructions for this discussion sheet. Allow participants a few minutes to read through the statements on the handout and mark the extent of their agreement with the statements. Then invite participants to discuss these statements with each other. Following pair/small-group discussion, the facilitator debriefs the whole group. Below are some comments that could be made in the debriefing. There may also be other comments the facilitator wishes to make.

Instructions: To what extent do you agree with the following statements? (Some of these are meant to be provocative!) Please rate them according to the following:

1 = Don't agree; 2 = Somewhat agree; 3 = Agree

1. All faculty and administrators need to be **actively engaged** in assessment for a department or program to really be "doing assessment." > *Perhaps not ALL faculty and administrators need to be actively engaged, but faculty play a key role in learning outcomes assessment efforts.*
2. The best way to build a campus culture of assessment is for top administration to be prescriptive in student learning outcomes as well as assessment measures and methods. > *This certainly depends on the institutional culture, but generally it's best to involve a wide range of stakeholders in the assessment process—although leadership is certainly a key component to success.*
3. All departments and programs should be moving ahead on assessment at the same pace, meeting specific goals within specified time frames. > *Generally, each department and program has separate assessment plans that may or may not be moving at the same pace. Assessment efforts are more tailored to the context.*
4. Assessment is a time-intensive add-on that will be a huge burden to faculty and staff who are already overburdened. > *This may appear to be true for some faculty and staff. However, if they can* adapt *what they're already doing, then it may not be seen as quite so onerous.*
5. The most effective assessment programs are ones in which the students are not aware they are being assessed. > *Students are major stakeholders in this effort, so it's generally best to involve them throughout the assessment process.*
6. Assessment is mainly about pre-/post- surveys. > *Assessment is about* much more than pre-/post- surveys, especially if it is to be done effectively and in providing feedback to the learners. Pre-/post- surveys provide a narrow picture of what is happening and could be considered part of a more robust assessment effort, aligned to goals and objectives and involving a mixed-methods approach.*

7. Good assessment practice is integrated throughout the program and is not something done at just one point in time. > *Yes, this statement adheres to principles of good assessment.*

8. It's sufficient for one office to primarily implement assessment. > *While one office or person may coordinate efforts, it takes a team to implement assessment (unless done by faculty in a course—and even then, it may be helpful to collaborate w others).*

9. Assessment is mostly a waste of time and is not very helpful. > *This is especially true if assessment information is not used—for feedback to learners, for program/ course improvement, and so on.*

10. Assessment is primarily about student learning. > *Based on the assessment literature, this statement is indeed true, which comes back to how assessment results are being used and who benefits from the assessment. Bottom line: Students should benefit and results should be used for their continued learning and development.*

HANDOUT: DISCUSSION QUESTIONS ON INTERCULTURAL ASSESSMENT

1. Why is it important to assess international learning and intercultural competence?

2. What specific goals and learning objectives do you wish to assess within intercultural learning?

3. How are you currently addressing and assessing intercultural learning and competence?

4. What do you feel has worked well in the assessment process? What would you like to change?

5. What are some challenges you face along with some lessons learned in assessing intercultural and international learning?

Reproduced from: Deardorff, D. K. (2015). *Demystifying outcomes assessment for international educators*. Sterling, VA: Stylus.

ASSESSING OUTCOMES IN INTERNATIONAL EDUCATION: STUDENT SUCCESS

- What does student success look like in your course or program in terms of intercultural learning?

- What learning processes and approaches lead to student success in your course or program?

- How will students know they've been successful in their intercultural learning?

- How would *others* know your students have been successful in their intercultural learning? In developing their intercultural competence?

Reproduced from: Deardorff, D. K. (2015). *Demystifying outcomes assessment for international educators*. Sterling, VA: Stylus.

ASSESSING OUTCOMES IN INTERNATIONAL EDUCATION: FORMING AN ASSESSMENT TEAM

Building a learning community involves many different people. "When forming a team for international learning outcomes and assessment, it is helpful to think in terms of building a learning community. . . . It is important to keep in mind that this team need not be static, but that rather the team structure should allow for the team to evolve, expand, or regroup as needed through the various stages of the process." From the *American Council on Education Web Guide.*

1. Who are your external stakeholders?

2. Who are your on-campus stakeholders?

3. Who are your on-campus collaborators?

4. Others you need to involve:

Reproduced from: Deardorff, D. K. (2015). *Demystifying outcomes assessment for international educators.* Sterling, VA: Stylus.

ASSESSING OUTCOMES IN INTERNATIONAL EDUCATION: APPLYING THE PROGRAM LOGIC MODEL

Program:

Mission Statement:

Goals:

- **Inputs (Resources):**

- **Activities (Learning opportunities):**

- **Outputs (Participants):**

- **Outcomes (Results):**

- **Impact (Long-term results):**

PROGRAM LOGIC MODEL WORKSHEET

Use this worksheet to ensure alignment between the five elements of the program logic model.

PROGRAM:
PURPOSE/MISSION:
GOALS:

Inputs	Activities	Outputs	Outcomes	Impact

Reproduced from: Deardorff, D. K. (2015). *Demystifying outcomes assessment for international educators*. Sterling, VA: Stylus.

ASSESSING OUTCOMES IN INTERNATIONAL EDUCATION: DEVELOPING AN ASSESSMENT PLAN

Key Questions to Explore in Developing an Assessment Plan:

1. What is the mission statement?
2. What are the learning needs?
3. What are the stated goals and objectives, based on mission and needs? How have international learning outcome(s) been defined and prioritized?
4. What are the specific measurable indicators for these outcomes? What will the student know or be able to do upon completion? What changes will occur?
5. What baseline data can be collected?
6. What evidence will demonstrate what students have learned or how they have changed? *Note: Map evidence to outcomes.*
7. What assessment tools and methods most effectively capture evidence of student learning, both during and at the end of the students' learning experience? Do these tools specifically measure the learning objectives?

   During (formative):
   After (summative):

   Note: Be sure to consider the cultural biases and limitations of tools and methods used. Know what each tool purports to measure and make sure it aligns with the learning outcome.

8. How will the learning processes be assessed?
9. How will these assessment tools and methods be implemented and by whom?
10. Who will collect the data from the assessment tools and methods used, and who will have access to data?
11. Who will provide multiple perspectives on analyzing and interpreting the data, how, and how often?
12. How will the data be used to provide feedback to students (Who will do this? When? How often?), how will the data be used to make changes, and who will make those changes?
13. How will the data be communicated to and among stakeholders (means of communication, schedule for reporting, etc.? How will stakeholders assist in making changes?
14. How will the assessment plan itself and the assessment team be reviewed (who will do this and how often—including external review)?

CREATING AN ASSESSMENT PLAN FOR YOUR PROGRAM OR COURSE

Organization:

Mission statement:

Your program:

Learning needs:

Goals:

Measurable objectives (1–3):

Indirect evidence/measures (aligned to objectives), including data already being collected:

Direct evidence/measures (aligned to objectives), including data already being collected:

Use of data collected:

Activities/resources/materials to support students' achievement of goals and objectives:

Communicating results to/among stakeholders (who, by whom, when, how):

OTHER:

Who
On-campus collaborators:
Off-campus collaborators:

When (timeline):

How:

Reproduced from: Deardorff, D. K. (2015). *Demystifying outcomes assessment for international educators*. Sterling, VA: Stylus.

INTERCULTURAL COMPETENCE FRAMEWORK:
FROM THEORY TO ASSESSMENT

A. **Overall goals in your context** (for example, "developing intercultural competence")

B. **Starting point: Developing outcome statements based on the ICC framework**
Select two or three elements from the Deardorff ICC model (see appendix B) that are
the highest priority for you in your program or course. List the elements here:

    1.

    2.

    3.

C. **Now write specific measurable outcomes statements for each of the above
elements** (ideally this would be done in dialogue with other stakeholders, including
students). See below for an example from the Association of American Colleges &
Universities' Intercultural VALUE Rubric:

EXAMPLE (from AAC&U Intercultural rubric)—For cultural self-awareness:
Identifies own cultural rules and biases (e.g., with a strong preference for those rules
shared with own cultural group and seeks the same in others).
    Outcome Statement #1:

    Outcome Statement #2:

    Outcome Statement #3:

These statements will need to be refined through dialogue with your stakeholders.
Discussion points include criteria or indicators that these have been reached, development of basic to advanced levels of these statements, and so on. Be sure to have
only one measurable element per statement and ensure that the outcome statement is
realistic and achievable given the parameters of your program or course (for example,
a reasonable time frame).

Reproduced from: Deardorff, D. K. (2015). *Demystifying outcomes assessment for international educators*. Sterling, VA: Stylus.

D. Given the above statements, what do you and your stakeholders believe to be **evidence that these statements have been achieved**? Be sure to consider both indirect evidence (self-report surveys/tools, interviews, focus groups, etc.) and direct evidence (student writing, portfolios, observation, testing, etc.). List below.

Outcome Statements	Outcome Statement #1	Outcome Statement #2	Outcome Statement #3
Which evidence shows achievement?	Indirect: Direct:	Indirect: Direct:	Indirect: Direct:

Note: Be sure to use a multi-measure, multi-perspective assessment approach.

E. Now you're at the point to begin putting together an **Assessment Plan**, which includes a mission, goals, objectives, evidence that objectives have been met (which determines assessment tools and methods), use of data collected (for example, details for student feedback, program improvement), communication of data collected (to all stakeholders involved), timeline for the plan's design and implementation, who is responsible, and so on.

Reproduced from: Deardorff, D. K. (2015). *Demystifying outcomes assessment for international educators*. Sterling, VA: Stylus.

ASSESSING OUTCOMES IN INTERNATIONAL EDUCATION: SELECTING ASSESSMENT TOOLS

Key Questions to Ask in Selecting Assessment Tools

1. What are the goals and objectives to be assessed?
2. What evidence is needed to indicate success at achieving the objectives?
3. What does the tool measure? Does it measure what it says it measures (content validity)?
4. Does the tool provide evidence that demonstrates successful completion of the objective(s)?
5. What are the limitations and cultural biases of the tool?
6. Is there a theoretical foundation for the tool? How was the tool developed? In what contexts?
7. Is the tool valid (accurate) and reliable (consistent)?
8. Are the administrative and logistical issues involved manageable?
9. How will the results of the tool be used (including for individual feedback)?
10. How does the tool fit into the comprehensive assessment strategy (since it's important for more than one tool or method to be used)?

Here is a sample template for selection of assessment tools and methods:

Course/ program objective	Tool	Purpose of tool	Alignment of objective to tool purpose*	Psychometrics of tool (validity/ reliability)	Theoretical foundation/ development of tool	Administrative/ logistical issues involved?	Limitations of tool	Use of results

*Note: If there is little or no alignment between the course or program objective and the purpose of the tool, then select a different tool that fits better with the stated objective. Otherwise the results will be invalid.

Other Notes:

WORKSHEET FOR SELECTING ASSESSMENT TOOLS

Here is a template for selection of assessment tools and methods:

Course/program objective	Tool	Purpose of tool	Alignment of objective to tool purpose?*	Psychometrics of tool (validity/reliability)	Theoretical foundation/development of tool?	Administrative/logistical issues involved?	Direct or indirect evidence?**	Limitations of tool	Use of results?

*Note: If there is little or no alignment between the course or program objective and the purpose of the tool, then select a different tool that fits better with the stated objective. Otherwise the results will be invalid.

** Note: Direct evidence refers to actual learning (performance, evidence of learning in the experience or course itself, and so on). Indirect evidence refers to perceptions of learning (most often through self-perspective), usually outside of the experience or course.

Reproduced from: Deardorff, D. K. (2015). *Demystifying outcomes assessment for international educators*. Sterling, VA: Stylus.

CHECKLIST FOR PROVIDING STUDENT FEEDBACK

Does feedback to students:

- Provide timely responses specific to the student?
- Prioritize the most important points (related to learning objectives)?
- Allow for dialogue with students when possible?
- Describe both the work and the process when possible?
- Comment on at least as many strengths as weaknesses?
- Take advantage of teachable moments?
- Use criterion-referenced feedback on the work itself (i.e., rubrics)?
- Use norm-referenced feedback about student processes and effort?
- Avoid personal comments, especially judgment?
- Provide positive suggestions (not prescriptions) for moving forward?
- Use vocabulary and concepts that the student will understand?
- Tailor the amount and content (of feedback) to each student's developmental level?
- Tailor the degree of specificity to the student and context (assignment/task)?
- Communicate respect for the student and the work?
- Position the student as the agent?
- Cause the students to think or wonder (i.e., ask questions)?

Ground rules for peer assessment:

- Review your peer's work carefully.
- Compare the work with the rubric.
- Talk about the work, not the person.
- Don't judge, but rather describe the strengths and make suggestions for improvement.

Adapted from S. Brookhart (2008)

Reproduced from: Deardorff, D. K. (2015). *Demystifying outcomes assessment for international educators*. Sterling, VA: Stylus.

CHECKLIST FOR ASSESSING INTERCULTURAL OUTCOMES IN PROGRAMS AND COURSES

This checklist can be used when embarking on the task of assessing students' intercultural learning in programs and courses. In using the questions presented in the checklist, educators can design and implement a quality assessment process that helps provide effective evidence of learning:

1. Has the "Why engage in assessment?" question been answered adequately?
2. Is assessment framed in terms of the learner, instead of the program or course? In other words, who benefits from the assessment information collected?
3. Are there clearly stated goals and measurable objectives based on the mission?
4. Do stated goals and objectives align with learners' needs and developmental stages?
5. Have terms such as *global competence* or *intercultural competence* been defined based on the literature and tailored to the specific context?
6. Are intercultural outcomes supported adequately by learning activities, methodologies, materials, and resources?
7. Are assessment tools and methods aligned with measurable objectives? Is more than one tool being used?
8. Is an assessment team in place comprising assessment experts, intercultural experts, and stakeholders—including learners, instructors, and administrators?
9. Is an assessment plan in place, including details as to how specific assessment data will be used?
10. Do instructors and administrators have an understanding of the complexities of intercultural learning and its development process?
11. Have baseline data been collected, including from a control group, if necessary?
12. Has the assessment process itself been reviewed?

Reproduced from: Deardorff, D. K. (2015). *Demystifying outcomes assessment for international educators*. Sterling, VA: Stylus.

Appendix B

Assessing Intercultural Competence as a Learning Outcome of International Education

Darla K. Deardorff

The following article is adapted from Darla K. Deardorff, "Assessing Intercultural Competence," in *Assessing Complex General Education Student Learning Outcomes*, ed. Jeremy D. Penn (San Francisco: Jossey-Bass, 2011), and includes results of a 2013 research survey conducted by the author.

One of the oft-noted learning outcomes of international education is intercultural and global competences. Once these have been identified as a goal, one of the first steps in assessment is in defining exactly what is to be assessed—in this case, in defining the actual concept of intercultural competence. If it is to be assessed, then it must first be defined, after which specific, measurable learning objectives can be articulated. Too often, this term or other similar terms are used without a concrete definition. As Fantini (2009) discusses, it is essential to arrive at a definition of intercultural competence before proceeding with any further assessment steps. Over five decades of scholarly effort have been invested in defining this concept within the United States, and such work should thus be considered when developing a working definition of intercultural competence. Two studies (Deardorff, 2006; Hunter, White, & Godbey, 2006) showed that in the case of postsecondary institutions, such definitions and scholarly work were often not utilized. Instead, definitions relied primarily on faculty discussions without any consultation of the literature.

Countless definitions and frameworks are published on intercultural competence. The article discusses the first study to document consensus among leading intercultural experts, primarily from the United States, on aspects of intercultural competence (Deardorff, 2006), as determined through a research methodology called the Delphi technique, an iterative process used to achieve consensus among a panel of experts. The aspects upon which these experts reached consensus were categorized and placed into a model, found in Figure B.1, which lends itself to assessment and to the further development of detailed measurable learning outcomes. Specifically, this model was derived from the need to assess this nebulous concept and hence its focus on internal and external outcomes of intercultural competence, based on the delineation of specific attitudes, knowledge, and skills inherent in intercultural competence. Follow-up research was conducted on the model in 2013, resulting in

131

further validation of this model by intercultural experts. Further, the 2013 research found that it remains important to emphasize the developmental process of intercultural competence (i.e., the Process Model).

Given that the items within each of these dimensions are still broad, each aspect can be developed into more specific measurable outcomes and corresponding indicators, depending on the context. The overall external outcome of intercultural competence is defined as *effective* and *appropriate* behavior and communication in intercultural situations, which again can be broken down into indicators of appropriate behavior in specific contexts.

Several key points to consider in this grounded-theory model have implications for assessment of intercultural competence. According to this grounded-research study, intercultural competence development is an ongoing process. Thus, it becomes important for individuals to have opportunities to reflect upon and assess the development of their own intercultural competence. Given the ongoing nature of intercultural competence development, incorporating integrated assessments throughout a targeted intervention is valuable. Critical thinking skills also play a crucial role (see the skills module of the model in Figure B.1) in an individual's ability to acquire and evaluate knowledge. As a result, critical thinking assessment could also be an appropriate part of intercultural competence assessment. Attitudes—particularly respect (which is manifested differently in different cultures), openness, and curiosity—serve as the basis of this model and affect all other aspects of intercultural competence. Addressing attitudinal assessment, then, becomes an important consideration. All the intercultural experts in this study agreed on only one aspect: the ability to see from others' perspectives; assessing global perspectives and the ability to understand other worldviews thus become important considerations as well. Deep cultural knowledge entails a more holistic, contextual understanding of that culture, including its historical, political, and social contexts. Thus, any assessment of culture-specific knowledge needs to go beyond the conventional surface-level knowledge of foods, greetings, customs, and so on. Further, knowledge alone is not sufficient for intercultural competence development. As Bok (2006) indicated, developing skills for thinking interculturally becomes more important than the actual knowledge acquired. (For further discussion of this process model of intercultural competence, see Deardorff, 2006, 2009).

Another model used prevalently in the international education field and beyond is Bennett's Developmental Model of Intercultural Sensitivity (M. J. Bennett, 1993). The key to this model is its developmental nature, emphasizing that the acquisition of intercultural sensitivity is a developmental process—six stages in this case. The first three stages of this model—denial, defense/polarization, and minimization of difference—are considered to be ethnocentric stages, focused on the individual's cultural lens, while the latter three stages—acceptance, adaptation, and integration of difference—are considered to be ethnorelative, moving beyond one way of seeing the world. Hammer (2012) later developed a psychometric measure, the Intercultural Development Inventory (IDI), based on this model, which measures an individual's

Figure B.1
Intercultural Competence Framework

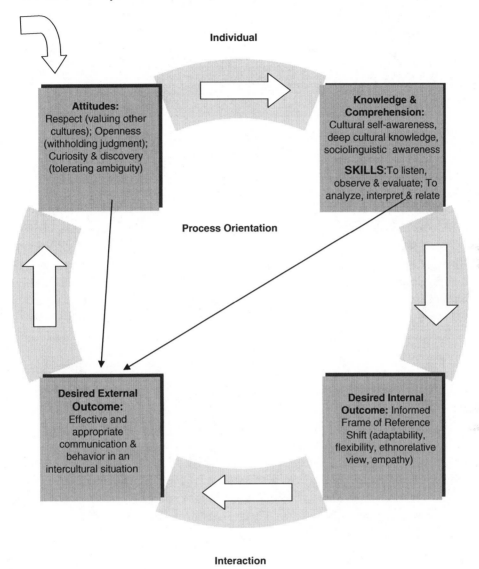

Source: Deardorff (2006)

perceived as well as actual stage of development, based on their responses to cultural difference statements.

Two other intercultural models highlighted in this article, those of King and Baxter Magolda (2005) and Cross (1988), are also developmental in nature and are used more within diversity and multi-cultural education, reflecting a grounding in diversity issues within the United States. Similar to Bennett's developmental model, King and Baxter Magolda (2005) propose a developmental model of intercultural maturity. They place their model within the context of a holistic approach based on the work of Kegan (1994), noting that such an approach "allows one to identify underlying capacities that may guide . . . a learner's ability to integrate knowledge, skills, and awareness, and to act in interculturally mature ways" (King & Baxter Magolda, 2005, p. 572). In their multidimensional framework, King and Baxter Magolda propose three domains of development: cognitive, intrapersonal, and interpersonal.

Terry Cross (1988) has developed a cultural competence continuum with six stages of cultural competence—for individuals and for agencies or groups. The six stages are cultural destructiveness, cultural incapacity, cultural blindness, cultural precompetence, basic cultural competence, and advanced cultural competence. In the advanced cultural competency stage, Cross sees one manifestation as advocating for cultural competence throughout the system and overall improved relations between cultures throughout society. Cross's model parallels those of Bennett and King and Baxter Magolda in delineating stages of development, which raises assessment-related questions such as the following: What direct evidence can be used to ascertain where individuals are in their intercultural developmental process? How do these stages of development reflect a person's actual competence in an intercultural situation? How do educators develop this competence in students, especially given the increased emphasis from employers on transferable skills?

Many other models and frameworks purport to define intercultural competence (see Spitzberg & Changnon, 2009, for a more thorough discussion); many, however, are not based on actual research. Regardless, in assessing intercultural competence, defining this concept within the context it will be used is highly important. Frameworks such as the ones highlighted in this article can become a key tool in laying the groundwork for assessing intercultural competence. These intercultural competence models can help educators specifically identify characteristics of intercultural competence development that can be translated into clear learning objectives that are actually measured or evaluated through assessment plans.

TRANSLATING INTERCULTURAL COMPETENCE DEFINITIONS AND FRAMEWORKS INTO ASSESSMENT EFFORTS

The important first step in assessing *intercultural competence* (ICC) is in defining the concept itself, using the existing literature as a basis. Most definitions and models tend to be general in terminology; thus, once a definition has been determined, one must develop a process that generates specific measurable outcomes and indicators within the context to be assessed. To begin that process, prioritize specific aspects of intercultural competence, based on the overall mission, goals, and purpose of the course, program, or organization. The definition used for intercultural competence determines the aspects that will be assessed as well as the level of assessment (i.e., individual, program, organization). As in the case of learning outcomes, the assessment level is usually that of the individual and the learning that occurs for each person. For example, based on the overall mission, "participants' ability to understand others' perspectives" may be an essential aspect of intercultural competence to assess and thus becomes a stated goal. From that point, one would engage other key persons in dialogue as to the best ways to achieve the specific measurable outcomes related to this goal. These ways of achieving the stated goal become the specified objectives, which are discussed in more detail shortly.

The process of prioritizing various aspects of intercultural competence is important and should not be done too quickly or taken lightly. The process itself often involves dialogue and discussion with key stakeholders to determine which specific elements of intercultural competence should be the focus of programmatic efforts and assessment endeavors. Prioritization is not a onetime discussion, but rather an ongoing process; needs and priorities may change from program to program or from year to year. Generally, choose two or three specific intercultural aspects to assess at any given time, due to the time, effort, and resources that the assessment efforts require.

Stating Goals and Measurable Objectives

Once the specific aspects of intercultural competence have been prioritized, the next step is writing goals and measurable objectives related to each of the prioritized aspects. First, let's look at what constitutes goals and objectives, or *learning outcomes*, as they are also called.

Goals are generally defined as the end destination. *Objectives*, on the other hand, are the means by which the goal or destination is reached. Objectives specify concrete learning expectations and how the learners will achieve the end goal. In stating goals, define success specifically for that particular program or course. What will success look like for this course or program participant? By the end of the program or course, what will the participant be able to do as a result of the learning that occurred? For example, a goal may be broadly stated as "Participants will be able to understand others' perspectives," "Learners will demonstrate the awareness, understanding, and skills necessary to live and work in a diverse world," or "Learners will become more interculturally competent." Specific, measurable objectives must then be articulated that state the learning expectations in achieving these goals. What will the learner need to be able to do in order to achieve the goal? The objectives become the road map for reaching the destination—the markers of important learning that ensure achievement of the goal.

What do measurable objectives or outcomes look like? In the assessment arena, a common way of thinking about measurable objectives is through the acronym

SMART: specific (what, why, how), measurable, action-oriented, realistic, and time-delineated. A key part of this statement is that the objective is realistic; it needs to fit what can realistically be accomplished with the course or program parameters. For example, it would not be realistic for a participant at a beginning language level to speak another language fluently after only two or three weeks in another country. For short-term study-abroad programs in postsecondary institutions, outcomes must realistically match the program length. For example, if the program exposes participants to another culture for six weeks, what can participants realistically be expected to achieve regarding intercultural competence development within that six-week period, given the level and quality of cultural preparation, the program parameters, and the way in which the intercultural experience has been set up? This in turn relates back to the overall priorities and which aspects of intercultural competence are deemed to be most important to that program or course.

In writing an assessment objective, usually only one action verb is used per outcome statement. Outcome statements (objectives) are focused on learning itself, not on the infrastructure, instructor, or activity. Examples of measurable outcomes under the general goal of "Understanding others' perspectives" are as follows: "By the end of the program, learners can articulate two different cultural perspectives on global warming," "By the end of this class, learners can define what a worldview is and three ways in which it impacts one's behavior." Writing specific outcomes statements (learning objectives) and developing indicators of the degree to which the statements can be assessed remains an area in need of further research, especially within specific fields such as engineering, law enforcement, and health care. The American Council on Education (Olson, Evans, & Schoenberg, 2007) provides a list of common intercultural learning outcomes found at the intersection of international and multicultural education. Those outcomes include ones found in appendix F, and even these statements can be tailored more specifically to a particular course or discipline.

IMPLEMENTING ICC ASSESSMENT—TOOLS AND METHODS

Spending adequate time on defining intercultural competence and developing clear, realistic, and measurable learning outcome statements based on the goals is an important step, since these outcome statements determine the assessment methods and tools to be used. Given the complexity of intercultural competence, a multi-method, multi-perspective assessment plan is desired. Advocating the use of multiple measures in assessing competence, Pottinger (1979) stresses that "how one defines the domain of competence will greatly affect one's choice of measurement procedures" (p. 30); he notes that pen-and-paper assessment tests have been widely criticized, due partly to the effect of the test format and partly to the limits such a test places on the complex phenomena being measured. Since competence varies by setting, context, and individual, using a variety of assessments ensures stronger measurement. Banta (2004) also advocates for multiple measures, stating that "multiple measures are essential because no single measure is perfectly reliable or valid; several measures of the same contract can furnish support for one another" (p. 5). In measuring intercultural competence, the variety of assessments should include *direct* and *indirect* measures. Direct measures are actual evidence of student learning (such as course assignments, performance, and capstone projects), usually collected during the learning experience, that illustrate *what* students know and can do (Banta, 2004). Indirect measures are *perceptions* of student learning (as collected through surveys, interviews and focus groups), usually collected outside of the learning experience, that help provide the *why* behind student performance (Banta, 2004)—the backstory. The key question to ask is, "What *evidence* of student learning exists regarding the stated objective?"

Further, using the definition of effective and appropriate behavior and communication in intercultural settings, measures need to be multi-perspective, beyond the learner's perspective. The learner can indicate to what degree he has been effective in an intercultural settings, but only the other person can determine the appropriateness of behavior or communication in the interaction, which emphasizes the need for multi-perspective assessments.

What does this all mean for assessing intercultural competence? Such assessment involves effort, and no "silver bullet" is available as an assessment tool; given the complexity of this concept, it would be challenging—if not impossible—for one tool to measure an individual's intercultural competence, especially a tool that yields a numerical score. In fact, Zessoules and Gardner (1991) conclude, "Norm-referenced, numerical scores do not yield detailed information about how a student has changed," adding that "isolated test scores tell us little or nothing about the ripening of processes and understandings students engage in" (p. 58), nor do they give a deeper and more complete picture of students' development of intercultural competence, which is vital in understanding this lifelong process. Furthermore, the concept's complexity gives rise to other questions such as, "Intercultural competence from whose perspective and according to whom?" or "Intercultural competence to what degree?" (See the Assessment Guide for Intercultural Competence at the end of this article for further questions to explore in the assessment process.) Research (Deardorff, 2006, 2009) found that a multi-measure, multi-perspective approach needs to be implemented when assessing intercultural competence in order to provide a more complete picture.

More than 100 intercultural assessment tools for collecting indirect evidence are available, in varying degrees of reliability and validity, with most being from a self-perspective. (For further detail on possible tools for assessing intercultural competence, see Fantini, 2009; Paige, 2004; and Stuart, 2008.) These tools should be combined with direct evidence (actual student learning or performance) to determine the degree to which the stated intercultural outcomes in students are achieved. A 2013 research survey by Deardorff examined the measures being used to assess intercultural competence–related outcomes at 190 higher education institutions (see Table B.1).

Table B.1
ICC Assessment Methods

ICC Assessment Method	Type of method	Percentage using method
Evaluation conducted by professors in individual courses	Direct	63%
Student paper or presentation	Direct	50%
Student journal/blogs/reflections	Direct	39%
Pre-/post- instrument	Indirect	36%
Interviews with students	Indirect	24%
Commercially developed self-report instrument	Indirect	24%
Custom-designed/adapted self-report instrument	Indirect	23%
Observation of students in specific situations (by professor, supervisor, host family, etc.)	Direct	21%
E-portfolios	Varies	18%
Ongoing assessment	Varies	17%
Longitudinal assessment	Varies	10%
Written test	Direct	8%

IMPLEMENTING ICC ASSESSMENT—GETTING STARTED

Given how daunting intercultural competence assessment can seem, one should start with manageable, bite-size portions, such as one or two clearly stated learning outcomes around aspects of intercultural competence. Then, one would design around those outcomes an assessment package consisting of at least one direct measure and one indirect measure for each of the learning outcomes (see chapters 6 and 7 for more). For each stated outcome, ask: What evidence do we need to demonstrate that this outcome has been achieved to some degree? To collect this evidence, explore first what is already being done to collect evidence of student learning and simply adapt data already being collected so that the data align with the stated outcomes. (Other measures can be added later, including ones from other perspectives.) For example, adapting existing data sources may involve adding a couple of questions on an institutional survey to students or on a study-abroad satisfaction survey that would collect evidence of student learning outcomes, which could be content-, process-, or practice-focused (e.g., "Give an example of a successful interaction you have had with someone from a different cultural background"). Another approach is to use data already collected, such as through the National Survey on Student Engagement

(NSSE), which has a global learning module that can be used for assessment purposes. For a worksheet that can be used to translate the Intercultural Competence Framework into practice, see appendix A.

SOME EXAMPLES OF PROGRAMS ASSESSING INTERCULTURAL COMPETENCE

Given the challenges of assessing intercultural competence, are there programs that indeed engage in such assessment? International education programs in postsecondary institutions provide some examples. On a broader scale, the American Council on Education has worked with numerous institutions within the United States in articulating global learning outcomes. Through this process, multiple assessments were used primarily through an e-portfolio method and a custom-developed self-report instrument. Other postsecondary institutions have also engaged in assessing intercultural competence through multiple measures, including self-report measures, journals, host family observations, supervisor observations, embedded in-class assignments, participant interviews, focus groups, and portfolios. These programs would often spend months—and in some cases up to two years—articulating the initial goals and objectives for developing and implementing an assessment plan on intercultural competence and global learning. In a 2013 study of nearly 200 higher education institutions, the most frequently used assessment method for intercultural competence outcomes was that of embedded classroom assessments (evaluations by professors, student papers, and presentations; see Table B.1), which is direct evidence of student learning. Of the institutions surveyed, a little over half were actively assessing intercultural competence using multiple methods.

In nonformal situations, ways to assess intercultural competence include observation by others, blogs, photo collages, and adaptation of satisfaction surveys to include questions on what was learned or gained as a result of participating in the experience. E-portfolios can also work in nonformal situations to collect evidence of intercultural learning. The challenge within this context is how the items in the e-portfolio would be evaluated and how to provide feedback to the learner.

The corporate world has examples of companies using a combination of self-report tools, 360° feedback instruments, and employee interviews to assess employees' intercultural competence development.

PRACTICES THAT LEAD TO DEVELOPMENT OF ICC

Regardless of the assessments used in measuring students' intercultural competence, the course or program should include actual practices and learning interventions that support and lead to intercultural competence development. How can students develop intercultural competence? (See J. M. Bennett [2009] and Berardo & Deardorff [2012] for more on this.) Two means are available in postsecondary education: through the curriculum and through co-curricular activities. These methods are often termed "internationalizing" the campus, which means bringing an intercultural and global dimension to students' education experiences.

What does it mean to infuse intercultural competence and global learning into courses? First, we should understand what intercultural competence and global learning are not; examples include a single international reading in a course or addressing this topic in one lecture, or even taking just one course in international studies or a related topic. Such cursory treatment is far too limited in guiding students through the developmental process of acquiring intercultural competence. To that end, intercultural competence needs to be addressed throughout many undergraduate courses, including STEM courses (science, technology, engineering, and mathematics). This infusion of intercultural competence and global learning into courses comprises finding multiple ways throughout a course to bring in diverse perspectives on issues, helping students begin to see from multiple cultural perspectives, using students' diverse backgrounds within a course, and requiring students to have either a local cultural immersion or study-abroad experience related to the major.

Given that intercultural competence manifests differently depending on the discipline, departments need to engage in reflection and collaboration around the following types of questions:

- What intercultural skills and knowledge are needed in this major?
- How does globalization affect this major, and what global learning should be required of graduates in this major?
- How can departmental assessments of students' intercultural competence go beyond one aspect, such as knowledge, to ensure that students have actually attained a degree of intercultural competence, and what will be the evidence?
- How can departments prepare their students to appreciate the multitude of countries and cultures that may affect their lives and careers?
- More broadly, what knowledge, skills, and attitudes do students need to be successful in the 21st century?

Beyond integrating intercultural competence outcomes within courses, educators and administrators need to understand that intercultural learning is transformational learning, requiring experiences that lead to this transformation. Consequently, developing intercultural competence does not unfortunately just happen because of learning knowledge about another culture or because persons from different backgrounds are in the vicinity of each other, or are even interacting with each other (Allport, 1954/1979). Intercultural competence "entails a more holistic, contextual understanding of that culture, including the historical, political, and social contexts

. . . beyond the conventional surface-level knowledge of foods, greetings, customs, facts, and so on to understanding the intricacies of these deeper contexts" (Deardorff, 2009, p. 480). Furthermore, intercultural competence involves a more holistic learning approach that takes into account students' emotional intelligence, personality characteristics (e.g., resiliency), and the actual situation and environment, among other factors. To that end, service learning and study abroad become two mechanisms by which students' intercultural competence can be further developed, ideally leading to students' transformation (see Deardorff & Edwards, 2012). In addition to transformative experiences, Bok (2006) outlines ways in which colleges can better equip students for a more global, interdependent world, including a well-constructed foundational course that provides a framework for understanding a variety of perspectives on global issues and the inclusion of foreign and comparative material into courses, as well as requiring foreign-language study.

Given that the only element that all the experts agreed on in the Deardorff study (2006) was the importance of being able to understand and see the world from others' perspectives, programs, when possible, need to address multiple worldviews and comparative perspectives. For example, speaker series that bring in speakers from diverse backgrounds can raise awareness of other perspectives on specific issues.

Programs also need to bring domestic and international students together in meaningful interactions. Such programs would include adequate preparation (such as a cross-cultural training) for domestic/international student interaction, have specific learning goals for all participants, and encourage meaningful domestic/international interactions through relationship-building opportunities. These opportunities can include programs such as community service, mentor programs, language partner programs, book clubs, and possibly even intramural sports.

Regardless of the context of intercultural learning, five design considerations should be taken into account to help make intercultural learning more meaningful to those involved, whether for students, staff, or faculty:

1. *Make it relevant.* What are the needs of the learners related to intercultural learning? In order for efforts to be relevant, learner needs must be addressed. What's important to learners? How can real-life examples and situations be incorporated so that all this information becomes more relevant? For example, if faculty are faced with increasingly intercultural classrooms, faculty need to know how to reach diverse students successfully.
2. *Involve stakeholders.* To what extent are stakeholders, especially students, involved in providing input and feedback? How much feedback are learners receiving on their own intercultural development?
3. *Incorporate experiential learning.* Beyond more static learning that occurs cerebrally in classrooms, how can learners engage in experiential activities and beyond (e.g., service learning, study abroad, co-curricular activities) so that they have opportunities to practice using the knowledge gained and honing

their skills? A key part of such experiential learning is the critical reflection that occurs.

4. *Go beyond the one-off exposure.* One intercultural workshop, lecture, or module is not enough. Intercultural competence needs to be intentionally addressed in an integrated, ongoing way throughout a course or program, or even throughout a student's college career.

5. *Focus on process, not results.* Unlike other areas of higher education, intercultural learning and intercultural competence development is much more about the process (the journey) than the end results, since the developmental process is lifelong. Learners are already at different places in their unique intercultural journeys, so a one-size-fits-all course or program does not meet learners where they are. Recognize where learners are (relevance!) and meet them where they are in terms of learning interventions. Feedback is crucial. Implications for assessment include the importance of using assessment information to provide feedback to learners so that they can continue their own development. Focusing on process also means looking at intercultural learning more holistically. How does this fit with other learning and development that occurs (academically, emotionally, personally, spiritually, and so on)?

CONCLUSION

Assessing intercultural competence as a learning outcome is not only possible but necessary as postsecondary institutions seek to graduate global-ready students. Given the complexity of assessing intercultural competence, questions such as the following can also be raised:

- How do educators avoid oversimplifying intercultural competence yet develop reliable methods with which to measure student outcomes for internationalization?
- How can educators navigate the inherent limits of formal assessment methods?
- How can assessment of intercultural competence be holistic and integrated? Should it be?
- How can unconscious competence be identified and assessed?
- Should *intercultural competence* be defined more generally or more specifically?
- What constitutes core intercultural competence?
- Is the identification of components or personal traits related to core intercultural competence too simplistic?
- How do educators assess the process of intercultural competence development, especially when research indicates that such development is lifelong?

- Given that other cultural definitions view intercultural competence more as about relationships than individuals, how are relationships assessed within intercultural competence?
- What roles do personal traits, identity, personality, emotional intelligence, conflict, self-authorship, and motives play in intercultural competence?
- How can intercultural competence be assessed as a "social judgment" made by persons involved in the interaction (Lustig & Koester, 2006)?
- Intercultural competence according to whom and to what end?

Pottinger (1979) also raises several other issues in regard to establishing competence: What are the best ways to establish minimal levels of competence? Conversely, is there a way to measure maximum competence? What is to be done with students who don't achieve minimal intercultural competence? Bowden and Marton (1998) raise the question of context: In which context is intercultural competence viewed and assessed?

This plethora of questions points to the need for further research on assessing intercultural competence. In the meantime, however, current research as discussed in this appendix suggests that intercultural competence assessment begins with a clear definition and framework derived from the literature, translated into concrete, specific goals and student learning outcomes. These prioritized learning outcomes are then assessed through direct and indirect measures. Ultimately, assessment and learning are integral to student development; such assessment goes beyond a score on a survey or simply documenting students' intercultural competence. Educators need to use the assessment information to guide students as well as to look more broadly at the collective impact of institutions on student learning in answering the question, "How well prepared are our students for the world in which we live and work?"

ASSESSMENT GUIDE FOR INTERCULTURAL COMPETENCE

Based on research and findings from Deardorff (2004, 2006, 2009), the following questions can be used in assessing intercultural competence:

- From whose perspective is intercultural competence being assessed? What are the cultural biases of the evaluator?
- Who is the locus of the evaluation?
- What is the context of the intercultural competence assessment?
- What is the purpose of the intercultural competence assessment?
- How will the assessment results be used? Who will benefit from the assessment?
- What is the time frame of the assessment (e.g., one point, ongoing)? In other words, does the assessment include formative and summative measures?
- What is the level of abstraction? In other words, will the assessment be more general, or will it assess more specific components of intercultural competence?
- Do the assessment methods match the working definition and stated objectives of intercultural competence?
- Have specific indicators been developed for intercultural competence assessment?
- Is more than one method being used to assess intercultural competence? Do the methods involve more than one evaluator's perspective?
- Are the degrees of intercultural competence being assessed? What is to be done with people not meeting the minimal level of intercultural competence?
- Does the assessment account for multiple competencies and multiple cultural identities?
- Has the impact of situational, social, and historical contexts been analyzed in the assessment of intercultural competence?
- How do the assessment methods impact the measurement outcomes? Have the limits of the instruments and measures been considered?
- Have student or participant goals been considered when assessing intercultural competence?
- Are assessment methods and measures appropriate to students' or participants' developmental process?

INTERCULTURAL COMPETENCE: SELF-REFLECTION

Part 1: The items listed below are invaluable in developing intercultural competence and in interacting effectively and appropriately with people from other cultures. Please rate yourself on the following:

5 = *Very high*; 4 = *High*; 3 = *Average*; 2 = *Below average*; 1 = *Poor*

1. Respect (valuing other cultures)	5	4	3	2	1
2. Openness (to intercultural learning and to people from other cultures)	5	4	3	2	1
3. Tolerance for ambiguity	5	4	3	2	1
4. Flexibility (in using appropriate communication styles and behaviors in intercultural situations)	5	4	3	2	1
5. Curiosity and discovery	5	4	3	2	1
6. Withholding judgment	5	4	3	2	1
7. Cultural self-awareness/understanding	5	4	3	2	1
8. Understanding others' worldviews	5	4	3	2	1
9. Culture-specific knowledge	5	4	3	2	1
10. Sociolinguistic awareness (awareness of using other languages in social contexts)	5	4	3	2	1
11. Skills to listen, observe, and interpret	5	4	3	2	1
12. Skills to analyze, evaluate, and relate	5	4	3	2	1
13. Empathy (do unto others as you would have others do unto you)	5	4	3	2	1
14. Adaptability (to different communication styles/behaviors, to new cultural environments)	5	4	3	2	1
15. Communication skills (appropriate and effective communication in intercultural settings)	5	4	3	2	1

Part 2: Reflect on situations requiring intercultural competence. What helped make you more appropriate and effective in your interactions? Now reflect on how you can continue to develop your intercultural competence, especially areas you rated as lower.

Note. Based on intercultural competence models developed by Deardorff, 2004; see also Deardorff, 2006.

Source: Darla K. Deardorff, "Framework: Intercultural Competence Model," in *Building Cultural Competence: Innovative Activities and Models*, ed. K. Berardo and D. K. Deardorff (Sterling, VA: Stylus, 2012), 45–52.

REFERENCES

Allport, G. (1979). *The nature of prejudice.* Reading, MA: Addison-Wesley. (Original work published in 1954)

Banta, T. (Ed.). (2004). *Hallmarks of effective outcomes assessment.* San Francisco: Jossey-Bass.

Bennett, J. M. (2009). Cultivating intercultural competence: A process perspective. In D. K. Deardorff (Ed.), *The SAGE handbook of intercultural competence* (pp. 121–140). Thousand Oaks, CA: SAGE.

Bennett, M. J. (1993). Towards ethnorelativism: A developmental model of intercultural sensitivity. In R. M. Paige (Ed.), *Education for the intercultural experience* (2nd ed., pp. 21–71). Yarmouth, ME: Intercultural Press.

Berardo, K., & Deardorff, D. K. (2012). *Building cultural competence: Innovative activities and models.* Sterling, VA: Stylus.

Bok, D. (2006). *Our underachieving colleges: A candid look at how much students learn and why they should be learning more.* Princeton, NJ: Princeton University Press.

Bowden, J., & Marton, F. (1998). *The university of learning: Beyond quality and competence.* London: Kogan Page.

Cross, T. (1988). Cultural and disability competence continuum [PowerPoint presentation]. Available from http://geriatrictoolkit.missouri.edu/multicultural/ CULTURAL_AND_DISABILITY_COMPETENCE_CONTINUUM.ppt

Deardorff, D. K. (2004). *The identification and assessment of intercultural competence as a student outcome of internationalization at institutions of higher education in the United States* (Unpublished dissertation). Raleigh: North Carolina State University.

Deardorff, D. K. (2006). The identification and assessment of intercultural competence as a student outcome of internationalization at institutions of higher education in the United States. *Journal of Studies in International Education, 10*(3), 241–266.

Deardorff, D. K. (Ed). (2009). *The SAGE handbook of intercultural competence.* Thousand Oaks, CA: SAGE.

Deardorff, D. K., & Edwards, K. (2012). Research on intercultural learning of students in service learning. In P. Clayton, R. Bringle, & J. Hatchers (Eds.), *Research on service learning: Conceptual frameworks and assessment* (pp. 157–186). Sterling, VA: Stylus.

Fantini, A. (2009). Assessing intercultural competence: Issues and tools. In D. K. Deardorff (Ed.), *The SAGE handbook of intercultural competence* (pp. 456–476). Thousand Oaks, CA: SAGE.

Hammer, M. (2012). The Intercultural Development Inventory: A new frontier in assessment and development of intercultural competence. In M. Vande Berg, R. M. Paige, & K. H. Lou (Eds.), *Student learning abroad: What our students are learning, what they're not, and what we can do about it* (pp. 115–136). Sterling, VA: Stylus.

Hunter, W., White, G., and Godbey, G. (2006, Fall). What does it mean to be globally competent? *Journal of Studies in International Education, 10*: 267–285.

Kegan, R. (1994). *In over our heads: The mental demands of modern life.* Cambridge, MA: Harvard University Press.

King, P. M., & Baxter Magolda, M. B. (2005). A developmental model of intercultural maturity. *Journal of College Student Development, 46*(6), 571–592.

Lustig, M. W., & Koester, J. (2006). *Intercultural competence: Interpersonal communication across cultures.* Boston: Pearson.

Olson, C. L., Evans, R., & Schoenberg, R. E. (2007). *At home in the world: Bridging the gap between internationalization and multicultural education.* Washington, DC: American Council on Education.

Paige, R. M. (2004). Instrumentation in intercultural training. In D. Landis, J. M. Bennett, & M. J. Bennett (Eds.), *Handbook of intercultural training* (3rd ed. pp. 85–128). Newbury Park, CA: SAGE.

Pottinger, P. S. (1979). Competence assessment: Comments on current practices. In P. S. Pottinger & J. Goldsmith (Eds.), *Defining and Measuring Competence* (pp. 25–39). San Francisco: Jossey-Bass.

Spitzberg, B., & Changnon, G. (2009). Conceptualizing intercultural competence. In D. K. Deardorff (Ed.), *The SAGE handbook of intercultural competence* (pp. 2–52). Thousand Oaks, CA: SAGE.

Stuart, D. K. (2008). Assessment instruments for the global workforce. In M. Moodian (Ed.), *Contemporary leadership and intercultural competence: Exploring the cross-cultural dynamics within organizations* (pp. 175–190). Thousand Oaks, CA: SAGE.

Zessoules, R., & Gardner, H. (1991). Authentic assessment: Beyond the buzzword and into the classroom. In V. Perrone (Ed.), *Expanding Student Assessment* (pp. 47–71). Alexandria, VA: Association for Supervision and Curriculum Development.

Appendix C

Some Thoughts on Assessing Intercultural Competence

Darla K. Deardorff

The following article is reprinted with permission from *Viewpoints*, National Institute of Learning Outcomes Assessment (NILOA), May 15, 2014, http://illinois.edu/blog/view/915/113048.

Intercultural competence is emerging as an important competency, not only within the United States but also around the world. It is especially relevant to employability, the increasing diversity of the world in which we live, and the pressing global challenges confronting us as humans. While other terms represent intercultural competence—global citizenship, cultural intelligence, global learning, and so on—they all infer the knowledge, skills, and attitudes needed to interact successfully with others from different backgrounds. The focus on intercultural competence is growing out of the internationalization movement, which is becoming more central in many colleges and universities, and which is driven by economic and social factors. Intercultural competence is often stated as one of the main goals of study-abroad experiences, as well as of internationalized curricula. In the United States, intercultural competence is seen as key to global workforce development and foundational to 21st-century skills.

What exactly is intercultural competence? Can it be assessed, and if so, how? Over the past half century, a considerable amount of scholarship has been produced on the concept of intercultural competence and its varying terms. In fact, Spitzberg and Changnon (2009) discussed more than 20 different definitions and frameworks. In 2006 the first research-based definition of intercultural competence appeared (Deardorff, 2006), followed by a synthesis of work published in the *SAGE Handbook of Intercultural Competence* (Deardorff, 2009) and a subsequent growing list of publications on this topic, not only in the United States but also in many other countries around the world. Various conferences focus on this topic, including a recent Intercultural Learner Conference at Duke University and the Association of International Educators (NAFSA) conference in San Diego in May 2014.

From all of this, several themes emerge:

- Intercultural competence is a complex, broad learning goal and must be broken down into more discrete, measurable learning objectives representing specific knowledge, attitude, or skill areas.
- The attainment of intercultural competence is a lifelong developmental *process*, which means there is no point at which one becomes fully interculturally competent.
- Language fluency is necessary but in itself insufficient to represent intercultural competence.
- Intercultural competence must be intentionally addressed throughout the curriculum and through experiential learning (such as study abroad, service learning, and so on).
- Faculty need a clearer understanding of intercultural competence in order to more adequately address it in their courses (regardless of discipline) and in order to guide students in developing this competence.

These emerging themes point to five implications for assessment of intercultural competence. The first is using the extant literature to define the concept. Intercultural competence is broadly about communication and behavior that is *effective* and *appropriate* in intercultural interactions—and all interactions can be considered intercultural.

Second, research results indicate that intercultural competence can, indeed, be assessed (Deardorff, 2011; Fantini, 2009; Stuart, 2008). The 140-plus existing assessment tools are predominantly self-report instruments, meaning that only half of the picture is measured. Often missing in intercultural competence assessment (at least in education and the humanities) is the other half of the picture: the *appropriateness* of communication and behavior, which, according to research studies, can only be measured through *others'* perspectives, not through self-report.

Third, most assessments of intercultural competence focus on *results* instead of *process* (i.e., how one *approaches* others, reflects critically, and thinks interculturally)—relying on indirect evidence only (often a survey instrument), which provides an incomplete picture of an individual's intercultural competence development. The Association of American Colleges & Universities provides a sample rubric—based on the intercultural competence framework from my research, as well as based on Bennett's Developmental Model of Intercultural Sensitivity—for measuring direct evidence of intercultural learning. Keep in mind, though, that even this rubric does not capture the full complexity of intercultural competence; rubrics must thus be developed that are aligned with specific learning objectives within intercultural competence development. For more, see *The SAGE Handbook of Intercultural Competence* (Deardorff, 2009).

Fourth, intercultural competence assessment must involve a multi-method, multi-perspective approach that focuses more on the process of intercultural competence than on an end result (Deardorff, 2012; Deardorff & Edwards, 2012; Gordon & Deardorff, 2013). Current examples of intercultural competence assessment include embedded course assessment, self-report instruments, reflection papers, critical incident analysis, interviews, observations (by professors, internship supervisors, host families, group members, etc.), simulations, and longitudinal studies. That more institutions are assessing intercultural competence outcomes is encouraging, but much work remains to be done on improving intercultural competence assessment. As such, there are currently no examples of best practices.

Fifth, determining whether students can *think and act interculturally* is essential (Bok, 2006). For example, are students living an intercultural lifestyle? Are students interculturally successful in their actions and interactions with others?

When all is said and done, the goal is to collect *evidence* of intercultural competence development and to use that information to guide students in their intercultural journey as well as for program improvement. In this sense, assessing intercultural competence is about much more than assessing a complex learning outcome; it's about developing an essential lifelong competence.

REFERENCES

Bok, D. (2006). *Our underachieving colleges: A candid look at how much students learn and why they should be learning more.* Princeton, NJ: Princeton University Press.

Deardorff, D. K. (2006). Identification and assessment of intercultural competence as a student outcome of internationalization. *Journal of Studies in International Education, 10*(3), 241–266. Retrieved from http://jsi.sagepub.com/content/10/3/241.full.pdf+html

Deardorff, D. K. (Ed.). (2009). *The SAGE handbook of intercultural competence.* Thousand Oaks, CA: SAGE.

Deardorff, D. K. (2011). Assessing intercultural competence. *New Directions for Institutional Research, 149.* Retrieved from http://onlinelibrary.wiley.com/doi/10.1002/ir.381/pdf

Deardorff, D .K. (2012). Intercultural competence in the 21st century: Perspectives, issues, application. In B. Breninger & T. Kaltenbacher (Eds.), *Creating Cultural Synergies: Multidisciplinary Perspectives on Interculturality and Interreligiosity* (pp. 7–23). Newcastle: Cambridge Scholars.

Deardorff, D. K., & Edwards, K. (2012). Research on intercultural learning of students in service learning. In P. Clayton, R. Bringle, & J. Hatchers (Eds.), *Research on service learning: Conceptual frameworks and assessment* (pp. 157–186). Sterling, VA: Stylus.

Fantini, A. (2009). Assessing intercultural competence: Issues and tools. In D. K. Deardorff (Ed.), *The SAGE handbook of intercultural competence* (pp. 456–476). Thousand Oaks, CA: SAGE.

Gordon, J., & Deardorff, D. K. (2013). Demystifying assessment: A critical component in student success. In W. Nolting, D. Donahue, C. Matherly, & M. Tillman (Eds.), *Successful models and best practices for internships, service learning and volunteering abroad* (pp. 74–81). Washington, DC: NAFSA.

Spitzberg, B. H., & Changnon, G. (2009). Conceptualizing multicultural competence. In D. K. Deardorff (Ed.), *The SAGE handbook of intercultural competence* (pp. 2–52). Thousand Oaks, CA: SAGE.

Stuart, D. (2008). Assessment instruments for the global workforce. In M. Moodian (Ed.), *Contemporary leadership and intercultural competence: Exploring the cross-cultural dynamics within organizations* (pp. 175–190). Thousand Oaks, CA: SAGE.

Appendix D

Checklist for Evaluating the Effectiveness of Outcomes Assessment in International Education

Readiness for Outcomes Assessment

1. ____ There are clearly stated goals and measurable objectives or outcome statements aligned with the mission or purpose.
2. ____ Assessment approaches are aligned with mission, goals, and objectives.
3. ____ The primary commitment to assess is improving student learning (although assessment can be used for external demands, too), and there is recognition that assessment is essential to learning.
4. ____ Assessment is an integral part of the strategic planning process and organizational decision-making.
5. ____ Stakeholders and on-campus collaborators (including assessment champions) have been identified who can be part of the assessment process.
6. ____ An assessment audit has been completed.
7. ____ A comprehensive assessment plan has been developed (through dialogue with stakeholders based on needs) *prior* to collection of data (which includes adapting current assessment efforts when possible).
8. ____ There are sufficient fiscal, infrastructure, and human resources available to support the implementation of the assessment plan.
9. ____ The assessment plan has been communicated to stakeholders, taking into account varying goals, needs, and backgrounds.
10. ____ Identified stakeholders, especially students and faculty, are included in all phases of the assessment process.

Implementing and Using Outcomes Assessment

1. ____ Assessment methods, aligned to goals and stated objectives, have been pilot-tested to ensure face validity of measures.

Reproduced from: Deardorff, D. K. (2015). *Demystifying outcomes assessment for international educators.* Sterling, VA: Stylus.

2. _____ Assessment is undertaken in a receptive and supportive environment.

3. _____ Evidence is collected in an ongoing manner to indicate progress toward and achievement of stated objectives and outcomes, as well as assessing the processes involved.

4. _____ Limitations and benefits of chosen assessment methods have been acknowledged—including existing cultural bias and language limitations—and threats to validity have been identified.

5. _____ Multiple assessment methods and tools (direct and indirect, qualitative and quantitative) have been used in collecting assessment data/evidence.

6. _____ Evidence has been triangulated to provide a more complete picture of student learning and to identify areas of consistency and inconsistency across different findings.

7. _____ Evidence has been interpreted from a variety of stakeholder perspectives, experiences, and backgrounds.

8. _____ Evidence is communicated in a variety of ways (written, oral, group meetings, etc.) to all stakeholder groups in an interactive and ongoing process. In particular, feedback is given directly to students.

9. _____ Gaps, limitations, and inconsistencies are addressed when communicating assessment evidence.

10. _____ Stakeholders are involved in discussing next steps and future directions, based on assessment evidence.

11. _____ Evidence is used in improving student learning, directly as feedback to students and indirectly through programmatic improvements.

12. _____ Decisions are made based on the relevant data collected.

13. _____ The assessment plan, usefulness of assessment efforts, and assessment infrastructure and resources are regularly evaluated (including through peer and external review).

14. _____ Assessment strategies and plans are changed and adapted to meet ongoing needs of those impacted, especially students.

Source: Adapted by Darla K. Deardorff from Banta, 2004; Braskamp & Engberg, 2014.

Appendix E

Some Assessment Tools for International Education Contexts

Appendix E contains several examples of assessment tools that can be used to collect or evaluate direct evidence of student learning in international education contexts.

Three Rubrics from the Association of American Colleges & Universities (AAC&U): Civic Engagement, Global Learning, and Intercultural Knowledge and Competence. These can and need to be adapted to specific goals and stated objectives (not necessarily used as is, unless strong alignment is present between these rubrics and stated goals or objectives). These rubrics were developed by faculty from across the United States through the Association of American Colleges & Universities and can be used as sample rubrics. These three and other VALUE rubrics are available online from the AAC&U.

Learner Contract/Agreement template. This template can be adapted and used with students in classrooms as well as in experiential learning programs, including study abroad, internships, and service learning. A learner contract is most often negotiated between the learner and the instructor, and is an excellent way to tailor the learning experience specifically to student needs and interests.

Embedded Course Assessments/Classroom Assessment Techniques (CATs). Given that embedded course assessments are the most prevalent method for gauging intercultural competence (see appendix B), international educators need to pay more attention to this formative evaluation method and partner with faculty in analyzing and using the information collected. Two examples are included here: K-W-L and 3-2-1, and many more CATs are available (see Angelo & Cross for an entire book on CATs: *Classroom Assessment Techniques: A Handbook for College Teachers*, 2nd ed. [San Francisco: Jossey-Bass, 1993]). These examples can be used not only in the classroom but also in international education programs such as orientations and training programs to collect formative evaluation evidence that can be used to provide feedback to students, as well as to adapt experiences to the learners' needs.

Autobiography of the Intercultural Encounters. This tool, developed by Michael Byram, has been used successfully within a European context as well as others, and can be used with those of any age, from children through adults.

List of resources for indirect intercultural assessment measures.

Research results in commonly used intercultural assessment methods.

CIVIC ENGAGEMENT VALUE RUBRIC

	Capstone	Milestones		Benchmark
	4	3	2	1
Diversity of Communities and Cultures	Demonstrates evidence of adjustment in own attitudes and beliefs because of working within and learning from diversity of communities and cultures. Promotes others' engagement with diversity.	Reflects on how own attitudes and beliefs are different from those of other cultures and communities. Exhibits curiosity about what can be learned from diversity of communities and cultures.	Has awareness that own attitudes and beliefs are different from those of other cultures and communities. Exhibits little curiosity about what can be learned from diversity of communities and cultures.	Expresses attitudes and beliefs as an individual, from a one-sided view. Is indifferent or resistant to what can be learned from diversity of communities and cultures.
Analysis of Knowledge	Connects and extends knowledge (facts, theories, etc.) from one's own academic study/ field/discipline to civic engagement and to one's own participation in civic life, politics, and government.	Analyzes knowledge (facts, theories, etc.) from one's own academic study/ field/discipline making relevant connections to civic engagement and to one's own participation in civic life, politics, and government.	Begins to connect knowledge (facts, theories, etc.) from one's own academic study/ field/discipline to civic engagement and to tone's own participation in civic life, politics, and government.	Begins to identify knowledge (facts, theories, etc.) from one's own academic study/ field/discipline that is relevant to civic engagement and to one's own participation in civic life, politics, and government.
Civic Identity and Commitment	Provides evidence of experience in civic-engagement activities and describes what she/he has learned about her or himself as it relates to a reinforced and clarified sense of civic identity and continued commitment to public action.	Provides evidence of experience in civic-engagement activities and describes what she/he has learned about her or himself as it relates to a growing sense of civic identity and commitment.	Evidence suggests involvement in civic-engagement activities is ge nerated from expectations or course requirements rather than from a sense of civic identity.	Provides little evidence of her/his experience in civic-engagement activities and does not connect experiences to civic identity.

(Continued)

	Capstone	Milestones		Benchmark
Civic Communication	Tailors communication strategies to effectively express, listen, and adapt to others to establish relationships to further civic action.	Effectively communicates in civic context, showing ability to do all of the following: express, listen, and adapt ideas and messages based on others' perspectives.	Communicates in civic context, showing ability to do more than one of the following: express, listen, and adapt ideas and messages based on others' perspectives.	Communicates in civic context, showing ability to do one of the following: express, listen, and adapt ideas and messages based on others' perspectives.
Civic Action and Reflection	Demonstrates independent experience and *shows initiative in team leadership* of complex or multiple civic engagement activities, accompanied by reflective insights or analysis about the aims and accomplishments of one's actions.	Demonstrates independent experience and *team leadership* of civic action, with reflective insights or analysis about the aims and accomplishments of one's actions.	Has clearly *participated in* civically focused actions and begins to reflect or describe how these actions may benefit individual(s) or communities.	Has *experimented with* some civic activities but shows little internalized understanding of their aims or effects and little commitment to future action.
Civic Contexts/ Structures	Demonstrates ability and commitment to *collaboratively work across and within community* contexts and structures *to achieve a civic aim.*	Demonstrates ability and commitment to work *actively within community* contexts and structures *to achieve a civic aim.*	Demonstrates experience identifying intentional ways *to participate in* civic contexts and structures.	Experiments with civic contexts and structures, *tries out a few to see what fits.*

Evaluators are encouraged to assign a zero to any work sample or collection of work that does not meet benchmark (cell one) level performance.

Note: For a definition of *civic engagement*, a discussion of framing language, and a glossary of terms used in the Civic Engagement VALUE rubric, please download the full version from the AAC&U website: http://www.aacu.org/value-rubrics. For more information, please contact value@aacu.org.

GLOBAL LEARNING VALUE RUBRIC

	Capstone	Milestones		Benchmark
	4	3	2	1
Global Self-Awareness	Effectively addresses significant issues in the natural and human world based on articulating one's identity in a global context.	Evaluates the global impact of one's own and others' specific local actions on the natural and human world.	Analyzes ways that human actions influence the natural and human world.	Identifies some connections between an individual's personal decision-making and certain local and global issues.
Perspective Taking	Evaluates and applies diverse perspectives to complex subjects within natural and human systems in the face of multiple and even conflicting positions (i.e. cultural, disciplinary, and ethical.).	Synthesizes other perspectives (such as cultural, disciplinary, and ethical) when investigating subjects within natural and human systems.	Identifies and explains multiple perspectives (such as cultural, disciplinary, and ethical) when exploring subjects within natural and human systems.	Identifies multiple perspectives while maintaining a value preference for own positioning (such as cultural, disciplinary, and ethical).
Cultural Diversity	Adapts and applies a deep understanding of multiple worldviews, experiences, and power structures while initiating meaningful interaction with other cultures to address significant global problems.	Analyzes substantial connections between the worldviews, power structures, and experiences of multiple cultures historically or in contemporary contexts, incorporating respectful interactions with other cultures.	Explains and connects two or more cultures historically or in contemporary contexts with some acknowledgement of power structures, demonstrating respectful interaction with varied cultures and worldviews.	Describes the experiences of others historically or in contemporary contexts primarily through one cultural perspective, demonstrating some openness to varied cultures and worldviews.

(Continued)

Personal and Social Responsibility	Takes informed and responsible action to address ethical, social, and environmental challenges in global systems and evaluates the local and broader consequences of individual and collective interventions.	Analyzes the ethical, social, and environmental consequences of global systems and identifies a range of actions informed by one's sense of personal and civic responsibility.	Explains the ethical, social, and environmental consequences of local and national decisions on global systems.	Identifies basic ethical dimensions of some local or national decisions that have global impact.
Understanding Global Systems	Uses deep knowledge of the historic and contemporary role and differential effects of human organizations and actions on global systems to develop and advocate for informed, appropriate action to solve complex problems in the human and natural worlds.	Analyzes major elements of global systems, including their historic and contemporary interconnections and the differential effects of human organizations and actions, to pose elementary solutions to complex problems in the human and natural worlds.	Examines the historical and contemporary roles, interconnections, and differential effects of human organizations and actions on global systems within the human and the natural worlds.	Identifies the basic role of some global and local institutions, ideas, and processes in the human and natural worlds.
Applying Knowledge to Contemporary Global Contexts	Applies knowledge and skills to implement sophisticated, appropriate, and workable solutions to address complex global problems using interdisciplinary perspectives independently or with others.	Plans and evaluates more complex solutions to global challenges that are appropriate to their contexts using multiple disciplinary perspectives (such as cultural, historical, and scientific).	Formulates practical yet elementary solutions to global challenges that use at least two disciplinary perspectives (such as cultural, historical, and scientific).	Defines global challenges in basic ways, including a limited number of perspectives and solutions.

Evaluators are encouraged to assign a zero to any work sample or collection of work that does not meet benchmark (cell one) level performance.

Note: For a definition of *global learning,* a discussion of framing language, and a glossary of terms used in the Global Learning VALUE Rubric, please download the full version from the AAC&U website: http://www.aacu.org/value-rubrics. For more information, please contact value@aacu.org.

INTERCULTURAL KNOWLEDGE AND COMPETENCE VALUE RUBRIC

| | Capstone | Milestones | | Benchmark |
	4	3	2	1
Knowledge *Cultural self-awareness*	Articulates insights into own cultural rules and biases (e.g. seeking complexity; aware of how her/his experiences have shaped these rules, and how to recognize and respond to cultural biases, resulting in a shift in self-description.)	Recognizes new perspectives about own cultural rules and biases (e.g. not looking for sameness; comfortable with the complexities that new perspectives offer.)	Identifies own cultural rules and biases (e.g. with a strong preference for those rules shared with own cultural group and seeks the same in others.)	Shows minimal awareness of own cultural rules and biases (even those shared with own cultural group(s)) (e.g. uncomfortable with identifying possible cultural differences with others.)
Knowledge *Knowledge of cultural worldview frameworks*	Demonstrates sophisticated understanding of the complexity of elements important to members of another culture in relation to its history, values, politics, communication styles, economy, or beliefs and practices.	Demonstrates adequate understanding of the complexity of elements important to members of another culture in relation to its history, values, politics, communication styles, economy, or beliefs and practices.	Demonstrates partial understanding of the complexity of elements important to members of another culture in relation to its history, values, politics, communication styles, economy, or beliefs and practices.	Demonstrates surface understanding of the complexity of elements important to members of another culture in relation to its history, values, politics, communication styles, economy, or beliefs and practices.
Skills *Empathy*	Interprets intercultural experience from the perspectives of own and more than one worldview and demonstrates ability to act in a supportive manner that recognizes the feelings of another cultural group.	Recognizes intellectual and emotional dimensions of more than one worldview and sometimes uses more than one worldview in interactions.	Identifies components of other cultural perspectives but responds in all situations with own worldview.	Views the experience of others but does so through own cultural worldview.

(Continued)

Skills *Verbal and nonverbal communication*	Articulates a complex understanding of cultural differences in verbal and nonverbal communication (e.g., demonstrates understanding of the degree to which people use physical contact while communicating in different cultures or use direct/indirect and explicit/implicit meanings) and is able to skillfully negotiate a shared understanding based on those differences.	Recognizes and participates in cultural differences in verbal and nonverbal communication and begins to negotiate a shared understanding based on those differences.	Identifies some cultural differences in verbal and nonverbal communication and is aware that misunderstandings can occur based on those differences but is still unable to negotiate a shared understanding.	Has a minimal level of understanding of cultural differences in verbal and nonverbal communication; is unable to negotiate a shared understanding.
Attitudes *Curiosity*	Asks complex questions about other cultures, seeks out and articulates answers to these questions that reflect multiple cultural perspectives.	Asks deeper questions about other cultures and seeks out answers to these questions.	Asks simple or surface questions about other cultures.	States minimal interest in learning more about other cultures.
Attitudes *Openness*	Initiates and develops interactions with culturally different others. Suspends judgment in valuing her/his interactions with culturally different others.	Begins to initiate and develop interactions with culturally different others. Begins to suspend judgment in valuing her/his interactions with culturally different others.	Expresses openness to most, if not all, interactions with culturally different others. Has difficulty suspending any judgment in her/his interactions with culturally different others, and is aware of own judgment and expresses a willingness to change.	Receptive to interacting with culturally different others. Has difficulty suspending any judgment in her/his interactions with culturally different others, but is unaware of own judgment.

Evaluators are encouraged to assign a zero to any work sample or collection of work that does not meet benchmark (cell one) level performance.

Note: For a definition of *intercultural knowledge and competence*, a discussion of framing language, and a glossary of terms used in the Intercultural Knowledge and Competence VALUE Rubric, please download the full version from the AAC&U website: http://www.aacu.org/value-rubrics. For more information, please contact value@aacu.org.

LEARNING CONTRACTS AND AGREEMENTS

Contract learning is, in essence, an alternative way of structuring a learning experience: It replaces a content plan with a process plan.—Malcolm S. Knowles (1991, p. 39)

Learning contracts are formal agreements negotiated between student and teacher or mentor on what will be learned, how it will be learned, and how the learning will be assessed and verified. Learning contracts have been used at all levels of education—from elementary through higher education. Note that the focus of the learning contract is on the learning—not on the logistics of an experience.

Here are some suggestions that may help your learning contracts/agreements be successful:

- Make sure the overall course or program goals and learning objectives are clearly stated and specific enough that you can assess and evaluate student learning, but broad enough that learners can adapt them for their own learning.
- You may want to require that all learners use one or two stated objectives and then add their own.
- Learners should be encouraged to limit the number of objectives they include on their contract to no more than four or five. The learning objectives they list must be specific and not too broad or general.
- Sometimes it helps to provide learners with resources, sample learning strategies, and rubrics. However, this depends on learning objectives.
- Sometimes it is helpful to match up learners of similar ability or interest to create peer collaboration.
- Make the layout of your learning contracts/agreements easy to follow and understand. Templates are often best to use.
- Allow for the possibility of renegotiating the contract, if feasible.
- Use the K-W-L method to determine what students already *know*, what they *want* to learn, and what they have *learned* as a starting point for students in developing their contracts. (See p. 165.)

Source: Adapted by D. K. Deardorff from Regina Public Schools and Saskatchewan Learning.

LEARNING CONTRACT

Student Name:

Course/Program:

I am contracting for the grade of _____ *and will do the following to achieve that grade:*
Course/Program Goals:

What are you going to learn? (objectives: what will be the change in knowledge, skills, attitudes, values)	*How are you going to learn it?* (resources/ strategies by which the changes will occur)	Target date for completion	How are *you* going to know you learned it? (specific evidence of learning)	How are you going to *prove* you learned it? (verification of learning—how *others* will know)

Student Signature _____ Instructor Signature _____ Date _____

Source: Adapted by D. K. Deardorff from Knowles (1986).

Reproduced from: Deardorff, D. K. (2015). *Demystifying outcomes assessment for international educators*. Sterling, VA: Stylus.

K-W-L

K-W-L is a tool that can be used for initial needs assessment as well as for summative assessment. K-W-L helps make learning relevant to learners, as well as tailor the course or experience to the learners. K-W-L determines what students already *know*, what they *want* to learn, and what they have *learned*. The information can be collected individually or via discussion, depending on the context, with the K-W collected in the beginning and the L at the end. K-W-L can be combined with 3-2-1 to determine what was actually learned (see p. 166).

K: What do learners already know about the particular topic to be explored?

W: What do learners want to understand, know, or be able to do as a result of exploring the particular topic? What questions do they have that they would like to investigate further about this topic?

L: What knowledge, skills, or attitudes did the learners gain as a result of exploring this particular topic? What changes occurred in the learners? What insights did learners gain?

3-2-1

3-2-1 is an assessment technique that can be used at the end of a topic/module to understand what insights learners have gained, to encourage them to apply knowledge to practice, and to determine what further questions learners may still have about the topic. This literally only takes about one minute and can be done with a small index card or piece of paper. Give learners the following instructions: "Please list 3 insights or takeaways you have from what we just covered, write 2 action steps you will do as a result of this learning, and then write 1 burning question you still have that you would like to investigate further. Complete sentences are not necessary." If you need a visual, you can use:

3	**Insights/takeaways**
2	**Action steps**
1	**Burning question**

Collect the cards/papers after a minute or two and then use this information to not only determine what learners got from the course or program (which can be compiled anonymously and given back to the learners), but also use the burning questions to tailor further learning interventions, if appropriate. This classroom assessment technique (CAT) is a variation on the "minute paper." Results of the 3-2-1 can also be reported at the meta-level through emerging patterns and themes.

AUTOBIOGRAPHY OF INTERCULTURAL ENCOUNTERS

This tool is designed to help analyze a specific intercultural encounter through a series of questions. The focus is on one encounter with one particular person from a different cultural background. The first question starts with self-definition. Other questions address the basics of the experience—what happened, when, where, and so on. The questions then go into some of the following issues:

- Why did you choose this experience?
- What were your feelings during this encounter?
- How would you describe the other's feelings during this encounter?
- What could you have done differently in this situation?
- How were your actions influenced by an idea you had about the other? What puzzled you?
- How did you adjust? How did the other person adjust?
- What did you understand only after reflecting on the experience?

This type of reflective tool can be used to address more of the process of intercultural development and not just the end results.

A set of materials for Autobiography of Intercultural Encounters can be found free online, in English, Italian, and French, at the URL in the source line.

Source: Council of Europe. (2009). *Autobiography of intercultural encounters.* Strasbourg: Council of Europe Publishing. http://ecep.ecml.at/Portals/26/training-kit/files/1_AIE_autobiography_en.pdf

---

INTERCULTURAL ASSESSMENT TOOLS

Given that numerous resources have already extensively outlined quite a few of the more than 140 intercultural assessments that exist, this book does not need to provide yet another list. The following resources contain lists of intercultural assessment tools. Be sure also to read chapter 2 as well as chapters 5 through 8 first, which explain more about why you need to use more than one tool to assess intercultural learning (including direct measures) and why it is crucial to start first with clearly stated measureable learning outcomes and then align assessment measures to the stated outcomes:

Book Chapters Listing Intercultural Assessment Tools

Bird, A., & Stevens, M. (2013). Assessing global leadership competencies. In M. Mendenhall, J. Osland, A. Bird, G. Oddou, M. Maznevski, M. Stevens, & G. Stahl (Eds.), *Global leadership: Research, practice, and development.* New York: Routledge.

Fantini, A. (2009). Assessing intercultural competence: Issues and tools. In D. K. Deardorff (Ed.), *The SAGE handbook of intercultural competence.* Thousand Oaks, CA: SAGE.

Paige, R. M., & Stallman, E. (2007). Using instruments for education abroad outcomes assessment. In M. Bolen (Ed.), *A guide to outcomes assessment in education abroad.* Carlisle, PA: Forum on Education Abroad.

Stuart, D. (2008). Assessment instruments for the global workforce. In M. Moodian, *Contemporary leadership and intercultural competence.* Thousand Oaks, CA: SAGE.

Web Resources Listing Intercultural Assessment Tools

Forum on Education Abroad Assessment Toolbox, http://www.forumea.org/research-outcomes.cfm (accessible to members only).

ICC Global, http://www.iccglobal.org (Online discussion forum on intercultural assessment)

Institute of Intercultural Communication, http://www.intercultural.org/tools.php

2013 RESEARCH SURVEY RESULTS: ASSESSMENT METHODS FOR MEASURING INTERCULTURAL COMPETENCE

Darla K. Deardorff

Following are some results from a 2013 research survey conducted by Darla K. Deardorff (see also appendix B). The survey asked higher education institutions which methods were used at their institution to assess students' intercultural competence. Based on the response of 190 higher education institutions, the following was reported:

ICC assessment method	Type of method	Percentage using this method
Evaluation conducted by professors in individual courses	Direct	63%
Student paper and/or presentation	Direct	50%
Student journal/blogs/reflections	Direct	39%
Pre/post instrument	Indirect	36%
Interviews with students	Indirect	24%
Commercially developed self-report instrument	Indirect	24%
Custom-designed/adapted self-report instrument	Indirect	23%
Observation of students in specific situations (by professor, supervisor, host family, etc.)	Direct	21%
E-portfolios	Varies	18%
Ongoing assessment	Varies	17%
Longitudinal assessment	Varies	10%
Written test	Direct	8%

The top three assessment methods involve embedded course assessments, which provide direct evidence of student learning related to intercultural competence development.

Reproduced from: Deardorff, D. K. (2015). *Demystifying outcomes assessment for international educators*. Sterling, VA: Stylus.

Appendix F
International Education Learning Outcomes Examples

When undertaking learning outcomes assessment in international education, it is helpful to look to others for examples. Within those examples, though, the best approach is to focus more on lessons learned rather than duplicating what was done or using some of the same tools and methods solely because they were used in that particular example (see chapter 8 on "Pitfalls"). International educators should follow principles of good assessment (see chapter 4 and appendix D) and spend adequate time in preparing and planning for assessment, which is the main thrust of this book (see "Introduction").

Despite the caveats just outlined, investigating examples of learning outcomes assessment in international education, especially for what works and doesn't, can be a useful exercise. In the investigation process, it is helpful to evaluate the examples based on the principles in chapter 4 and using the checklist in appendix D. Highlighted in this appendix are some assessment efforts at the national level (e.g., the American Council on Education and the Association of American Colleges & Universities, both in the United States), the international organizational level (e.g., IES Abroad and the Council on International Educational Exchange), the accrediting body level (e.g., those with quality enhancement plans that focus on internationalization, cultural diversity, global learning, global citizenship, or multi-culturalism), and the institutional level (e.g., Duke University and Purdue University, both in the United States). This discussion is not meant to be exhaustive, nor meant to somehow indicate good or best practice. Readers are encouraged to delve into these further if they are interested in learning more about these assessment efforts.

NATIONAL LEVEL—UNITED STATES

Some efforts have been made at the U.S. national level to focus on global learning outcomes, namely through the American Council on Education and the Association of American Colleges & Universities.

American Council on Education

The American Council on Education has been a national leader in global learning outcomes. Two projects in recent years are highlighted here: Assessing International Learning and At Home in the World.

Lessons Learned in Assessing International Learning

Sponsored through a FIPSE (Fund for the Improvement of Postsecondary Education) grant, this multi-institutional project focused on holistic assessment of students' actual work, instead of using a onetime, indirect measure. The pioneering collaboration utilized an e-portfolio, combined with an online student survey, in order to measure the breadth and depth of student learning. This was one of the first efforts to apply e-portfolio to learning that occurs through international experiences, both on and off campus. The following six institutions were involved in the project:

Michigan State
Portland State (OR)
Dickinson College (PA)
Kalamazoo College (MI)
Palo Alto Community College (CA)
Kapi'olani Community College (HI)

Together, these six institutions co-developed a standardized rubric that could be used with the e-portfolios, allowing for longitudinal collection of data to be compared across courses, experiences, and institutions. Artifacts were collected from a variety of international student experiences, including coursework (including in foreign languages), study abroad, and on-campus participation in internationally focused events. A minimum of five learning artifacts included course papers, photo journals, personal essays (including study-abroad application essays and return reflection essays), journal entries, videos of interviews or student performance, and audio demonstrating foreign language competency. Rubrics including the ACE/FIPSE Assessing International Learning Rubric, the Attitude Rubric, and anchor samples can be found online at the American Council on Education website: www.acenet.edu/news-room/Pages/ACEFIPSE-Project-on-Assessing-International-Learning.aspx.

At Home in the World: Educating for Global Connections and Local Commitments

At Home in the World (AHITW) is "a collaborative initiative of the American Council on Education's Inclusive Excellence Group and Center for Internationalization and Global Engagement," as described on the AHITW website. At its core is the emerging centrality of intercultural competence as not only one of the key outcomes of multi-cultural as well as international education efforts but also one of the key competences of the 21st century. Following are learning outcomes that were identified as the "common ground" between diversity/multi-cultural education and international education through ACE's At Home in the World project. These learning outcomes were generated by participants at an ACE roundtable when looking at learning outcomes shared between internationalization and multi-cultural education.

Institutional participants in the three-year At Home in the World project were

Alliant International University (CA)
Arcadia University (PA)
Bennett College for Women (NC)
Grossmont-Cuyamaca Community College District (CA)
Mercy College (NY)
North Carolina State University
University of Colorado at Colorado Springs
Washington State University

An At Home in the World Toolbox produced from this project is available at www.acenet.edu/news-room/Pages/AHITW-Toolkit-Main.aspx.

Common Intercultural Learning Outcomes

Students should be able to:

Knowledge/Content Oriented

- Understand the interconnectedness and interdependence of global systems
- Understand the historical, cultural, economic, and political forces that shape society and explain their own situation in this context
- Develop a nuanced/complex understanding of culture as a concept and the deep/complex/dynamic nature of culture
- Understand various cultures and how culture is created
- Understand the relationship of power and language, and how language interacts with culture
- Understand the connections between power, knowledge, privilege, gender, and class (locally and globally)

- Understand conflict and power relationships
- Understand how language frames thinking and perspective
- Recognize how stereotypes develop and where they come from

Attitudinal/Mode of Being

- Develop a sense of perspective and social responsibility
- Overcome provincial/parochial thinking
- Reduce their own prejudice
- Appreciate difference; value and acknowledge other cultures as legitimate
- Improve cultural self-awareness and understanding of one's self in the global context
- Demonstrate greater appreciation of or an interest in learning about different cultures
- Develop empathy and perspective consciousness
- Demonstrate open-mindedness and an understanding of complexity

Skills

- Think, work, and move across boundaries—in diverse environments
- Develop and use skills in conflict resolution
- Develop and use intercultural communication skills
- Demonstrate language proficiency
- Take informed responsibility for actions in a globally connected world
- Link theory and practice through own experience both as citizens and professionals
- Internalize and apply cultural understandings and knowledge
- Seek out multiple perspectives

Source: Christa Olson, Rhodri Evans, and Robert E. Schoenberg, *At Home in the World: Bridging the Gap Between Internationalization and Multicultural Education* (Washington, DC: American Council on Education, 2007). Copyright 2014, American Council on Education. Adapted with permission.

Association of American Colleges & Universities

AAC&U has been another key national leader in global learning outcomes assessment. Following are descriptions of two AAC&U projects: Shared Futures and VALUE Rubrics.

Shared Futures

According to Hovland (2006), the Association of American Colleges & Universities (AAC&U) has worked with higher education institutions to make global learning a key characteristic of undergraduate education" for two decades (p. vii). Launched in 2001 AAC&U's multi-project Shared Futures initiative attempted to weave together elements of a global learning agenda and worked with institutions to move from theory to practice in implementing global learning in the curriculum. AAC&U's research in working with liberal arts institutions through the Shared Futures Initiative indicated that learning outcomes were "poorly defined," not well integrated in the curriculum, and that better alignment was needed in regard to assessment (Hovland, 2006; McTighe Musil, 2006). Shared Futures advocated for sharing the responsibility of global learning goals across the curriculum, instead of making this a requirement in a few courses.

VALUE Rubrics

VALUE stands for Valid Assessment of Learning in Undergraduate Education and served as a campus-based project sponsored by AAC&U. As stated in the VALUE materials, "VALUE builds on a philosophy of learning assessment that privileges multiple expert judgments of the quality of student work over reliance on standardized tests administered to samples of students outside of their required courses." Based on the VALUE materials, some of the assumptions underlying the VALUE Project include the following—that learning develops over time, "that good practice in assessment requires multiple assessments," and that well-planned "e-portfolios and the assessment of the work in them can inform programs and institutions on progress toward achieving expected goals." Derived from College Learning for the New Global Century (AAC&U, 2007), the VALUE rubrics assess outcomes in the following 16 areas: Inquiry and Analysis, Critical Thinking, Creative Thinking, Written Communication, Oral Communication, Quantitative Literacy, Information Literacy, Reading, Teamwork, Problem Solving, Civic Knowledge and Engagement, Intercultural Knowledge and Competence, Ethnical Reasoning and Action, Foundations and Skills for Lifelong Learning, Integration, and Global Learning.

Institutions that were directly engaged with the VALUE Project were the following:

Alverno College (WI)
Bowling Green State University (OH)
City University of New York–LaGuardia Community College
College of San Mateo (CA)
George Mason University (VA)
Kapi'olani Community College (HI)
Portland State University (OR)
Rose-Hulman Institute of Technology (IN)
San Francisco State University (CA)
Spelman College (GA)
St. Olaf College (MN)
University of Michigan

See appendix E for examples of these VALUE rubrics used in evaluating direct evidence of student learning that are most closely related to international education outcomes (intercultural knowledge, global learning, and civic engagement). Other rubrics such as teamwork, oral communication, problem solving, and critical thinking are also closely aligned with anticipated outcomes of international education. Note that these VALUE rubrics, developed jointly by faculty from across the United States, need to be *adapted* to fit within specific course and institutional contexts and not necessarily used as is. For more on the VALUE project, and to view all of the VALUE rubrics, go to www.aacu.org/value.

INTERNATIONAL EDUCATION ORGANIZATIONAL EXAMPLES

Assessment efforts within an organization include pioneering efforts by IES Abroad and the Council for International Educational Exchange (CIEE).

IES MAP (Model Assessment Practice)

The Institute for the International Education of Students (IES Abroad) is a not-for-profit consortium with more than 95 study-abroad programs in 34 cities around the world, involving over 195 institutional partners and around 6,000 students. In 1999 IEA Abroad introduced the IES Abroad Model Assessment Practice for Study Abroad Programs, "the first evaluation tool of its kind" (p. 1). In 2011 IES Abroad introduced guidelines for assessing language and cultural communication outcomes in study abroad programs.

According to the *IES Abroad Map for Language and Intercultural Communication*, this MAP "sets forth realistic goals and objectives for language learners and teachers, and charts a course to greater proficiency." The five discrete levels of language learning and cultural communication identified by MAP are Novice Abroad, Emerging Independent Abroad, Independent Abroad, Emerging Competent Abroad, Competent Abroad. These five levels help students observe their own progress, as well as assist instructors. Each level defines specific outcomes for intercultural communication and for the four key language competencies: listening, speaking, reading, and writing.

Examples of Student Goals in Intercultural Communication
- Novice Abroad: "Observes and describes hosts' behavior (roles, relationships, meal times)."
- Emerging Independent Abroad: "Challenges self to get involved in host interactions and to express emotions when appropriate."
- Independent Abroad: "Thoughtfully handles critical incidents between hosts and self."
- Emerging Competent Abroad: "Tries to personally solve awkward situations by talking with conversation participants (requesting information, explanations, or clarifications, offering excuses, apologizing)."
- Competent Abroad: "Can share observations on the host culture with locals, showing sensitivity as well as good critical thinking."

Council on International Education Exchange (CIEE)

CIEE'S INTERCULTURAL DEVELOPMENT/LEARNING ASSESSMENT MEASURES

Tara Harvey, CIEE

CIEE currently focuses primarily on assessing the intercultural development of those students that enroll in the company's targeted intercultural learning initiatives. CIEE has historically offered a two-credit course called the Seminar on Living and Learning Abroad (SLL) to students on more than 40 study abroad programs. In fall 2014, the organization started a process of transitioning this seminar to a three-credit course entitled Intercultural Communication and Leadership. Both versions of the semester-long intercultural course use the Intercultural Development Inventory (IDI) pre- and post-semester to assess students' development; the data are also used to help the resident staff teaching the course tailor their approach to their students' developmental worldview. In addition to this quantitative assessment, the course includes numerous formative and summative assessments that are more qualitative in nature, such as regular assignments, journaling, and a final Digital Storytelling project. CIEE also collects IDI data on a small number of study abroad participants not enrolled in these courses in order to have a point of comparison and a better understanding of wider intercultural development on their programs, and plans to expand these efforts in the future.

ACCREDITATION

Professional accrediting bodies such as those for business, education, engineering, nursing, and social work have accrediting standards related to some dimension of global or intercultural competence.

The following chart outlines postsecondary institutions within the southern region of the United States that have focused on some aspects of global learning for re-accreditation purposes, done through an institution-initiated effort known as a Quality Enhancement Plan (QEP). These QEPs have assessment plans with each, and readers are encouraged to further investigate the ways in which learning outcomes are measured in the following QEPs related to international education.

Quality Enhancement Plans With Focus on Internationalization, Cultural Diversity, Global Learning, Global Citizenship, or Multi-culturalism (Sample Institutional Listing)

Institution	Location	Quality Enhancement Plan
Anderson University	Anderson, SC	Global Engagement: Anderson University Abroad
Appalachian State University	Boone, NC	Global Learning: A World of Opportunities for Appalachian Students
Austin College	Sherman, TX	The Global Program
Bellarmine University	Louisville, KY	Liberal Education in an International Context
Bellhaven College	Jackson, MS	Worldview Curriculum
Cabarrus College of Health Sciences	Concord, NC	Enhancing Cultural Competence in Healthcare Delivery
Covenant College	Lookout Mountain, GA	Quality Enhancement Plan for Intercultural Competencies
Duke University	Durham, NC	Global Duke: Enhancing Students' Capacity for World Citizenship
Florida International University	Miami, FL	Global Learning for Global Citizenship
Georgia Gwinnett College	Lawrenceville, GA	Internationalization of the Curriculum
Georgia Institute of Technology	Atlanta, GA	Strengthening the Global Competence and Research Experiences of Undergraduate Students

Institution	Location	Quality Enhancement Plan
Kennesaw State University	Kennesaw, GA	Get Global
Mary Baldwin College	Staunton, VA	Learning for Civic Engagement in a Global Context
Motlow State Community College	Lynchburg, TN	Internationalizing the Curriculum—Improving Learning Through International Education: Preparing Students for Success in a Global Society
Randolph College	Lynchburg, VA	Bridges Not Walls
Regent University	Decatur, GA	Developing Globally Competent Christian Leaders
Rollins College	Rollins, FL	Education for Citizenship and Leadership in Local and Global Communities
Saint Augustine's College	Raleigh, NC	Global Learning for Success
Spelman College	Atlanta, GA	Spelman Going Global! Developing Intercultural Competence
University of Tampa	Tampa, FL	Building International Competence: An Integrated Approach to International Education
University of Tennessee	Knoxville, TN	The International and Intercultural Awareness Initiative
University of Texas at Tyler	Tyler, TX	GATE: Global Awareness Through Education
Wake Forest University	Winston-Salem, NC	Beyond Boundaries: Preparing Students to Become Global Citizens
Winthrop University	Rock Hill, SC	The Global Learning Initiative

INSTITUTIONAL EXAMPLES

In the end, learning outcomes assessment is context-specific within a course or program. On the following pages, you will find two examples of learning outcomes assessment within an institutional context (Duke University) and within an international education course (Purdue University) using the assessment plan worksheet from appendix A (p. 122).

KEY QUESTIONS TO EXPLORE IN DEVELOPING AN ASSESSMENT PLAN: DUKE UNIVERSITY

Submitted by Dr. Matt Serra, director of Office of Assessment, Trinity College of Arts and Sciences, Duke University

What is the mission statement?

The Quality Enhancement Plan (QEP) for the university is focused on global citizenship. Specifically, we aim *to enhance our students' capacity for global citizenship*. In this context, we define "capacity" as competence (knowing how to do something in theory) and capability (the ability to put competence into practice). The QEP is made up of three parts. The Winter Forum is a two-and-one-half-day immersive experience focused on a particular global issue. In the Global Semester Abroad, a group of undergraduates study a specific global issue from multiple perspectives, global regions, and cultures. The Global Advisors is a cadre of professional advisors tasked with aiding undergraduates as they navigate the growing options in terms of global experiences, loosely defined. The following are the student learning goals for the overall QEP:

1. Knowledge: an awareness of significant contemporary issues and their scope, including the history, differences, and perspectives of different global regions and cultures.
2. Skills: the ability to engage positively with and learn from people of different backgrounds and in different environments.
3. Attitudes: self-awareness as both national and global citizens.
4. Group-identity (program objective): the development of bonds within the student body through shared experiences that will serve to strengthen the sense of Duke as a learning community.

What are the learning needs?

To increase undergraduate understanding of how they fit, interact with, and flourish in an ever increasingly connected world comprising a variety of cultural, historical, and disciplinary views and issues.

What are the stated goals and objectives, based on mission and needs? How have international learning outcome(s) been defined and prioritized?

The Winter Forum is one of three parts to the QEP and has the following stated goals.

(a) Evaluate a global issue from perspectives of multiple disciplines.
   Relates to QEP Objectives: 1, 2
(b) Evaluate a global issue from multiple cultural perspectives.
   Relates to QEP Objectives: 1, 2
(c) Engage in collaborative group work, centered on a global issue that serves to deepen their understanding of that issue.
   Relates to QEP Objectives: 2, 4
(d) Relate the Winter Forum experience to classroom coursework and co-curricular experiences.
   Relates to QEP Objectives: 2, 4

What are the specific measurable indicators for these outcomes? (What will the student know or be able to do upon completion? What changes will occur?)

Participants will demonstrate an increasingly sophisticated understanding, both across disciplines and across cultures, of the material covered in the Forum.

Students will demonstrate the ability to be self-aware about the growth they have made during the forum in relation to the stated learning objectives.

Participants will demonstrate an increased knowledge of the issues specific to the forum topic.

What baseline data can be collected?

There will be both a pre-test of basic topical knowledge and a pre-forum self-report survey of current levels of awareness, understanding, and dispositions toward the forum topic. Scores on standardized instruments designed to measure global perspective will be gathered on a subset of the participants at the time of their matriculation to the college. This same instrument will be administered in the penultimate term of the subsets' tenure at Duke as a post-measure.

What evidence will demonstrate what students have learned or how they have changed? (*Note: Map evidence to outcomes.*)

Student Presentations

At the end of the Winter Forum, students will be expected to complete a group presentation that demonstrates their understanding, both across disciplines and across cultures, of the material covered in the Forum. To facilitate the cooperative learning aspects and to maximize the student learning from different disciplinary and cultural perspectives, careful planning will go into the makeup of each group. We will use rubric-based scoring by designated three-person teams for each presentation. At the beginning of the Forum, students will be provided a set of topic-relevant areas and issues (aligned with the four learning outcomes) that will need to be addressed in the end-of-Forum presentation. The rubric will look at each of these general areas/ issues for level of coverage, information brought to bear, and other relevant indicators in light of the specified learning objectives.

Relates to Winter Forum Outcomes: (a), (b), (c)

Student Surveys

Prior to the Winter Forum, students will be surveyed about expected gains in relation to the four learning outcomes as well as other topic-relevant issues. At the conclusion of the Winter Forum, students will be asked to assess their perceived gains.

Relates to Winter Forum Outcomes: (a), (b), (c), (d)

Tests of Student Knowledge

Tests of student knowledge will be designed by the faculty and administered prior to participation in the Winter Forum. This test will include questions designed to elicit information about the student's sense of the interdisciplinary and intercultural complexity of the issue, the student's factual knowledge in relation to the global issue that is the topic of the Forum, and the student's ability to engage in rigorous analytical thinking on the issue. To assure a high response rate, the pre-participation tests will be made part of the application for enrollment in the Forum. After the end of the Forum, the participants will be sent via the Web a complementary test. Completion of this post-test will be voluntary (although it will be modestly incentivized). This post-test would serve double duty. First, it can give the students immediate feedback concerning gains in their level of knowledge, and so on. Also, it can be used by the program coordinators to assess the Winter Forum's impact on students and program issues.

Relates to Winter Forum Outcomes: (a), (b)

Forum Activities Assessed by Rubric

Trained raters will attend randomly selected activities and score, using a standard rubric, the level to which the participants in the selected activity are actually integrating the stated learning outcomes into the activity. To ensure consistency and reliability of scoring, a cohort of raters will be trained in development and use of rubrics. This training will take place in the term leading up to the Forum. This cohort will be made up of Office of Assessment, Trinity College (OATC) and Office of Institutional Research (IR) personnel.

Relates to Winter Forum Outcomes: (a), (b), (c)

What assessment tools and methods most effectively capture evidence of student learning, both during and at the end of the students' learning experience? Do these tools specifically measure the learning objectives?

During (formative): See Item immediately prior
After (summative): See Item immediately prior

Note: Be sure to consider the cultural biases and limitations of tools/methods used. Know what each tool purports to measure and make sure it is aligned with the learning outcome.

How will the learning processes be assessed?

All rubrics will be based on a developmental model. In this case we will rely on Bloom's taxonomy to judge depth and sophistication of discussions and presentations.

How will these assessment tools and methods be implemented and by whom?

All assessment activities will be administered and performed by trained personnel out of the OATC and IR offices.

Who will collect the data from the assessment tools/methods used (and who will have access to data)?

All raw data will be collected by OATC and IR personnel and will be reported out in de-identified and aggregate form only.

Who will analyze the data (need multiple perspectives on analyzing and interpreting the data), how, and how often?

Data analysis will be done by the associate director of the OATC. Report production will be done by the director of the OATC with support and editing done by the associate director of the OATC and the OATC project manager associated with the Forum. This report is only a reporting of the findings and is not meant as an interpretation. Both the WF and QEP advisory boards will receive the reports and discuss them as they see fit.

How will the data be used to provide feedback to students (Who will do this? When? How often?), how will the data be used to make changes, and who will make those changes?

Students will receive personalized and contextualized reports for all standardized instruments each time they are taken via the OATC. The overall report will be made available for viewing by any member of the university committee. Midterm following the Forum, the report is made available to both the QEP and WF advisory committees for their consumption.

How will the data be communicated to and among stakeholders (means of communication, schedule for reporting, etc.)? How will stakeholders assist in making changes?

See Item immediately above. Each report is used to inform the next Forum planning committee to ensure that each successive Forum builds on the successes and hurdles of the previous Forum.

How will the assessment plan itself and the assessment team be reviewed (who will do this, how often—including external review)?

The advisory committees for the WF and QEP review all reports, methods, and so forth once a year to determine if the necessary information is being provided by the current assessment plan.

KEY QUESTIONS TO EXPLORE IN DEVELOPING AN ASSESSMENT PLAN: PURDUE UNIVERSITY

Submitted by Dr. Charles Calahan, assistant director of Global Learning Faculty Development Purdue University
Introduction to Intercultural Learning

I. What is the mission statement?

The intercultural learning mission of "The University" is to equip graduates with personal and social responsibility that empowers success as global citizens in a global society and international marketplace.

II. What are the learning needs?

The learning needs are that students be introduced to Intercultural Knowledge and Effectiveness, which is defined as the attitudes, skills, and knowledge that come together to support the effective and appropriate interaction in a variety of diverse and cultural contexts.

IIIa. What are the stated goal or course description, student learning outcomes, and the student learning objectives, based on mission and needs?

Course Description

Introduction to Intercultural Learning: In the context of transformative education, this course contributes to a person's developmental process in intercultural attitudes, skills, and knowledge that evolve over an extended time. The course focuses on introducing the constructs of intercultural openness, curiosity, empathy, communication, cultural self-awareness, and cultural worldview.

Student Learning Outcomes (SLO)

Attitudes

1. Students identify, reflect on, and self-evaluate their own *Attitude of Intercultural Openness*, representing their interactions with culturally different others. (SLO1)

2. Students identify, reflect on, and self-evaluate their own *Attitude of Intercultural Curiosity*, asking questions about other cultures and seeking out information about other cultures. (SLO2)

Skills

3. Students identify, reflect on, and self-evaluate their own *Skill of Intercultural Empathy*: an adequate understanding of the complexity of values of persons from a different culture, and interpretation of experiences or perspectives from their own and more than one worldview. (SLO3)
4. Students identify, reflect on, and self-evaluate their own *Skill of Intercultural Communication*: an understanding of and adaptation to cultural differences in verbal and nonverbal communication. (SLO4)

Knowledge

5. Students identify, reflect on, and self-evaluate their own *Knowledge of Cultural Self-Awareness*, pertaining to their new perspectives, and insights into their own cultural rules and biases. (SLO5)
6. Students identify, reflect on, and self-evaluate their own *Knowledge of Cultural Worldview*: an understanding of other cultures in relation to history, values, politics, communication styles, economy, or beliefs and practices. (SLO6)

Student Learning Objectives (OBJ):

Attitudes

1.1 *Intercultural Openness*: Students exchange answers to a list of questions with persons from another culture, record the responses, create a collage or concept map of "selfie" photos, and answer four reflection questions in which they describe, interpret/analyze, evaluate, and set a goal. (OBJ1.1)
2.1 *Intercultural Curiosity*: Studying the Cultural Iceberg Theory model, students create a crossword puzzle composed of 30 cross-cultural questions. Afterward, they answer four reflection questions in which they describe, interpret/analyze, evaluate, and set a goal. (OBJ2.1)

Skills

3.1 *Intercultural Empathy*: Students interpret the *Cross the River Parable* exercise from at least two totally different perspectives, discuss and write the two perspectives, and answer four reflection questions in which they describe, interpret/analyze, evaluate, and set a goal. (OBJ3.1)
4.1 *Intercultural Communication*: Students observe the verbal and nonverbal communication behavior in a public place where persons of different cultures interact,

respond to two questions in a prompt, and answer four reflection questions in which they describe, interpret/analyze, evaluate, and set a goal. (OBJ4.1)

Knowledge

5.1 *Cultural Self-Awareness*: Students complete an Identity Dialogue exercise, discuss and write six short essay responses, and answer four reflection questions in which they describe, interpret/analyze, evaluate, and set a goal. (OBJ5.1)

6.1 *Knowledge of Cultural Worldview*: Students research the answers to a list of cross-cultural questions, locate corresponding images on the Internet, and produce a document of their findings. Then they answer four reflection questions in which they describe, interpret/analyze, evaluate, and set a goal. (OBJ6.1)

IIIb. How have international learning outcome(s) been defined and prioritized?

Intercultural Knowledge and Effectiveness learning outcomes were defined and prioritized by a University Task Force, University Curriculum Committee, Faculty Senate, University Office of Assessment, College Curriculum Committees, and Departmental Curriculum Committees.

The Association of American Colleges & Universities Intercultural Knowledge VALUE Rubric was identified, vetted, and adopted by the university committees mentioned above. The six constructs comprising the rubric are the basis of the six student learning outcomes.

IV. What are the specific measurable indicators for these outcomes? What will the student know or be able to do upon completion? What changes will occur?

Indicators

Attitudes

1.1.1 Intercultural Openness: Did the student welcome interactions with persons culturally different from them?

1.1.2 Intercultural Openness: Did the student suspend judgment during interactions with persons culturally different from them?

2.1.1 Intercultural Curiosity: Did the student ask questions, without seeking answers, about other cultures regarding cultural differences?

2.1.2 Intercultural Curiosity: Did the student not only ask questions but also seek the answers to these questions about other cultures regarding cultural differences?

Skills

3.1.1 Intercultural Empathy: Did the student use a worldview different from their own to interpret the views or actions of persons from other cultures?

3.1.2 Intercultural Empathy: Did the student demonstrate the ability to act in a supportive manner that recognizes the feelings of another cultural group?

4.1.1 Intercultural Communication: Did the student understand the cultural aspects of differences in nonverbal and verbal communication?

Knowledge

5.1.1 Cultural Self-Awareness: Did the student describe their own insights into their own personal cultural rules or biases?

5.1.2 Cultural Self-Awareness: Did the student seek to improve their understanding of the complicated differences between cultures?

5.1.3 Cultural Self-Awareness: Was the student aware of how their own experiences have shaped their own personal rules or biases?

6.1.1 Cultural Worldview: Did the student understand the complex variety of elements important to members of another culture? *(Elements may include history, values, politics, economics, communication styles, beliefs, or practices)*

V. What baseline data can be collected?

Students reflect on, discuss, and self-critique their completion of a pre-survey— A.S.K.S^2 PLUS—in addition to completing pre-reflections prior to starting assignments.

Optional: Students complete the Intercultural Development Inventory (IDI) as a pre-survey followed by an IDI post-survey.

VI. What evidence will demonstrate what students have learned and/or how they have changed? (*Note: Map evidence to outcomes.*)

Attitudes

Student Learning Outcome

1. Students identify, reflect on, and self-evaluate their own *Attitude of Intercultural Openness*, representing their interaction with culturally different others. (SLO1)

Student Learning Objective

1.1 Intercultural Openness: Students exchange answers to a list of questions with persons from another culture, record the responses, create a collage or concept map of selfies, and answer four reflection questions in which they describe, interpret/analyze, evaluate, and set a goal. (OBJ1.1)

Indicators

1.1.1 Intercultural Openness: Did the student welcome interactions with persons culturally different from themselves?

1.1.2 Intercultural Openness: Did the student suspend judgment during interactions with persons culturally different from them?

Student Learning Outcome

2. Students identify, reflect on, and self-evaluate their own *Attitude of Intercultural Curiosity*—that is, they ask questions about other cultures and seek out information about other cultures. (SLO2)

Student Learning Objective

2.1 Intercultural Curiosity: Studying the Cultural Iceberg Theory model, students create a crossword puzzle composed of 30 cross-cultural questions. Afterward, they answer four reflection questions in which they describe, interpret/analyze, evaluate, and set a goal. (OBJ2.1)

Indicators

2.1.1 Intercultural Curiosity: Did the student ask questions, without seeking answers, about other cultures regarding cultural differences?

2.1.2 Intercultural Curiosity: Did the student not only ask questions but also seek the answers to these questions about other cultures regarding cultural differences?

Skills

Student Learning Outcome

3. Students identify, reflect on, and self-evaluate their own Skill of Intercultural Empathy that is an adequate understanding of the complexity of what can be important to persons from a different culture and to interpret experiences or perspectives from their own and more than one worldview. (SLO3)

Student Learning Objective

3.1 Intercultural Empathy: Students interpret the Cross the River Parable Exercise from at least two totally different perspectives, discuss/write two perspectives and answer four describe, interpret/analyze, evaluate, and set a goal reflection questions. (OBJ3.1)

Indicators

3.1.1 Intercultural Empathy: Did the student use a worldview different from their own to interpret the views or actions of persons from other cultures?

3.1.2 Intercultural Empathy: Did the student demonstrate the ability to act in a supportive manner that recognizes the feelings of another cultural group?

Student Learning Outcome

4. Students identify, reflect on, and self-evaluate their own Skill of Intercultural Communication that is an understanding of and adaptation to cultural differences in verbal and nonverbal communication. (SLO4)

Student Learning Objective

4.1 Intercultural Communication: Students observe both the verbal and nonverbal communication behaviors in a public place where persons of different cultures interact, respond to two prompting questions in a written document, and answer four reflection questions in which they describe, interpret/analyze, and evaluate and set a goal. (OBJ4.1)

Indicators

4.1.1 Intercultural Communication: Did the student understand the cultural aspects of differences in nonverbal and verbal communication?

Knowledge

Student Learning Outcome

5. Students identify, reflect on, and self-evaluate their own Knowledge of Cultural Self-Awareness, involving their new perspectives and insights into their own cultural rules and biases. (SLO5)

Student Learning Objective

5.1 Cultural Self-Awareness: Students complete an Identity Dialogue Exercise, discuss/write six short essay items, and answer four describe, interpret/analyze, evaluate, and set a goal reflection questions. (OBJ5.1)

Indicators

5.1.1 Cultural Self-Awareness: Did the student describe their own insights into their own personal cultural rules or biases?

5.1.2 Cultural Self-Awareness: Did the student seek to improve their understanding of the complicated differences between cultures?

5.1.3 Cultural Self-Awareness: Was the student aware of how their own experiences have shaped their own personal rules or biases?

Student Learning Outcome

6. Students identify, reflect on, and self-evaluate their own Knowledge of Cultural Worldview: their understanding of other cultures in relation to history, values, politics, communication styles, economy, or beliefs and practices. (SLO6)

Student Learning Objective

6.1 Knowledge of Cultural Worldview: Students research the answers to a list of cross-cultural questions; locate corresponding images, photos, and links on the Internet; produce a document; and answer four describe, interpret/analyze, evaluate, and set a goal reflection questions. (OBJ6.1)

Indicator

6.1.1 Cultural Worldview: Did the student understand the complex variety of elements important to members of another culture? *(Elements may include history, values, politics, economics, communication styles, beliefs, or practices)*

VII. What assessment tools and methods most effectively capture evidence of student learning, both during and at the end of the students' learning experience? Do these tools specifically measure the learning objectives?

The first assessment tool to capture evidence of intercultural learning is A.S.K.S^2 PLUS, used as a pre-survey. A.S.K.S^2 PLUS is a hybrid tool to collect a small and very limited measure of quantitative data and also qualitative data. Used as a pre-survey, it is a teaching tool for the instructor to interview students and collect baseline data in order to guide the teaching and learning process. The instructor uses the self-reported levels of Bloom's Affective Domain on the A.S.K.S^2 PLUS to learn the degree that students see themselves on attitudes, skills, and knowledge of intercultural competency.

For the Affective Domain, the lower-to-higher hierarchy consists of

- Not aware of behavior or values
- Aware of and recognizes behavior or values
- Cooperates or complies with values
- Prefers behavior and values
- Behavior or values are a priority
- Behavior and values are habitual and natural

Student artifacts and reflective writing are used to formatively assess and to finally evaluate student learning. Rubrics for each of the six assignments facilitate and standardize the assessment process.

For example, for formative assessment using Bloom's Affective Domain, if half of the class consider themselves to be unaware of how to interact with culturally different others and the other half of the class consider themselves as able to recognize and to value intercultural openness, the instructor structures the openness assignment with a scaffolding of teaching and learning with consideration of each group as distinct. The expectation for each of the two groups is different. The unaware group may only move up on the Affective Domain scale to having some awareness. The valuing group may move up on the Affective Domain hierarchy to making their intercultural behavior a priority. Both groups progress developmentally up the hierarchy.

Using a standardized assessment, such as the Intercultural Development Inventory (IDI), assists the instructor in tailoring teaching and learning to best achieve student learning outcomes. This information helps the instructor target and scaffold the learning to individual students or specific levels of intercultural development. For example, a student who developmentally is in denial when dealing with difference will produce a different level of intercultural student learning artifact than a student who is developmentally at a higher level of accepting differences. Students are best served by an instructor who recognizes differences in ways of learning and stages of intercultural development.

Baseline assessment data provide the means to gauge improvement on intercultural learning on the attitudes, skills, and knowledge of interacting with difference at the end of the course. This can be done using both the A.S.K.S^2 PLUS post-survey and a standardized assessment post-survey to compare with the pre-surveys. In order to report the progress of intercultural learning, the professor may create a bar chart showing the comparison of pre- and post-mean scores for intercultural attitudes, skills, and knowledge, along with examples or artifacts of student class intercultural learning assignments to pass along to the Department Curriculum Committee or even the College Curriculum Committee. The Department Curriculum Committee and the College Curriculum Committee review the instructor's report and student artifacts. The Curriculum Committee may make recommendations to the instructor, as well as forwarding their report to the University Curriculum Committee.

Example of Indirect Evidence

Using A.S.K.S^2 PLUS, the following chart provides indirect formative assessment of what the instructor needs to focus on relating to teaching and learning. If communication is the lowest mean on the pre-survey, the instructor may elect to spend more time and make additional assignments on verbal and non-verbal communication.

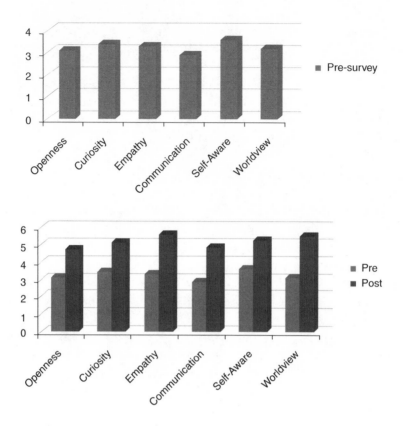

The chart also provides indirect summative assessment showing the self-reported intercultural learning gain by students.

Examples of Indirect Evidence From Reflective Writing Predicting Potential Behavior

Upon completing each of the six assignments targeting the constructs identified on the AAC&U Intercultural Knowledge and Competency VALUE Rubric, students are assigned to answer four reflection questions in the form of one sentence per question. The four reflection questions are

1. Please *describe* and define in one sentence the specific intercultural competency topic (i.e., openness, curiosity, empathy . . . etc.) of this assignment.
2. *Interpret or analyze* the experience and the importance of this assignment in one sentence.
3. Please *evaluate* the experience of this assignment.

4. In one sentence, as a result of this assignment, experience, and writing reflection, what *goal* related to your intercultural development will you make?

Following are examples of ways the goal statements for each of the six assignments are potentially used for both the formative assessment and the summative evaluation of individual students and meeting the student learning objectives in the course.

INTERCULTURAL ATTITUDES

Intercultural Openness

1.1 The Intercultural Openness assignment includes student artifacts of transformative student learning in the forms of reflection, written description, photo collage, or concept map.

Examples:
The productive reflection goal statement of **Student A** for the assignment was: *"I will meet one new person from another culture or country each week of this semester."*
Instructor's Rating of Intercultural Development: **High**   Medium   Low

Not the best goal statement from **Student B** was, *"When I do study abroad during semester break, I will meet some people from another country."*
Instructor's Rating of Intercultural Development: High   Medium   **Low**

Intercultural Curiosity

2.1 The Intercultural Curiosity assignment includes student artifacts of transformative student learning in the forms of reflection; research on thirty questions, with correct answers, based on Cultural Iceberg Theory; and a crossword puzzle.

Examples:
Student A said, *"My goal is to read, study, and understand the What's Up with Culture website this next month."*
Instructor's Rating of Intercultural Development: High   **Medium**   Low

A less productive goal statement from **Student B** was, *"I plan to visit one of the campus cultural centers."*
Instructor's Rating of Intercultural Development: High   Medium   **Low**

For formative assessment purposes, the instructor may wish to rate the goals of students as high, medium, and low in potential to develop intercultural competency. As formative feedback, students may take this initial feedback and be given the opportunity to rewrite and resubmit their goal statements. Depending on the quality of student work, the instructor may decide to spend more or less time addressing a specific intercultural construct in the course.

As summative evaluation, as a follow-up to the final goal statements by the students, the instructor may consider surveying the students at the end of the semester or study abroad regarding their actual behavior and ask if indeed they did meet their goals. This may also present the opportunity to collect some evidence from logs, reflections, or journals.

Examples of Direct Evidence

Intercultural Attitudes

1.1 The Intercultural Openness assignment includes student artifacts of transformative student learning in the forms of reflection, written description, photo collage, or concept map.

Student A for the assignment on Intercultural Openness answered twenty relationship-building questions. Some of the questions were, *"When are you the happiest?" "Describe your family." "What one word describes you as a child?"* Student A exchanged answers to these twenty questions with four persons from another culture, compiled the answers into a complete and clear report, and took four selfies to produce a photo collage to document the interaction with culturally different others.

Rubric:

	High	**Medium**	**Low**
Selfies	4 or more	2 to 3 photos	1 photo
Questions	20 to 25 questions each answered clearly and completely for all photos	16 to 20 questions each answered for all photos	Fewer than 16 questions with some answers not clear or incomplete

2.1 The Intercultural Curiosity assignment includes student artifacts of transformative student learning in the forms of reflection; research on thirty questions, with correct answers, based on Cultural Iceberg Theory; and a crossword puzzle.

Student A, to fulfill the assignment on Intercultural Curiosity, searched the Internet and, after analysis, selected an image of "Cultural Iceberg Theory." She next identified thirty topics from below the waterline or out of awareness, wrote these topics up as questions with one-word answers, and then constructed an online crossword puzzle with the thirty correct answers.

Rubric:

	High	**Medium**	**Low**
Image selection	Image provided was high quality with excellent content	Image provided was high quality with adequate content	Image was provided but poor quality or content was inadequate
Questions	30 questions provided	30 questions provided	Fewer than 30 questions provided
Answers	All answers correct	All answers correct	Some answers correct

Standardized Assessment Tools

Some instructors, curriculum committees, and universities may elect to use a standardized assessment. Direct evidence may also include the results, pre- and post-assessments, of a psychometrically sound assessment that can be used for both formative assessment and summative evaluation.

In summary, the instructor collects baseline data on the intercultural attitudes, skills, and knowledge of the students to guide the teaching and learning in the course. The instructor collects indirect evidence of self-reported data from students on their self-perceptions of developing intercultural values using Bloom's Affective Domain of moving from unawareness to adopting values to inculcating the values of intercultural attitudes, skills, and knowledge into their lives. Direct evidence of students developing intercultural competency is collected in assignments on intercultural openness and curiosity, skills of empathy and communication, and knowledge of self-awareness and worldview. Self-reported post-survey or summative assessment data are collected at the end of the course. Comparisons of pre-survey and post-survey data and direct evidence from examples of student assignments are passed on to the responsible Curriculum Committees to review and, if needed, to make recommendations. Curriculum Committees also request a final report from the instructor describing the intercultural learning outcomes, evidence of achieving these learning outcomes, and recommendations for improvement in meeting the student learning outcomes.

VIII. How will the learning processes be assessed?

Learning processes will be assessed by examination of the reflections and self-evaluations of students based upon the six constructs from the AAC&U Intercultural Knowledge VALUE Rubric as associated with both of the learning hierarchies, Bloom's Cognitive and Affective Domains. The lower to higher hierarchy of the Cognitive Domain is remembering, understanding, applying, analyzing, evaluating, and creating. Lower-order thinking is often associated with remembering, such as memorizing answers for a multiple-choice, true-false, or fill-in-the-blank exam. Higher-order thinking is linked to some application, analyzing, evaluating, and creating. Generally speaking, the student learning on the six assignments in this course, Introduction to Intercultural Learning, taps into the higher-order thinking levels of Bloom's Cognitive Domain.

For the Affective Domain, the lower-to-higher hierarchy consists of:

- Not aware of behavior or values
- Aware of and recognizes behavior or values
- Cooperates or complies with values
- Prefers behavior and values
- Behavior or values are a priority
- Behavior and values are habitual and natural

Student artifacts and reflective writing are used to formatively assess and to finally evaluate student learning. Rubrics for each of the assignments facilitate and standardize the assessment process. Behavior associated with student learning can be measured by the instructor using the behavior goal statements of students and asking students at the end of the semester about the degree to which they met their behavioral goal statements relating to the six intercultural learning assignments.

IX. How will these assessment tools and methods be implemented and by whom?

The instructor and graduate teaching assistants of the course collect baseline data on the developmental levels of intercultural competency of the students. Baseline data may be from A.S.K.S^2 PLUS or a standardized assessment such as the Intercultural Development Inventory. A.S.K.S^2 PLUS is used, as a hybrid tool, to collect a small and very limited measure of quantitative data and also qualitative data specifically correlated to the six assignments in the course. These data are used for formative assessment, to improve teaching and learning during the semester, and summative evaluation.

The instructor assigns the six assignments, which correspond to the six constructs of openness, curiosity, empathy, communication, self-awareness, and worldview on the AAC&U Intercultural Knowledge and Competency VALUE Rubric. Each assignment is completed by students. Instructors provide feedback for each assignment, and students may have the opportunity to revise their work and resubmit based on instructor feedback. Each assignment includes reflective writing, which may also be reviewed and, with instructor feedback, provide opportunity for students to resubmit their reflection.

As a result of these assignments, students produce the artifacts of the six specific assignments and reflections of their learning, including behavioral goal statements. The behavioral goal statement potentially provides assessment of actual intercultural behavior at the end of the semester.

X. Who will collect the data from the assessment tools/methods used, and who will have access to data?

Examples and artifacts of student work, including reflections and goal statements, are provided to departmental, college, and university curriculum committees for review and feedback. The university assessment group provides a final review.

XI. Who will analyze the data (need multiple perspectives on analyzing and interpreting the data), how, and how often?

Same as above and scheduled every two years for review of the stakeholders above who provide feedback back down through the chain of evidence.

XII. How will the data be used to provide feedback to students? (Who will do this? When? How often?) How will the data be used to make changes, and who will make those changes?

First, the instructor uses the assignments to provide feedback to students after the completion of each assignment. In some cases, the instructor may elect to permit students to resubmit their work after feedback. The number of times is up to the instructor and based on the resources allocated to the course.

Feedback from the curriculum committees and assessment group provides the opportunity to the instructor to make changes and to improve the achieving of student learning outcomes, to improve student learning, and to meet the intercultural learning mission of The University.

XIII. How will the data be communicated to and among stakeholders (means of communication, schedule for reporting, etc.)? How will stakeholders assist in making changes?

Same as above.

XIV. How will the assessment plan itself and the assessment team be reviewed (who will do this, how often—including external review)?

All the above is reviewed by the Vice Provost for Undergraduate Education. External review is up to the discretion and timetable of the Provost's Office and The University Office of Assessment.

Appendix G

Selected Assessment Resources for International Educators

The resources included in this appendix are meant to serve as a starting point for individuals to delve deeper into the topics raised in this book. This list is not meant to be exhaustive in any way but merely serves to highlight a few of the many available resources. Some important ones may have inadvertently not been included in this list. Nonetheless, this list provides at least some selected resources for further learning about the topic of outcomes assessment within the context of international higher education.

Recommended Reading

A wealth of assessment literature is available. International educators are strongly encouraged to read some assessment books to learn more in-depth information on outcomes assessment. Following are just a few of the many excellent books on learning assessment.

Angelo, T., & Cross, P. (1993). *Classroom assessment techniques: A handbook for faculty.* San Francisco: Jossey-Bass.

Banta, T. (2004). *Hallmarks of effective outcomes assessment.* San Francisco: Jossey-Bass.

Banta, T., & Palomba, C. (2014). *Assessment essentials: Planning, implementing, and improving assessment in higher education.* San Francisco: Jossey-Bass.

Boak, G. (1998). *A complete guide to learning contracts.* Brookfield, VT: Gower.

Bresciani, M. (2006). *Outcomes-based academic and co-curricular program review: A compilation of institutional and good practices.* Sterling, VA: Stylus.

Bresciani, M., Gardness, M., & Hickmott, J. (2009). *Demonstrating student success: A practical guide to outcomes-based assessment in learning and developing in student affairs.* Sterling, VA: Stylus

Driscoll, A., & Wood, S. (2007). *Developing outcomes-based assessment for learner-centered education: A faculty introduction.* Sterling, VA: Stylus.

Hernon, P., & Dugan, R. (2013). *Higher education outcomes assessment in higher education for the 21st century.* Westport, CT: Libraries Unlimited.

Huba, M. E., & Freed, J. E. (2000). *Learner-centered assessment on college campuses: Shifting the focus from teaching to learning.* Boston: Allyn and Bacon.

Knowles, M. (1986) *Using learning contracts.* San Francisco: Jossey-Bass.

Maki, P. L. (2004). *Assessing for learning: Building a sustainable commitment across the institution.* Sterling, VA: Stylus.

Maki, P. L. (Ed.) (2010). *Coming to terms with student outcomes assessment: Faculty and administrators' journeys to integrating assessment in their work and institutional culture.* Sterling, VA: Stylus.

Palomba, C., & Banta, T. (2001). *Assessing student competence in accredited disciplines: Pioneering approaches to assessment in higher education.* Sterling, VA: Stylus.

Schuh, J. (2008). *Assessment methods for student affairs.* San Francisco: Jossey-Bass.

Secolsky, C., & Denison, D. (2011). *Handbook on measurement, assessment and evaluation in higher education.* New York: Routledge.

Stevens, D. (2012). *Introduction to rubrics: An assessment tool to save grading time, convey effective feedback, and promote student learning.* Sterling, VA: Stylus.

Suskie, L. (2009). *Assessing student learning: A common sense guide.* San Francisco: Jossey-Bass.

Walvoord, B. E. (2004). *Assessment clear and simple: A practical guide for institutions, departments, and general education.* San Francisco: Jossey-Bass.

Program Evaluation–Related Resources

Fitzpatrick, J., Sanders, J., & Worthen, B. (2010). *Program evaluation: Alternative approaches and practical guidelines* (4th ed). Boston: Pearson.

Knowlton, L., & Phillips, C. (2013). *The logic model guidebook: Better strategies for great results.* Thousand Oaks, CA: SAGE.

Wholey, J., Hatry, H., & Newcomer, T. (2010). *Handbook of practical program evaluation.* San Francisco: Jossey-Bass.

Assessment Conferences

Several assessment conferences take place each year, including the long-running Assessment Institute that occurs each October in Indianapolis, hosted by Indiana University–Purdue University Indianapolis, and the annual conference of the Association for Authentic, Experiential and Evidence-Based Learning (AAEEBL), held in July. Other assessment-related conferences include the Association of Institutional Research Forum, the International Assessment in Higher Education Conference, and the World Congress on Education, the latter two being international in scope. International educators are encouraged to participate in such assessment conferences to gain perspectives from the assessment field as well as to share insights from international education.

Other Selected Publications Related to International Education Assessment

Numerous articles have been published, especially in education abroad, on assessment efforts. Fewer books and book chapters are available. Following is a selected list of publications that may be of interest to those who wish to learn more about the international education context and some examples.

Bennett, J. (2009). Cultivating intercultural competence: A process perspective. In D. K. Deardorff (Ed.), *The SAGE handbook of intercultural competence* (pp. 121–140). Thousand Oaks, CA: SAGE.

Berardo, K., & Deardorff, D. (2012). *Building cultural competence: Innovative activities and models.* Sterling, VA: Stylus.

Bok, D. (2006). *Our underachieving colleges: A candid look at how much students learn and why they should be learning more.* Princeton, NJ: Princeton University Press.

Bolen, M. C. (Ed.). (2007). *Guide to outcomes assessment in education abroad.* Carlisle, PA: Forum on Education Abroad.

Brown, S., & Kysilka, M. (2002). *Applying multicultural and global concepts in the classroom and beyond.* Boston: Allyn & Bacon.

Byram, M. (1997). *Teaching and assessing intercultural communicative competence.* Clevedon: Multilingual Matters.

Clayton, J. (2003). *One classroom, many worlds: Teaching and learning in the cross-cultural classroom.* Portsmouth, NH: Heinemann.

Deardorff, D. K. (2006). The identification and assessment of intercultural competence as a student outcome of internationalization at institutions of higher education in the United States. *Journal of Studies in International Education, 10*(3), 241–266.

Deardorff, D. K. (2007, Spring). Principles of international education assessment. *IIE Networker,* 51–52.

Deardorff, D. K. (2008). Intercultural competence: A definition, model and implications for education abroad. In V. Savicki (Ed.), *Developing intercultural competence and transformation: Theory, research, and application in international education* (pp. 32–52). Sterling, VA: Stylus.

Deardorff, D. K. (2009a). Implementing intercultural competence assessment. In D. K. Deardorff (Ed.), *The SAGE handbook of intercultural competence* (pp. 477–491). Thousand Oaks, CA: SAGE.

Deardorff, D. K. (Ed.). (2009b). *The SAGE handbook of intercultural competence.* Thousand Oaks, CA: SAGE.

Deardorff, D. K., de Wit, H., Heyl, J., & Adams, T. (Eds.). (2012). *The SAGE handbook of international higher education.* Thousand Oaks, CA: SAGE.

De Wit, H. (2009). *Measuring success in the internationalization of higher education.* Amsterdam: EAIE.

Fantini, A. (2009). Assessing intercultural competence: Issues and tools. In D. K. Deardorff (Ed.), *The SAGE handbook of intercultural competence* (pp. 456–476). Thousand Oaks, CA: SAGE.

Green, M. (2012a). *Improving and assessing global learning.* Washington, DC: NAFSA.

Green, M. (2012b). *Measuring and assessing internationalization.* Washington, DC: NAFSA.

Musil, C. (2006). *Assessing global learning: Matching good intentions with good practice.* Washington, DC: AAC&U.

Paige, R. M. (Ed.). (1993). *Education for the intercultural experience.* Yarmouth, ME: Intercultural Press.

Pedersen, P. (1994). *A handbook for developing multicultural awareness.* 2nd ed. Alexandria, VA: American Counseling Association.

Savicki, V. (Ed.). (2007). *Developing intercultural competence and transformation: Theory, research, and application in international education.* Sterling, VA: Stylus.

Spitzberg, B., & Changnon, G. (2009). Conceptualizing intercultural competence. In D. K. Deardorff (Ed.), *The SAGE handbook of intercultural competence* (pp. 2–52). Thousand Oaks, CA: SAGE.

Stuart, D. (2008). Assessment instruments for the global workforce. In M. Moodian (Ed.), *Contemporary leadership and intercultural competence* (pp. 175–190). Thousand Oaks, CA: SAGE.

Vande Berg, M., Paige, M., & Lou, K. (2012). *Student learning abroad.* Sterling, VA: Stylus.

Some Online Resources for International Educators

American Council on Education. *Assessing international learning outcomes.* Retrieved from http://www.acenet.edu/news-room/Pages/Internationalization-Toolkit.aspx#curriculum

Association of American Colleges & Universities. AAC&U VALUES rubric for intercultural competence. Retrieved from http://www.aacu.org/value/rubrics/InterculturalKnowledge.cfm

Forum on Education Abroad. Outcomes Assessment and Research Toolbox. http://www.forumea.org/resources/member-resources/outcomes-tool-box (accessible to members only).

Internet Resources for Higher Education Outcomes Assessment. Hosted by
    North Carolina State University. http://www2.acs.ncsu.edu/UPA/archives/
    assmt/resource.htm (one of the most extensive assessment websites available).
NAFSA. Assessment and evaluation for international educators report. www.nafsa.
    org/assessmentbasics

Some Assessment-Related Associations and Organizations

Accreditation Organisation of the Netherlands and Flanders
American Evaluation Association
Association for the Assessment of Learning in Higher Education
Association for Authentic, Experiential and Evidence-Based Learning
Association for Educational Assessment (Europe)
Association for Institutional Research
Centro Nacional de Evaluacion para la Educación Superior (Mexico)
Council for Higher Education Accreditation
European Association for Quality Assurance in Higher Education
International Association for Education Assessment
International Association for Research on Service Learning and Community
    Engagement
National Institute for Learning Outcomes Assessment
Quality Assurance Agency for Higher Education (United Kingdom)
Tertiary Education Quality and Standards Agency (Australia)

References

Aerden, A. (2014). *A guide to assessing the quality of internationalisation*. European Consortium for Accreditation in Higher Education Occasional Paper.

Allport, G. (1954). *The nature of prejudice*. Cambridge, MA: Addison-Wesley.

Alverno College Faculty. (1994). *Student assessment-as-learning at alverno College* (3rd ed.) Milwaukee: Alverno College.

American Council on Education. (2008). *Mapping internationalization on U.S. campuses*. Washington, DC: American Council on Education.

Anderson, L., & Krathwohl, D. (Eds.). (2001). *A taxonomy for learning, teaching, and assessing: A revision of Bloom's taxonomy of educational objectives*. New York: Longman.

Ashizawa, S. (2012). Recent trends in university internationalization in Japan. In D. K. Deardorff, H. de Wit, J. Heyl, & T. Adams (Eds.), *The SAGE handbook of international higher education* (pp. 177–178). Thousand Oaks, CA: SAGE.

Astin, A. W. (1972). The measured effects of higher education. *Annals of the American Academy of Political and Social Science, 404*(1), 1–20.

Banta, T. (Ed.). (2004). *Hallmarks of effective outcomes assessment*. San Francisco: Jossey-Bass.

Banta, T. (2005). How much have we learned? *BizEd, 4*(6), 35–38.

Banta, T., & Palomba, C. (2014). *Assessment essentials: Planning, implementing, and improving assessment in higher education* (2nd ed.). San Francisco: Jossey-Bass.

Bennett, J. M. (1993). Cultural marginality: Identity issues in intercultural training. In R. Paige (Ed.), *Education for the intercultural experience* (2nd ed., pp. 109–135). Yarmouth, ME: Intercultural Press.

Bennett, J. M. (2009). Cultivating intercultural competence: A process perspective. In D. Deardorff (Ed.), *SAGE Handbook of Intercultural Competence* (pp. 121–140). Thousand Oaks, CA: SAGE.

Bennett, M. J. (1993). Towards ethnorelativism: A developmental model of intercultural sensitivity. In R. Paige (Ed.), *Education for the intercultural experience* (2nd ed., pp. 21–71). Yarmouth, ME: Intercultural Press.

Bennett, N. (1976). *Teaching styles and pupil progress*. Cambridge, MA: Harvard University Press.

Bennett, R. (2009). *Formative assessment: A critical review.* Presentation at the University of Maryland, College Park, MD.

Bloom, B. (1956). *Taxonomy of educational objectives, Handbook I: The cognitive domain.* New York: David McKay Co.

Bok, D. (2006). *Our underachieving colleges: A candid look at how much students learn and why they should be learning more.* Princeton, NJ: Princeton University Press.

Bolen, M. C. (2007). *A guide to outcomes assessment in education abroad.* Carlisle, PA: Forum on Education Abroad.

Braskamp, L. A., & Engberg, M. E. (2014, February 11). Guidelines to consider in being strategic about assessment [blog post]. Retrieved from the National Institutes for Learning Outcomes Assessment website: http://illinois.edu/blog/view/915/109546

Bresciani, M. J., Gardner, M. M., & Hickmott, J. (2009). *Case studies for implementing assessment in student affairs: New directions for student services, No. 127.* San Francisco: Jossey-Bass.

British Council. (2013). *Culture at work.* London: Author.

Brookhart, S. (2008). *How to give effective feedback to your students.* Alexandria, VA: Association for Supervision and Curriculum Development.

Brookhart, S. (2010). *How to assess higher-order thinking skills in your classroom.* Alexandria, VA: Association for Supervision and Curriculum Development.

Camacho, M. (2004). Power and privilege: Community service learning in Tijuana. *Michigan Journal of Community Service Learning, 10*(3), 31–42.

Cambridge, D. (2010). *E-portfolios for lifelong learning and assessment.* San Francisco: Jossey-Bass.

Chen, H. (2005). *Practical program evaluation: Assessing and improving planning, implementation, and effectiveness.* Thousand Oaks, CA: SAGE.

Clayton, P., Ash, S., & Jameson, J. (2009). Assessing critical thinking and higher-order reasoning in service-learning enhanced courses and course sequences. In T. Banta, B. Jones, & K. Black (Eds.), *Planning, implementing, and sustaining assessment: Principles and profiles of good practice* (pp. 58–62). San Francisco: Jossey-Bass.

Cohen, A. (1994). *Assessing language ability in the classroom* (2nd ed.). Boston: Heinle & Heinle.

Cross, T. (1988). *Cross-cultural continuum for agencies and individuals.* http://www.cfilc.org/atf/cf/%7BFF5A65B0-F157-496A-80B2-D0F5B1AE44C2%7D/CULTURAL%20AND%20DISABILITY%20COMPETENCE%20CONTINUUM.ppt

Deardorff, D. K. (2005). A matter of logic? *International Educator, 14*(3), 26–31.

Deardorff, D. K. (2006). The identification and assessment of intercultural competence as a student outcome of internationalization at institutions of higher education in the United States. *Journal of Studies in International Education, 10*(3), 241–266.

Deardorff, D. K. (2007, Spring). Principles of international education assessment. *IIE Networker*, 51–52.

Deardorff, D. K. (2008). Intercultural competence: A definition, model, and implications for education abroad. In V. Savicki (Ed.), *Developing intercultural competence and transformation: Theory, research, and application in international education* (pp. 32–52). Sterling, VA: Stylus.

Deardorff, D. K. (Ed.). (2009). *The SAGE handbook of intercultural competence*. Thousand Oaks, CA: SAGE.

Deardorff, D. K. (2011). Assessing intercultural competence as a learning outcome. *New Directions in Institutional Research*, *2011*(149), 65–79.

Deardorff, D. K., de Wit, H., Heyl, J., & Adams, T. (Eds.). (2012). *The SAGE handbook of international higher education*. Thousand Oaks, CA: SAGE.

Deardorff, D. K., & van Gaalen, A. (2012). Outcomes assessment in the internationalization of higher education. In D. Deardorff, H. de Wit, J. Heyl, & T. Adams (Eds.), *The SAGE handbook of international higher education* (pp. 167–191). Thousand Oaks, CA: SAGE.

Della Chiesa, B., Scott, J., & Hinton, C. (2012). *Languages in a global world: Learning for better cultural understanding*. Paris: OECD.

De Wit, H. (2009). *Measuring success in the internationalisation of higher education*. Amsterdam: European Association for International Education.

Driscoll, A., & Wood, S. (2007). *Developing outcomes-based assessment for learner-centered education: A faculty introduction*. Sterling, VA: Stylus.

Dwyer, M. M., & Peters, C. K. (2004, March/April). The benefits of study abroad. *Transitions Abroad, 37*(5). Retrieved from http://www.transitionsabroad.com/publications/magazine/0403/benefits_study_abroad.shtml

Egron Polak, E., & Hudson, R. (2014). *Internationalization of higher education: Growing expectations, fundamental values*. Paris: International Association of Universities.

Eisner, E. W. (2002). What can education learn from the arts about the practice of education? *The Encyclopedia of Informal Education*. Retrieved from http://www.infed.org/biblio/eisner_arts_and_the_practice_of_education.htm

Erickson, J., & O'Connor, S. (2000). Service-learning's effect on prejudice: Does it reduce or promote it? In C. O'Grady (Ed.), *Transforming education, transforming the world: The integration of service-learning and multicultural education into higher education*. Mahwah, NJ: Lawrence Erlbaum Associates.

Ewell, P. (2005). Can assessment serve accountability? It depends on the question. In J. C. Burke and Associates (Eds.), *Achieving accountability in higher education: Balancing public, academic, and market demands*. San Francisco: Jossey-Bass.

Fantini, A. (2009). Assessing intercultural competence: Issues and tools. In D. K. Deardorff (Ed.), *The SAGE handbook of intercultural competence* (pp. 456–476). Thousand Oaks, CA: SAGE.

Fitch, P. (2004). Effects of intercultural service-learning experiences on intellectual development and intercultural awareness. In S. H. Billig & M. Welch (Eds.),

New perspectives in service-learning: Research to advance the field (pp. 107–126). Greenwich, CT: Information Age.

Fitch, P. (2005). In their own voices: A mixed methods approach to studying of intercultural service-learning with college students. In S. Root, J. Callahan, & S. H. Billig (Eds.), *Improving service-learning practice: Research on models to enhance impacts* (pp. 187–211). Greenwich, CT: Information Age.

Gardiner, L., Anderson, C., & Cambridge, B. (1997). *Learning through assessment: A resource guide for higher education.* Washington, DC: American Association for Higher Education.

Green, M. F. (2012). *Measuring and assessing internationalization.* Retrieved from the NAFSA website: http://www.nafsa.org/_/File/_/downloads/measuring_assessing .pdf

Green, M. F. (2013). *Improving and assessing global learning.* Retrieved from the NAFSA website: http://www.nafsa.org/_/File/_/downloads/improving_assessing .pdf

Green, M. F., Marmolejo, F., & Egron-Polak, E. (2012). *The internationalization of higher education: Future prospects.* In D. K. Deardorff, H. de Wit, J. Heyl, & T. Adams (Eds.), *The SAGE handbook of international higher education* (pp. 439–457). Thousand Oaks, CA: SAGE.

Green, M. F., & Olson, C. (2008). *Internationalizing the campus: A user's guide.* Washington, DC: American Council on Education.

Gronlund, N. E. (2006). *Assessment of student achievement* (8th ed.). Boston: Pearson.

Hammer, M. (2012). The Intercultural Development Inventory: A new frontier in assessment and development of intercultural competence. In M. Vande Berg, R. M. Paige, & K. H. Lou (Eds.), *Student learning abroad: What our students are learning, what they're not, and what we can do about it* (pp. 115–136). Sterling, VA: Stylus.

Hatfield, S. (2005, November). *Assessment 101: The core curriculum.* Presentation at University of North Carolina–Wilmington.

Heyl, J. (2007). *The SIO as change agent.* Durham, NC: Association of International Education Administrators.

Heyl, J., & Tullbane, J. (2012). Leadership in international higher education. In D. K. Deardorff, H. de Wit, J. Heyl, & T. Adams (Eds.), *The SAGE handbook of international higher education* (pp. 113–130). Thousand Oaks, CA: SAGE.

House, R. J., Dorfman, P., Javidan, M., Hanges, P. J., & Sully de Luque, M. F. (2014). *Strategic leadership across cultures: The GLOBE study of CEO leadership behavior and effectiveness in 24 countries.* Thousand Oaks, CA: SAGE.

House, R. J., Hanges, P. J., Javidan, M., Dorfman, P. W., & Gupta, V. (2004). *Culture, leadership, and organizations: The GLOBE study of 62 societies.* Thousand Oaks, CA: SAGE.

Huba, M., & Freed, J. (2000). *Learner-centered assessment on college campuses: Shifting the focus from teaching to learning.* Boston: Allyn and Bacon.

Hudzik, J. (2012). *Leading comprehensive internationalization: Strategy and tactics for action*. Washington, DC: NAFSA.

Hudzik, J., & Stohl, M. (2009). Modeling assessment of outcomes and impacts from internationalization. In H. de Wit (Ed.), *Measuring success in the internationalization of higher education* (EAIE Occasional Paper 22). Amsterdam: European Association for International Education.

Hughes, A. (2002). *Testing for language teachers*. Cambridge: Cambridge University Press.

Institute of International Education. (2013). *Open doors report on international educational exchange*. Retrieved from http://www.iie.org/opendoors

International Education Association of South Africa. (2014). *Global dialogue 2014: Nelson Mandela Bay declaration of the future of internationalization in higher education*. Port Elizabeth, South Africa: Nelson Mandela Metropolitan University. Retrieved from http://www.nafsa.org/_/File/_/ieasa_2014.pdf

Jankowski, N., Hutchings, P., Ewell, P., Kinzie, J., & Kuh, G. (2013, November/December). The degree qualifications profile: What it is and why we need it now. *Change: The Magazine of Higher Learning*. Retrieved from http://www.changemag.org/Archives/Back%20Issues/2013/November-December%202013/Degree_full.html

Kegan, R. (1994). *In over our heads: The mental demands of modern life*. Cambridge, MA: Harvard University Press.

Kettner, P., Moroney, R., & Martin, L. L. (2013). *Designing and managing programs: An effectiveness-based approach* (4th ed.). Thousand Oaks, CA: SAGE.

Kiely, R. (2004). A chameleon with a complex: Searching for transformation in international service-learning. *Michigan Journal of Community Service Learning, 10*(2), 5–20.

Kiely, R. (2005). A transformative learning model for service-learning: A longitudinal case study. *Michigan Journal of Community Service Learning, 12*(1), 5–22.

King, P. M., & Baxter Magolda, M. B. (2005). A developmental model of intercultural maturity. *Journal of College Student Development, 46*(6), 571–592.

Kneffelcamp, L. (1989, June). *Assessment as transformation*. Speech to the American Association for Higher Education Fourth National Conference on Assessment in Higher Education, Atlanta.

Knight, J. (2004). Internationalization remodeled: Definition, approaches, and rationales. *Journal of Studies in International Education, 8*(5), 5–31. doi: 10.1177/1028315303260832

Knight, J. (2012). Student mobility and internationalization: Trends and tribulations. *Research in Comparative and International Education, 7*(1), 20–33.

Knowles, M. (1986). *Using learning contracts*. San Francisco: Jossey-Bass.

Knowles, M. (1991). Introduction: The art and science of helping adults learn. In M. Knowles (Ed.), *Andragogy in action: Applying modern principles of adult learning*. San Francisco: Jossey-Bass.

Knowlton, L., & Phillips, C. (2013). *The logic model guidebook: Better strategies for great results* (2nd ed.). Thousand Oaks, CA: SAGE.

Kyllonen, P. (2013). *Beyond the common core (soft skills, noncognitive skills, 21st century skills and competencies, interpersonal & intrapersonal skills, social-emotional skills)* [PowerPoint presentation]. Retrieved from the National Center for the Improvement of Educational Assessment website: http://www.nciea.org/wp-content/uploads/Kyllonen-RILS-2013.pdf

Levin, H. M. (2012). The utility and need for incorporating noncognitive skills into large-scale educational assessments. In M. von Davier, E. Gonzalez, I. Kirsch, & K. Yamamoto (Eds.), *The role of international large-scale assessments: Perspectives from technology, economy, and educational research* (pp. 67–86). New York: Springer.

Lewin, R. (2009, Fall). Transforming the study abroad experience into a collective priority. *Peer review, 11*(4). Retrieved from https://www.aacu.org/peerreview/2009/fall/lewin

Light, T. P., Chen, H., & Ittelson, J. C. (2011). *Documenting learning with ePortfolios: A guide for college instructors.* San Francisco: Jossey-Bass.

Maki, P. (2004). *Assessing for learning: Building a sustainable commitment across the institution.* Sterling, VA: Stylus.

Merrill, M., & Pusch, M. (2007). Apples, oranges, and kumys: Models for research on students doing intercultural service learning. In S. B. Gelmon and S. H. Billig (Eds.), *From passion to objectivity: International and cross-disciplinary perspectives on service learning research* (pp. 21–40). Greenwich, CT: Information Age.

Muffo, J. (2001). Institutional effectiveness, student learning, and outcomes assessment. In R. Howard (Ed.), *Institutional research: Decision support in higher education.* Tallahassee, FL: Association for Institutional Research.

Musil, C. (2006). *Assessing global learning: Matching good intentions with good practice.* Washington, DC: American Association of Colleges and Universities.

Nilsson, B. (2003, March). Internationalisation at home from a Swedish perspective: The case of Malmö. *Journal of Studies in International Education, 7*(1), 27–40.

O'Grady, C. (2000). *Integrating service learning and multicultural education in colleges and universities.* Mahwah, NJ: Lawrence Erlbaum Associates.

Olson, C. L., Evans, R., & Schoenberg, R. E. (2007). *At home in the world: Bridging the gap between internationalization and multicultural education.* Washington, DC: American Council on Education.

Paige, R. M., & Goode, M. L. (2009). Cultural mentoring: International education professionals and the development of intercultural competence. In D. K. Deardorff (Ed.), *The SAGE handbook of intercultural competence* (pp. 333–349). Thousand Oaks, CA: SAGE.

Palloff, R. M., & Pratt, K. (2009). *Assessing the online learner: Resources and strategies for faculty.* San Francisco: Jossey-Bass.

Palomba, C., & Banta, T. (1999). *Assessment essentials: Planning, implementing, and improving assessment in higher education*. San Francisco: Jossey-Bass.

Palomba, C., & Banta, T. (Eds.). (2011). *Assessing student competence in accredited disciplines: Pioneering approaches to assessment in higher education*. Sterling, VA: Stylus.

Parker, B., & Dautoff, D. (2007). Service-learning and study abroad: Synergistic learning opportunities. *Michigan Journal of Community Service-Learning, 13*(2), 40–53.

Penn, J. (Ed.). (2011). *Future directions for assessing complex general education student learning outcomes*. San Francisco: Jossey-Bass.

Perry, W. (1970). *Forms of intellectual and ethical development in the college years*. New York: Holt, Reinhart and Winston.

Pottinger, P. S. (1979). Competence assessment: Comments on current practices. *New Directions for Experiential Learning, 1979*(3), 25–39.

Putnam, R. D. (2007). *E Pluribus Unum:* Diversity and community in the twenty-first century: The 2006 Johan Skytte Prize lecture. *Scandinavian Political Studies, 30*(2), 137–174.

Rhodes, T. L. (2010). *Assessing outcomes and improving achievement*. Washington, DC: Association of American Colleges and Universities.

Rice, K., & Pollack, S. (2000). *Developing a critical pedagogy of service learning: Preparing self-reflective, culturally aware, and responsive community participants.* In C. O'Grady (Ed.), *Integrating service learning and multicultural education in colleges and universities*. Mahwah, NJ: Lawrence Erlbaum Associates.

Riordan, T., & Doherty, A. (1999). *Student learning outcomes in baccalaureate education: Report of the Alverno College Institute*. Milwaukee, WI: Alverno.

Rogers, P. J. (2000). Causal models in program theory evaluation. *New Directions in Evaluation, 2000*(87), 47–55. doi:10.1002/ev.1181

Rossi, P., Lipsey, M., & Freeman, H. (2004). *Evaluation: A systematic approach* (7th ed.). Thousand Oaks, CA: SAGE.

Shulman, L. S. (2007). Counting and recounting: Assessment and the quest for accountability. *Change, 39*(1), 20–25.

Sinek, S. (2009). *Start with why: How great leaders inspire everyone to take action*. New York: Portfolio.

Slimbach, R. (1996). Connecting head, heart, and hands: Developing intercultural service competence. In R. Sigmon (Ed.), *Journey to service-learning: Experiences from independent liberal arts colleges and universities* (pp. 99–111). Washington, DC: Council of Independent Colleges.

Stefani, L., Mason, R., & Pegler, C. (2007). *The educational potential of e-portfolios: Supporting personal development and reflective learning*. London: Routledge.

Steinke, P., & Fitch, P. (2011). Outcome assessment from the perspective of psychological science: The TAIM approach. *New Directions for Institutional Research, 2011*(149): 15–26. doi:10.1002/ir.377

Stiggins, R. J. (2008). *Assessment manifesto: A call for the development of balanced assessment systems.* Princeton, NJ: Educational Testing Service.

Stuart, D. K. (2008). Assessment instruments for the global workforce. In M. Moodian (Ed.), *Contemporary leadership and intercultural competence: Exploring the cross-cultural dynamics within organizations* (pp. 175–190). Thousand Oaks, CA: SAGE.

Thorndike, R. M. (2005). *Measurement and evaluation in psychology and education* (7th ed.). Upper Saddle River, NJ: Prentice Hall.

Tyler, R. W. (1949). *Basic principles of curriculum and instruction.* Chicago: University of Chicago Press.

Urraca, B., Ledoux, M., & Harris, J. (2009). Beyond the comfort zone: Lessons of intercultural service. *Clearing House, 82*(6), 281–289.

Vande Berg, M., & Paige, R. (2009). Applying theory and research: The evolution of intercultural competence in U.S. study abroad. In D. K. Deardorff (Ed.), *The SAGE handbook of intercultural competence* (pp. 404–418). Thousand Oaks, CA: SAGE.

Vande Berg, M., Paige, R. M., & Lou, K. H. (Eds.). (2012). *Student learning abroad: What our students are learning, what they're not, and what we can do about it.* Sterling, VA: Stylus.

Walvoord, B. (2004). *Assessment clear and simple: A practical guide for institutions, departments, and general education.* San Francisco: Jossey-Bass.

Zessoules, R., & Gardner, H. (1991). Authentic assessment: Beyond the buzzword and into the classroom. In V. Perrone (Ed.), *Expanding Student Assessment* (pp. 47–71). Alexandria, VA: Association for Supervision and Curriculum Development.

INDEX

215

Building Cultural Competence presents the latest work in the intercultural field and provides step-by-step instructions for how to effectively work with the new models, frameworks, and exercises for building learners' cultural competence. Featuring fresh activities and tools from experienced coaches, trainers, and facilitators from around the globe, this collection of over 50 easy-to-use activities and models has been used successfully worldwide in settings that range from Fortune 500 corporations to the World Bank, non-profits, and universities.

Sty/us

22883 Quicksilver Drive
Sterling, VA 20166-2102

Subscribe to our e-mail alerts: www.Styluspub.com

Also by Darla K. Deardorff

Building Cultural Competence

Innovative Activities and Models

Edited by Kate Berardo and Darla K. Deardorff

Foreword by Fons Trompenaars

"A new book of training activities is always welcome, but this volume offers something more: a thoughtful, careful analysis of how to design and execute relevant cultural training. You get the toolkit, in short, as well as guidance from some of the master builders."

—*Craig Sorti, author, trainer, and consultant in intercultural communications*

"This book brings creativity and innovativeness to training tools, models, and activities. I fully agree with the authors that it is amazing that this important field of endeavor has made so little progress in the last 30 years. The cry for intercultural competence becomes louder at a time when we don't have to travel to find an increasingly diverse population, and thus training is needed now more than ever."

—*Fons Trompenaars, founder of Trompenaars Hampden-Turner, a major multinational consulting firm with offices in The Netherlands, Japan, Singapore, and the United States*

"*Building Cultural Competence* makes a valuable contribution to intercultural trainers by presenting 50+ innovative activities designed specifically for the development of intercultural competence and framing the use of these activities in terms of intercultural facilitation and intercultural development."

—*R. Michael Paige, author of* Education for the Intercultural Experience *and Professor of International and Intercultural Education, University of Minnesota*

For HR directors, corporate trainers, college administrators, diversity trainers, and study abroad educators, this book provides a cutting-edge framework and an innovative collection of ready-to-use tools and activities to help build cultural competence—from the basics of understanding core concepts of culture to the complex work of negotiating identity and resolving cultural differences.

(continued)